THE CONTESTED PARTERRE

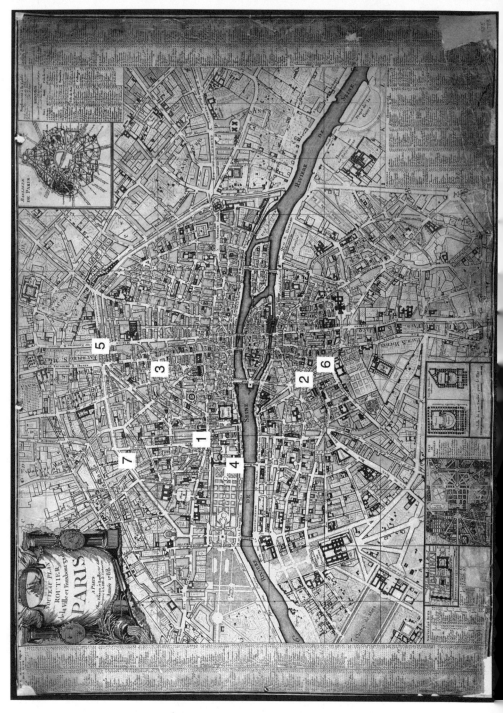

Frontispiece. 1788 street map of the city and suburbs of Paris. Note the overhead views of the new Comédie-Française and Comédie-Italienne playhouses in the inset at the bottom of the map. Key: (1) Opera, 1673–1763, 1770–81. (2) Comédie-Française, 1689–1770. (3) Comédie-Italienne, 1680–97, 1716–83. (4) Opera, 1763–70; Comédie-Française, 1770–82. (5) Opera, 1781–94. (6) Comédie-Française, 1782–93. (7) Comédie-Italienne, 1783–1801. (Courtesy of the Harvard Map Collection, Harvard University.)

THE CONTESTED PARTERRE

Public Theater and French Political Culture, 1680–1791

JEFFREY S. RAVEL

CORNELL UNIVERSITY PRESS

Ithaca and London

First published 1999 by Cornell University Press.

First printing, Cornell Paperbacks, 1999.

Printed in the United States of America.

Library of Congress Cataloging-in-Publication Data

Ravel, Jeffrey S.
    The contested parterre : public theater and French political
culture, 1680–1791 / Jeffrey S. Ravel.
       p.   cm.
    Includes bibliographical references and index.
    ISBN 0-8014-3544-7 (cloth : alk. paper). — ISBN 0-8014-8541-X
(paper : alk. paper)
      1. Theater—France—Paris—History—18th century. 2. Theater-
-France—Paris—History—17th century. 3. Theater audiences-
-France—Paris. I. Title.
PN2636.P3R28 1999
792'.09443'61—dc21   99-10072
                                                            CIP

Cornell University Press strives to use environmentally responsible suppliers and materials to the fullest extent possible in the publishing of its books. Such materials include vegetable-based, low-VOC inks and acid-free papers that are recycled, totally chlorine-free, or partly composed of nonwood fibers.

Cloth printing   10 9 8 7 6 5 4 3 2 1
Paperback printing   10 9 8 7 6 5 4 3 2 1

Contents

Illustrations

Acknowledgments

It is a pleasure to acknowledge the rich network of mentors, colleagues, friends, and institutions that has made this book possible. Lynn Hunt directed the dissertation version of this project with characteristic incisiveness, promptness, and good cheer; her confidence in my work since the doctorate has been invaluable. Randolph and Frances Starn have provided food, shelter, wise counsel, and a *cassone*, each at the appropriate moment. Two communities of astute readers, Susanna Barrows' 1990–91 dissertation group and the 1996 Newberry Library Fellows, offered criticism on significant portions of this manuscript. In France, my *remerciements* begin with Roger Chartier, who has graciously assisted an entire generation of American students of French history. Arlette Farge, Christian Jouhaud, Jacques Revel, and Martine de Rougemont also gave me the benefit of their knowledge of French history, French theater, and the French archives. Fabienne Queyroux swiftly and expertly responded to every cry for archival help I made from this side of the Atlantic. In the United States, Dena Goodman, Gregory Brown, and two anonymous university press readers offered excellent comments on the penultimate draft of the book. Other colleagues who provided encouragement and advice include Adrianna Bakos, David A. Bell, Daniel Borus, Alice Conklin, Paula Findlen, Paul Friedland, Daniel Gordon, Lisa Graham, Basil Guy, Carla Hesse, Jeff Horn, James Johnson, Steven Kaplan, Wendy Kozol, Sheryl Kroen, Laura Mason, Sarah Maza, Anne McCants, Brendan McConville, Jeffrey Merrick, Len Smith, Ken Straus, Regina Sweeney, Charles Walton, William Weber, and Abby Zanger.

I worked in a number of libraries and archives to prepare this study. My greatest debt is to Mme Muzarelle and the staff at the Bibliothèque de l'Arsenal, who met my demands to look at endless boxes of Bastille documents with professionalism and good humor. The librarians, archivists, and staff members at the following institutions all assisted me in my forays into Parisian repositories: the Archives Nationales, the Bibliothèque Nationale, the Service Historique des Armées de la Terre, and the Bibliothèque Historique de la Ville de Paris.

A fellowship from the American Council of Learned Societies and a National Endowment for the Humanities (NEH) Newberry Library Fellowship, both received in the academic year 1995–96, allowed me to revise this study. Grants from the Dean of the Humanities and Social Sciences and the Kelly-Douglas Fund at the Massachusetts Institute of Technology facilitated publication of the book. At earlier stages of this project I received generous financial assistance from the following sources: the Doreen B. Townsend Center for the Humanities at the University of California, Berkeley; the California Alpha chapter of Phi Beta Kappa; the Hans Rosenberg Fellowship Trust Fund and the Heller Grant-in-Aid Fund, both of which are administered by the Berkeley History department; the Graduate Division at Berkeley; the Josephine de Kármán Fellowship Trust Fund; the Ministère des Services Culturelles de l'Embassade de France, which administers the Bourses Chateaubriand; the American Historical Association, which provided a Bernadotte E. Schmidt Travel Grant; and the NEH, which awarded me a Summer Research Grant.

I save my most important thanks for last. Two long-time teachers and friends, Bill Weatherford and Pierrette Spetz, first inspired my interest in the theater and in France. My parents, Frances and Ira Ravel, and my brother, Bruce, have supported without qualification all that I have done, and left undone. Gabriel Ravel, a newcomer to my ruminations on performance, has taught me a great deal about acting and audiences in four short years. I dedicate *The Contested Parterre* to Cristelle Baskins, my best editor, my parenting partner, and my perpetual muse.

J.S.R.

Cambridge, Massachusetts

Abbreviations

AD	Abbé Jean-Barthélemy de la Porte and Jean-Marie-Bernard Clément. *Anecdotes dramatiques*. 3 vols. Paris: Veuve Duchesne, 1775.
ADML	Archives départementales de Maine-et Loire
AHR	*American Historical Review*
AMB	Archives municipales de Bordeaux
AN	Archives Nationales, Paris
BA	Bibliothèque de l'Arsenal, Paris
BN	Bibliothèque Nationale de France, Paris
CL	Friedrich Melchior Grimm et al. *Correspondance littéraire, philosophique et critique*. 16 vols. Paris: Garnier frères, 1877–82.
CS	François Métra et al. *Correspondance secrète, politique et littéraire, ou mémoires pour servir à l'histoire des cours, des sociétés, et de la littérature en France, depuis la mort de Louis XV*. 12 vols. London: John Adamson, 1787–88.
ECS	*Eighteenth-Century Studies*
FHS	*French Historical Studies*
JMH	*Journal of Modern History*
MF	*Mercure de France*
MS	Louis Petit de Bachaumont et al. *Mémoires secrets pour servir à l'histoire de la république des lettres en France*. 36 vols. London: Adamson, 1777–89.
RHMC	*Revue d'histoire moderne et contemporaine*
SHAT	Service Historique des Armées de la Terre, Chateau de Vincennes
SVEC	*Studies on Voltaire and the Eighteenth Century*

THE CONTESTED PARTERRE

The theaters of aristocratic nations have always been filled with spectators not belonging to the aristocracy. At the theater alone the higher ranks mix with the middle and lower classes; there alone do the former consent to listen to the opinion of the latter, or at least to allow them to give an opinion at all. At the theater, men of cultivation and of literary attainments have always had more difficulty than elsewhere in making their taste prevail over that of the people, and in preventing themselves from being carried away by the latter. The parterre has frequently made laws for the loges.

—Alexis de Tocqueville,
Democracy in America

Introduction:
Political Culture,
Print, and Performance

Writing in the 1830s, only two generations removed from the fall of the absolutist monarchy, Tocqueville had in mind a critical point: the public theaters of the Old Regime were not simply an extension of the court at Versailles. The durable image of the Sun King's performances of power, first formulated by Louis's own propagandists and then reinscribed in the memoirs of the Duc de Saint-Simon and subsequent commentators, has tended to obscure other prerevolutionary configurations of theater and politics. Louis himself staged these rituals of absolutist power from the first festive cycles celebrated at the royal chateau in the 1660s and 1670s down to his death in 1715. In spite of the reluctance of his less theatrically flamboyant successors, the many set pieces in which the French King represented his power to quiescent courtiers and subjects continued until the Revolution at the end of the century. Only 1789 and its aftermath, it is commonly thought, with its revolutionary *journées* and civic festivals, broke the Bourbon stranglehold on the official theatrics of power. Since then, French regimes have continued to rely on theatrical formulae to legitimize their use of power, as Marx suggested when he labeled the 1799 coup d'état of Napoleon Bonaparte a tragedy and the 1851 coup of Napoleon III a farce. But these performances have used props and scripts different from those used at Versailles; most significantly, they have often claimed to blur the distinction between performers and observers on which the legitimacy of the Sun King rested. The huge bicentennial Bastille Day parade, for example, commissioned by the Mitterand government and designed by an advertising guru, depended on modern technology to carry its inclusive message of liberty, equality, and universal solidarity to every corner of the globe.[1]

---

[1] See the account in Steven L. Kaplan, *Farewell Revolution: Disputed Legacies* (Ithaca, 1995), 270–330.

1

The absolutist theater of Versailles has in recent years renewed its "run" in the writings of historians interested in the passage from monarchical assumptions to republican experiments in late eighteenth-century France. This movement, understood until a generation ago as the product of Marxist class struggle, is today often explained as the outcome of changes in French "political culture." Historians have broadly defined this term to include not only printed debates about increasingly politicized topics, but also visual images, rhetorical practices, and collective symbolic actions with more or less explicitly political content.[2] Cultural historians such as Joan Landes, Sarah Maza, and Roger Chartier have led the way in forging a particularly suggestive account of these transformations; their narratives originate in the theatrical politics of Louis XIV's Versailles. Landes, for example, in her classic account of gender and politics in the age of the French Revolution, characterizes the court as "a vast visual and theatrical spectacle, a machinery whose royal retinue functioned to authorize the king's superior and indivisible power. Like a god, the monarch was memorialized and imaged in ceremonial court practices." The rise of a new "print order" throughout the eighteenth century, however, particularly as embedded in the works of Jean-Jacques Rousseau, led to "an implicit opposition between the old and new forms of representation, that is, . . . between the iconic spectacularity of the Old Regime and the textual and legal order of the bourgeois public sphere."[3] Maza, in her influential analysis of Parisian trial briefs in the final two decades of the Old Regime, builds on Landes' schema by focusing specifically on the world of law. For her, the central transformation in French political culture at the end of the eighteenth century is that from a playhouse metaphor to a courtroom one: "In the old symbolic order, the spotlight was on the stage, on the theatrical display of power at the core of which was the sacred body of the king; in the new, the focus was on the public [that read legal briefs], which was both the ultimate repository of power and that which needed to be taught, convinced, controlled."[4] And Chartier, in his synthetic discussion of the cultural origins of the Revolution, also relies on the spectacle of Versailles to represent the vision of political culture

---

[2] Revisionists and postrevisionists, however, have not readily agreed on a definition of political culture. See, for example, the definition given by Keith Baker in his introduction to *The French Revolution and the Creation of Modern Political Culture*, vol. 1, *The Political Culture of the Old Regime* (Oxford, 1986), xi–xiii; and the review of this volume, by Sarah Maza, "Politics, Culture, and the Origins of the French Revolution," *JMH* 61 (December 1989): 704–23.

[3] Joan Landes, *Women and the Public Sphere in the Age of the French Revolution* (Ithaca, 1988), 18, 67.

[4] Sarah Maza, *Private Lives and Public Affairs: The Causes Célèbres of Prerevolutionary France* (Berkeley, 1993), 314.

discarded by the revolutionaries: "In the age of 'baroque' politics the traits that defined the public were the same as those that typified the theater public: heterogeneous, hierarchized, and formed into a public only by the spectacle they were given to see and believe." In contrast, he argues, the "new political culture" that made the Revolution possible was one in which the passive spectators of the baroque theater had been replaced by an active, participatory public of readers and thinkers.[5]

Each of these historians makes a compelling case for the revolutionary passage from theatricality to textuality, from effeminate passivity to masculine aggression, from the overwhelming splendor of court spectacle to the persuasive capacity of reasoned argument. They argue that spectators wanted to participate in the performance of politics. When the Revolution granted these wishes to some of the King's former subjects in the form of elections, written constitutions, and representative political institutions, it acknowledged this shift in French political culture; the theatrical metaphor had ceased to describe the politics of the new regime. Power was no longer performed before a passive audience, as it was at Versailles; it was now rendered abstract and textual, susceptible to endless revision and reappropriation by attentive readers. Politics became a masculinized editorial exercise, which left behind the spontaneities and imperfections of the effeminate stage.

Those familiar with current trends in eighteenth-century studies will already have recognized the theoretical presence of Jürgen Habermas in the work of the scholars just described. In *The Structural Transformation of the Public Sphere*, first published in German in 1962 and issued in English translation in 1989, Habermas argued that eighteenth-century western Europe was distinguished by the emergence of a "bourgeois," or "authentic" public sphere in which individuals suppressed their private interests and motivations to debate issues of public concern in a critical, rational fashion.[6] This new public sphere, according to Habermas, superseded the older, "representative" public sphere in which monarchs represented their unchallenged sovereignty to docile subjects. Although eighteenth-century specialists have certainly profited from Habermas's insights, they have also

---

[5] Roger Chartier, *The Cultural Origins of the French Revolution*, trans. Lydia G. Cochrane (Durham, 1991), 33.

[6] Jürgen Habermas, *The Structural Transformation of the Public Sphere*, trans. Thomas Burger and Frederick Lawrence (Cambridge, MA, 1989). For provocative summaries of Habermas's impact on eighteenth-century studies, see Dena Goodman, "Public Sphere and Private Life: Toward a Synthesis of Current Historiographical Approaches to the Old Regime," *History and Theory* 31 (1992): 1–20; Anthony La Vopa, "Conceiving a Public: Ideas and Society in Eighteenth-Century Europe," *JMH* 64 (March 1992): 79–116; and Margaret C. Jacob, "The Mental Landscape of the Public Sphere: A European Perspective," *ECS* 28 (Fall 1994): 95–113.

registered discontent with various aspects of his synthesis.[7] In the case of eighteenth-century France, some historians have proposed a chronology that situates the political emergence of "public opinion," formulated in the "public sphere," in the 1750s.[8] From this decade down to the Revolution, these scholars argue, public opinion replaced the will of the King as the source of sovereign political authority within the French kingdom; royal ministers, Jansenist magistrates, and enlightened philosophes alike had to plead their cases before the tribunal of public opinion. This narrative of French public opinion at the end of the eighteenth century, which offers a subtle analysis of Old Regime political culture in its final throes, is the major contribution since the mid-1980s to our understanding of the origins of the French Revolution.[9]

An argument that advances the "reign of public opinion" in France after 1750, however, begs other historiographical questions important to the study of eighteenth-century France and Europe as a whole. As it has been characterized, French public opinion after 1750 was primarily a print affair; it was formulated, we are told, in the disembodied world of author-ial intentions, typographical conventions, and readerly inventions. Occa-sionally, in institutions such as the salon, the academy, or the Masonic lodge, the public sphere in which opinions were formed became tangible. But the rules of sociability that governed such gatherings worked to mini-mize conflict; what Chartier has elsewhere called "the order of books" extended itself into these gatherings of the *literati* and their followers.[10]

---

[7] For class-based criticism of Habermas, see Arlette Farge, *Subversive Words: Public Opinion in Eighteenth-Century France*, trans. Rosemary Morris (University Park, PA, 1995). On the gendering of the public sphere (absent from Habermas's 1962 essay), in addition to Landes, see Keith Michael Baker, "Defining the Public Sphere in Eighteenth-Century France: Variations on a Theme by Habermas" in *Habermas and the Public Sphere,* ed. Craig Calhoun, (Cambridge, MA, 1992), 181–211; Daniel Gordon, "Philosophy, Sociology, and Gender in the Enlighten-ment Conception of the Public Sphere," *FHS* 17 (Fall 1992): 882–911; Sarah Maza, "Women, the Bourgeoisie, and the Public Sphere: Response to Daniel Gordon and David Bell," ibid., 935–50; and Gordon's response, ibid., 951–53; and Elizabeth C. Goldsmith and Dena Good-man, eds., *Going Public: Women and Publishing in Early Modern France* (Ithaca, 1995).

[8] Mona Ozouf, "'Public Opinion' at the End of the Old Régime," *JMH* 60, suppl. (Septem-ber 1988): S1–S21; Ozouf, "Public Spirit," in *A Critical Dictionary of the French Revolu-tion,* ed. François Furet and Mona Ozouf (Cambridge, MA, 1989), 771–80; Keith Baker, "Public Opinion as Political Invention," in *Inventing the French Revolution: Essays on French Political Culture in the Eighteenth Century* (Cambridge, 1990), 167–99.

[9] In addition to the works already cited, see David A. Bell, *Lawyers and Citizens: The Making of a Political Elite in Old Regime France* (New York, 1994); Dena Goodman, *The Republic of Let-ters: A Cultural History of the French Enlightenment* (Ithaca, 1994); and Daniel Gordon, *Citizens without Sovereignty: Equality and Sociability in French Thought, 1670–1789* (Princeton, 1994); one might list many other useful studies. For a review of some of this work, see Dale K. van Kley, "In Search of Eighteenth-Century Parisian Public Opinion," *FHS* 19 (Spring 1995): 215–26.

[10] Roger Chartier, *The Order of Books*, trans. Lydia Cochrane (Stanford, 1994).

Two problems exist with this construction of public opinion for those who wish to understand not only the roots of 1789, but politics and culture in France throughout the eighteenth century. First, as a variety of scholars have noted, appeals to a "public," if not to a "public opinion" that foreshadows a Rousseauian General Will enshrined in the Terror, appeared in Paris and the provinces well before 1750.[11] The existence of these "publics," many of them independent of the court and the person of the King, suggests that an "authentic public sphere" functioned in some fashion before 1750, and that it shaped the subsequent formation of public opinion in the final decades of the Old Regime. Second, and more critical, is the need to distinguish between print constructions and the material world. On the one hand, as Habermasian-influenced scholars have demonstrated, the useful fiction of an authentic public sphere in which enlightened, yet disinterested, individuals rationally discussed affairs of public interest was an eighteenth-century creation. On the other hand, in the eighteenth century just as in the twentieth, it was exceedingly difficult in any materially precise sense to locate the "public" that constituted spheres and rendered opinions. This problem should not permit us, however, to abandon all scrutiny of the experiential world in favor of uniquely discursive conceptions of the public; Habermas himself drew attention to the physical meeting spaces of the eighteenth-century public, including salons, art exhibits, concert halls, and public theaters.[12]

In light of these objections, one might reasonably return to the initial question: Did French political culture shift from theatrical metaphors to editorial ones during the eighteenth century? Landes, Maza, and Chartier, citing their own work as well as that of Robert Darnton and others, are right to point to the incredible expansion in print material and the significant rise in literacy rates during the eighteenth century; surely these factors were responsible for the new emphasis on the textual and the judicial in French political culture toward the end of the eighteenth century. But theater and the theatrical metaphor also increased in importance as the century progressed. In the cap-

---

[11] Jeffrey Sawyer, *Printed Poison: Pamphlet Propaganda, Faction Politics, and the Public Sphere in Early Seventeenth-Century France* (Berkeley, 1990), argues for the importance of a public sphere in the period immediately before the rise of Richelieu. Other books concerned with a seventeenth-century public sphere are Alain Viala, *Naissance de l'écrivain: Sociologie de la littérature à l'âge classique* (Paris, 1985); Michèle Fogel, *Les Cérémonies de l'information dans la France du XVIe au XVIIIe siècles* (Paris, 1989); and Hélène Merlin, *Public et littérature en France au XVIIe siècle* (Paris, 1994). Farge, *Subversive Words,* discusses "public opinion" as it was formulated by the *menu peuple* of Paris and recorded by police spies as early as the 1660s. Bell, *Lawyers and Citizens,* 67–104, suggests that by the 1730s Parisian barristers were already exploiting the political possibilities of the public sphere in their religious and constitutional struggles.

[12] Habermas, *Structural Transformation,* 31–43.

ital, public theatrical venues expanded from three at midcentury to seven by 1789; in the provinces, twenty-seven towns constructed new public theaters between 1750 and the outbreak of the Revolution.[13] Many more individuals in Paris and the provinces built theaters in their private residences during this period, following the lead of Louis XV, who approved the construction of an opulent indoor opera house at Versailles, an expense his seventeenth-century predecessor had not undertaken.[14] Theatrical publishing statistics reinforce the evidence for the spread of theater mania in France in the decades before the Revolution: approximately three thousand works, or half of the French-language plays written and published from 1610 to 1789, first appeared in print between 1760 and 1789.[15] Only a fraction of these were intended for the public stages of Paris and the provinces; the remainder were meant for private performance. French interest in books, periodicals, judicial briefs, "forbidden bestsellers," and many other forms of print production was an outstanding feature of French political culture in 1789, but the passion for live theater was also strong at the end of the Old Regime.

The ongoing popularity of theater and the theatrical metaphor in French political culture suggests the need to rethink the understanding of the transformations in French political culture in the eighteenth century. Live theater combines the discursive and the performative aspects of political cultures; playwrights require bodies, voices, movement, and gestures to animate their ideas, and eighteenth-century audiences responded to performance in a vivid, often visceral fashion. These performances, staged nightly in Parisian playhouses in the eighteenth century, have much to teach about theatrical concerns in the period, to be sure. But they also provide insight into aspects of French political culture that the current concern with texts and readers has obscured. An important performative aspect to political and cultural negotiations existed in the eighteenth century, as Arlette Farge and others have reminded us.[16] The King's subjects expressed discontent with the

---

[13] On the Parisian public theaters, see Martine de Rougemont, *La Vie théâtrale en France au XVIIIe siècle* (Paris, 1988), 235–78; and Michèle Root-Bernstein, *Boulevard Theater and Revolution in Eighteenth-Century Paris* (Ann Arbor, 1984), 13–39. On theatrical construction in the provinces, see Max Fuchs, *La Vie théâtrale en province au XVIIIe siècle* (Geneva, 1933).

[14] On private theaters in the eighteenth century, a relatively unknown topic outside the court and the upper aristocracy, see the suggestive chapter in Rougemont, *Vie théâtrale*, 297–314.

[15] I base these figures on calculations derived from Jacques Scherer, *La Dramaturgie classique en France* (Paris, 1959), 457–59; and Clarence D. Brenner, *A Bibliographical List of Plays in the French Language, 1700–1789* (Berkeley, 1947), *passim*.

[16] Arlette Farge, *Fragile Lives: Violence, Power, and Solidarity in Eighteenth-Century Paris*, trans. Carol Shelton (Cambridge, MA, 1993), 1–6; Lisa Jane Graham, "Crimes of Opinion: Policing the Public in Eighteenth-Century Paris," in *Visions and Revisions of Eighteenth-Century France*, eds. Christine Adams et al. (University Park, PA, 1997), 79–84.

monarchy through their cries, gestures, and collective actions; and the Crown, through its network of spies and other policing agents, paid close attention to what these dissatisfied individuals said and did.

The public theaters of Paris are central to a fully integrated study of eighteenth-century French political culture because they combine, in the same space, the rituals and concerns of the court, the ideas of philosophes and others, and the everyday actions of Parisians. The workings of these playhouses have been difficult to analyze, however, because they are not easily studied outside the theoretical writings of Rousseau, Diderot, and their interlocutors or beyond the realm of the printed word. In other words, how does one write a history of theater audience behavior, a notoriously ephemeral subject? And how does one use that behavior to interpret a political culture? I address these questions here by studying the activity of theater spectators who stood in the parterres, or pits, of the three privileged Parisian public theaters, the Comédie-Française, the Comédie-Italienne, and the Opera, from 1680 to 1791. In the chapters that follow, I analyze police archives, memoirs, periodicals, and other sources to get at the difficult problem of spectator behavior.

Beyond questions of historical reconstruction, though, some readers may wonder why one would look at audiences in privileged theaters to address the question of anti-absolutist tendencies in French political culture. Might not the marginal fair theaters and the boulevard playhouses, where the King and the court did not control the content of the plays or the personnel of the troupes, prove more likely candidates for a study of the politicization of eighteenth-century French theater? Although these sites are not without political importance, I argue that the privileged theaters, because they attracted significant financial and administrative commitments from the monarchy, were more important to the form and content of eighteenth-century French political culture.[17] In the last third of the seventeenth century, Louis XIV had designated three troupes as the sole producers of opera, French-language plays, and Italian-language plays at court and in the public playhouses of the capital. The royal decrees establishing the Académie royale de musique (the Opera), the Comédie-Française, and the Comédie-Italienne specified that the goal of their monopolies was to perfect the representation of the lyric and dramatic arts for the greater glory of the French state. In practice, this desire led to productions that implicitly, and at times quite explicitly, emphasized

[17] On the marginal theaters, in addition to Root-Bernstein, see Robert Isherwood, *Farce and Fantasy: Popular Entertainment in Eighteenth-Century Paris* (Oxford, 1986).

the power and magnificence of the Bourbon monarchy; when the Comédie-Italienne began to deviate from this goal at the end of the seventeenth century by presenting plays filled with scatological humor that mocked figures at court, the Crown revoked its privilege and exiled its performers from the capital.

Contemporary accounts and subsequent historical analysis of the eighteenth century have usually stressed the extent to which these theaters perpetuated the rituals of absolutist theater as practiced at Versailles.[18] Supposedly, the crowds in the theaters were primarily wealthy members of the nobility or the upper middle classes, as Choderlos de Laclos suggested in the climactic scene of *Les Liaisons dangéreuses* in which an audience of her peers jeered the Marquise de Merteuil out of the theater and, implicitly, *le monde.* The performances they enjoyed, until the time of Figaro on the eve of the Revolution, staged variations on stories that had entertained French and European elites since the classical revival of the fourteenth and fifteenth centuries. And these elites interacted with each other according to norms of courtly comportment, as James H. Johnson argued in his study of musical audiences.[19] There would seem to be little, at first glance, that authorizes one to proclaim these theaters as sites of opposition to the Crown.

Beyond the world of the wings and the loges, however, where elites mingled with the celebrated performers of these public spectacles, was a second theatrical milieu, one that was not an extension of the court at Versailles. For the privileged theaters of Paris also counted on the socially heterogeneous male spectators who crowded into the parterre, or pit, area of the theaters to supply between one-half to two-thirds of their audience on any given night. The strategy of representing royal majesty to quiescent courtiers at Versailles worked relatively well under Louis XIV and was continued under his eighteenth-century successors. But the affective constraints that bound courtiers at Versailles did not apply in the parterres of the capital, where curious theatergoers could purchase admission for twenty *sous,* or approximately a day's wages for a laborer.[20] Spectators seated in the

---

[18] See John Lough, *Paris Theatre Audiences in the Seventeenth and Eighteenth Centuries* (London, 1957); and Henri Lagrave, *Le Théâtre et le public à Paris de 1715 à 1750* (Paris, 1972).
[19] Choderlos de Laclos, *Les Liaisons dangéreuses* (Paris, 1784); Henry Carrington Lancaster, *The Comédie-Française, 1680–1701: Plays, Actors, Spectators, Finances* (Baltimore, 1941); Lancaster, *The Comédie-Française, 1701–1774: Plays, Actors, Spectators, Finances* (Philadelphia, 1951); Brenner, *The Théâtre Italien. Its Repertory, 1716–1793* (Berkeley, 1961); James H. Johnson, *Listening in Paris: A Cultural History* (Berkeley, 1995). On Opera audiences, see also William Weber, "L'Institution et son public. L'Opéra à Paris et à Londres au XVIIIe siècle," *Annales ESC* 48 (November–Dember 1993): 1519–39.
[20] On court etiquette, see Norbert Elias, *The Court Society,* trans. Edmund Jephcott (New York, 1983); and the interesting critique of Elias in Gordon, *Citizens without Sovereignty,* 88–94.

more expensive seats in the loges or on the stage often did follow the rules of courtly etiquette articulated at Versailles, but parterre denizens, always the majority of spectators, felt little compulsion to follow suit. The result was that the King's Players *(les comédiens du roi)* performed before raucous, interventionist crowds of parterre spectators who had little use for courtly *politesse*. Their refusal to bear quiet testimony to the spectacle staged before them implied, at the very least, a healthy disrespect for the ceremonials of absolutism in which the privileged troupes figured prominently at court. In the eighteenth century, observers sympathetic to the behavior of parterre spectators and hostile to the tenants of French absolutism took these implications further, attributing "frondeur," "patriotic," and "republican" sentiments to the actions of parterre audience members. The theater, and the parterre in general, provided fodder for those who wished to imagine alternatives to absolutist culture.

The disorderliness of parterre spectators was a problem that exercised government officials and theatrical reformers outside the state's bureaucracy for more than a century before the Revolution. The King and his ministers turned first to the Parisian police force and later to royal soldiers stationed in the Paris garrison to contain the parterre. By the second half of the eighteenth century, some philosophes, playwrights, and other advocates of material and moral progress also actively sought to tame the disruptive parterre; they envisioned the kingdom's public theaters as schools of civic virtue that would contribute to the education of the populace and the betterment of the nation. These individuals argued for the installation of benches in the open area of the parterre, a development that they believed would fix the attention of the men in the pit on the didactic spectacle staged before them. Thus, both absolutist bureaucrats and enlightened reformers attempted to bend the will of disorderly parterre spectators to their own political and cultural agendas. The space of the parterre became a contested terrain where issues basic to French political culture in the seventeenth and eighteenth centuries came into play. The disciplinary efforts of the government and of certain philosophes evoked responses from parterre spectators and other observers that called into question the legitimacy of absolutist authority and enlightened notions of progress; parterre defenders argued that incursions from either camp impinged on the liberties a paying spectator at the theater naturally enjoyed. By the end of the Old Regime, contentious debates over the parterre, and large-scale, violent riots within its confines, revealed some of the limitations of an absolutist political culture that had incorporated many aspects of Enlightenment thought without according political liberty to the King's subjects.

The privileged theaters, therefore, provide an outstanding location for the study of conflict within the political culture of eighteenth-century

France. The theatricalized etiquette of Versailles existed paradoxically alongside a form of spectatorship that insisted on its noisy, raucous right to intervene in the spectacle of French theater, and, implicitly, of French politics. The walls of the Comédie-Française, the Comédie-Italienne, and the Opera housed these contradictory visions of French political culture; each night, a spectacle based on absolutist assumptions took place before an audience that insisted on its right to intervene in the proceedings.

This book, then, offers a history of the parterres in the privileged playhouses of seventeenth- and eighteenth-century Paris.[21] The word "parterre" has two meanings in this study. In its literal sense, it refers to the open space on the ground floor of these theaters where male spectators stood to watch dramatic performances. The other sense of the term refers to the group of men who stood in the space of the parterre as spectators. Old Regime observers endowed this collective entity with agency: the parterre misbehaved, it caused a play to fail, it adored a certain actress. It is this second, more contested, meaning that animates the argument of the book, for attempts to collapse the socially heterogeneous male spectators who stood in the parterre into a univocal entity influenced, and were influenced by, efforts to redefine French political sovereignty in terms of the nation.

The first chapter offers a synchronic view of parterre spectators' practices in the eighteenth century. It follows these theatergoers from the time they left their homes or workplaces in the late afternoon to attend the theater until their return home after the play, but it concentrates particularly on their behavior in the theater during performance. In so doing, it presents the case for the audiences' engagement with the spectacle staged before them in terms of eighteenth-century expectations. These theatergoers did not sit quietly and appreciatively during the performance as we do today; neither did they ignore the spectacle. Instead, they used cries and gestures to intervene in a frequently decisive manner.

The remaining five chapters provide a diachronic perspective on the history of the parterre from Louis XIV to the Revolution. Chapter 2 looks at the origins of the contested parterre in the reigns of Louis XIII and Louis XIV. Chapter 3 studies the crucial juncture (1680–1725) when parterre spectators, for a number of commercial and institutional reasons, found their critical voices in the theater; it also details the way in which contemporary observers from the police to playwrights acknowledged the growing potency of the parterre. The state's decision to police the parterres of

---

[21] For an earlier study of the parterre, uncritical of its sources but emphatic about the political overtones of the pit, see Aristide Prat, "Le Parterre au XVIIIe siècle," *La Quinzaine* 68 (February 1906): 388–412.

the privileged theaters, the subject of chapter 4, attested to the concern generated among the King and his ministers by developments in the public theater after the founding of the Comédie-Française in 1680. By the mid-eighteenth century, however, the policing system created under Louis XIV no longer met the perceived challenges of the parterre. A new policing system, detailed in chapter 5, staffed by soldiers stationed at the royal garrison in Paris, began to operate in the theaters. The new system, however, exacerbated conflict between spectators and local and royal policing agents in the final decades of the Old Regime, indicating that neither absolutist nor enlightened policies were adequate to deal with the political and aesthetic demands of parterre spectators by the time of the Revolution. Although these developments generated new tensions in the playhouses after 1750, other observers began to conceive of the parterre as representative of larger, more politicized notions such as the "public" or the "nation." I study this trend in the final chapter through a careful consideration of theatrical anecdotes and the debate regarding the installation of benches in the parterres. Revolutionary legislators acknowledged the political, social, and educational importance of the theater in January 1791, when they passed laws that dismantled the theatrical Old Regime created by the Bourbon monarchy.

"The parterre has frequently made laws for the loges." Tocqueville's dictum should be read on at least two levels: both as a statement about the theater and as a statement about politics. As a theater historian, Tocqueville refused to be taken in by the claims of philosophes and others who argued for theater's didactic potential. He recognized that in the theater the will of the majority triumphed and that neither the aristocracy nor the intelligentsia could foist their agendas on an independent, theatergoing public. As a political theorist writing in the 1830s, Tocqueville also saw the parterre as a metaphor for the masses whom he thought would inevitably achieve political ascendancy. Tocqueville was neither the first nor the last to convert the heterogeneous group of men who gathered in Paris's eighteenth-century parterres into a symbol of some larger social or political idea: the crowd, the public, the nation. In the chapters that follow, I oscillate between imposing my own agenda on the men who gathered in the pit and bearing witness to their spontaneity and exuberance within the playhouse, an experience lost to twentieth-century theatergoers. In this sense, I can do no better than contemporary observers of the parterre, who chastised it, applauded it, avoided it, and tried to seat it, but who could never entirely circumscribe it within the regime of the printed word.

1

Parterre Practices in Eighteenth-Century Paris

—"Well, Fleury," cried the Chevalier Richard after his tale, "do you understand your parterre now? Did you follow the progression? Did I fill in all the blanks?"

—"Perfectly," I told him.

—"Now isn't it true," he began with his comic enthusiasm, "that you have seen those people applaud you and torment you, cry 'Bravo' and destroy your playhouse? Tell me, isn't the history of the parterre to be found in the streets?"

—*Mémoires de Fleury*

Social Composition

Observers in the eighteenth century and after have often associated the world of the three privileged theaters, the Comédie-Française, the Comédie-Italienne, and the Académie royale de musique, or the Opera, with the court at Versailles. Each theater maintained boxes for the sovereign and his family members, whose entries invariably halted any performance. Other important functional and ceremonial members of the court aristocracy leased boxes at the privileged playhouses in which they frequently appeared. In these semi-private loges, often furnished by their annual occupants and equipped with screens to offer their inhabitants relief from the roving lorgnettes of the parterre and other loges, courtly rules of social intercourse applied. The wings of these stages, as well as the foyers and balconies of the theaters, sheltered discussions of affairs of state alongside the amorous intrigues that entertained Old Regime elites and their would-be imitators among the middling classes.[1]

Yet it would be historically inaccurate and needlessly impoverishing to characterize the privileged public playhouses of Paris solely as extensions of

[1] Lagrave, *Le Théâtre et le public*, 207–13, 220–21, 499–512; Johnson, *Listening in Paris*, 9–17, 30–34.

13

the Bourbon court. These three theaters, in each of their eighteenth-century locations, were also enmeshed in the densely populated, rapidly metamorphosing neighborhoods of the eighteenth-century capital.[2] They consistently drew their audiences from all sectors of the city's population, save perhaps the manual laborers, whose wages and work schedules usually prohibited them from attending the theater. By the time the curtain rose on a performance at five in the afternoon, tax farmers, students, propertied women, shopkeepers, magistrates, clerks, prostitutes, intellectuals, and many others had gathered in the playhouses. And each night, more than half of this assembly crowded into the parterre, a rectangular open space on the ground floor of the theater in which one stood for three to four hours to watch the evening's performance.[3] The numerical majority of parterre spectators corresponded to their critical predominance; from the beginning of the century to its revolutionary end, playwrights and performers knew that they would be judged, in the final resort, by the spectators who jostled each other for elbow room on a nightly basis in the pit.

The first question one might ask about the eighteenth-century parterre, therefore, is who stood there? However, it is no easy task to determine the social composition of audiences that gathered two to three centuries ago. Records, imprecise to begin with, have partially disappeared; current social categories do not correspond to eighteenth-century distinctions; and the number of theater admissions over the course of the century is in the millions. Given these overwhelming limitations, the French theater historian Henri Lagrave has offered the most complete, nuanced discussion of the social identity of public theater audiences in all areas of the eighteenth-century playhouse.[4] His work, based on careful

---

[2] Pioneering work in the social history of eighteenth-century Paris by Georges Rudé, Richard Cobb, and Jeffrey Kaplow has been followed more recently by Daniel Roche, *The People of Paris: An Essay in Popular Culture in the Eighteenth Century*, trans. Marie Evans (Berkeley, 1987); Annik Pardailhé-Galabrun, *The Birth of Intimacy: Privacy and Domestic Life in Early Modern Paris*, trans. Jocelyn Phelps (Philadelphia, 1991); David Garrioch, *Neighbourhood and Community in Paris, 1740–1790* (Cambridge, 1986); Thomas Brennan, *Public Drinking and Popular Culture in Eighteenth-Century Paris* (Princeton, 1988); Farge, *Fragile Lives*; Farge, *Subversive Words*; Farge and Jacques Revel, *The Vanishing Children of Paris: Rumor and Politics before the French Revolution*, trans. Claudia Miéville (Cambridge, MA, 1991); and Lisa Jane Graham, *If the King Only Knew: On the Margins of Absolutism in Eighteenth-Century France* (Charlottesville, VA, forthcoming).

[3] Lancaster, *The Comédie-Française, 1680–1701*, 17–18; Lagrave, *Le Théâtre et le public*, 245–46; Guy Bosquet, "La Comèdie-Italienne sous la régence: Arlequin poli par Paris (1716–1725)," *RHMC* 24 (April–June 1977), 196–97.

[4] Lagrave, *Le Théâtre et le public*, 207–58. Although Lagrave's work is limited to the first thirty-five years of the reign of Louis XV, much of what he says holds true for the rest of the reign, as well as for the last fifteen years of the reign of Louis XIV. Lough, *Paris Theater Audiences*, deals exclusively with the Comédie-Française.

consideration of descriptions of theater crowds left behind in a variety of
sources, posits a two-tiered audience. One level of this audience, which
Lagrave calls *le public riche*, consisted primarily of men and women of
noble origin, military officers, pages, *petits-maîtres*, priests, men of law,
financiers, provincials, and foreigners. Because of their financial standing and daily schedules, Lagrave suggests that these spectators were unre-
stricted in their theater attendance.[5] The other tier of this theatergoing
public, *le public populaire*, faced financial and temporal restrictions on
their theater attendance. The cheapest tickets at the Comédie-Française
and the Comédie-Italienne, those offering admission to the parterre,
often cost the equivalent of a day's wages for most manual laborers.[6] Furthermore, the five o'clock curtain time traditionally observed in the privileged theaters meant that many workers and *petit bourgeois* could only
attend the theater on Sundays or on one of the dozens of Church holidays
scattered throughout the calendar. Given these constraints, however,
Lagrave still demonstrates the presence of merchants, artisans, shop-
keeper's assistants, apprentices, low-level bureaucrats and Old Regime
paper pushers, and students and intellectuals in the privileged theater
audience.

He qualifies their attendance at the theater, however, by arguing for the
existence of a *public du dimanche*, which was more "popular" than that
which attended the theater on other days. Box office receipts show that the
percentage of total paying spectators who bought parterre tickets was on
average 5 to 10 percent higher on Sundays than on other days of the week,[7]
and that the second loges, the preferred seating of the *petit bourgeois* and
his family, were more crowded on Sundays than on other days of the
week.[8] In addition, the Comédie-Française rarely performed works new to
the repertory on Sundays, preferring not to risk the disapprobation of the
more "popular" crowd.[9]

In the specific case of the parterre, Lagrave suggests that the pit accommodated people of the highest distinction and men of lesser social stand-

[5] This "rich public" seated itself throughout the playhouse; see the account in the early-
eighteenth-century German travel guide by J. C. Nemeitz quoted in Lagrave, *Le Théâtre et le
public*, 232.
[6] Lagrave, *Le Théâtre et le public*, 234–36, for calculations on the average worker's salary.
[7] Ibid., 245. These calculations are somewhat complicated. In essence, he discards Tuesdays,
Thursdays, and Saturdays, days of generally lower attendance owing to competition from the
Opera and other reasons. On the remaining days, Monday, Wednesday, and Saturday, the percentage of parterre tickets sold was 54 percent, 57 percent, and 52 percent, respectively, compared to 62 percent on Sunday.
[8] Ibid., 246.
[9] Ibid., 247–50.

ing.[10] In doing so, he follows the lead of eighteenth-century contemporaries who commented on the social heterogeneity of the parterre, but he does not push his analysis of the social composition of the parterre any further. Using police records, however, a source underexploited by Lagrave, one can expand on these speculations.[11] These archives provide information on two types of spectators. First, the surviving papers of the Paris lieutenant general of police contain details regarding the arrest and imprisonment of spectators detained for unruly behavior. Second, the files of the *commissaires*, or district commissioners, include declarations made by individuals who had their pockets picked while attending the theater.[12] Taken together, these two sources permit us to identify 303 individuals who attended public theaters in the fifty-year period from 1717 to 1768. From this group, 207 stood in the parterre (see table 1 and Appendix).

How does this evidence expand on Lagrave's brief remarks concerning the social composition of the parterre? A quick glance at table 1 confirms the social diversity of the parterre; according to this sample, military officers, Parisian barristers, and high financiers stood alongside students, apprentices, and clerks in the crowded pits of the privileged theaters. At the same time, the distinction between a "rich" public and a "popular" one loses its usefulness for the parterre. The wealth of men who claimed to be financiers or military officers, for example, fluctuated wildly; many of these men stood in the parterre because they could not afford a ticket elsewhere in the theater. To take the example of financiers (from the Appendix), there was a great deal of difference between François Louis Lattainant de Bainville, a forty-three-year-old *chevalier grande trésorier des ordres militaires et hospitaliers;* Alexandre Despueche, a sixty-eight-year-old *banquier à Paris;* and Michel Patrice Maulny de la Toussière, the *vérificateur des douanes du Roy de la généralité de Bourges*, who was visiting Paris; all of whom had items stolen while standing in the parterre of the Comédie-Italienne in the late 1750s or early 1760s.[13]

Thus, even broadly defined categories suggest the diversity of the parterre crowd and the difficulty of attributing any sort of unified theatrical taste to

---

[10] Ibid., 233–34. He suggests that men of high standing were joined in the parterre by "[le] gros public, celui des 'gens de pied.'"

[11] Lagrave, *Le Théâtre et le public*, 241–44, relies solely on the work of Frantz Funck-Brentano, *La Bastille des comédiens. Le For l'Evêque*, esp. 258–302, which is an anecdotal treatment of spectator arrests based on selected material from the Archives de la Bastille.

[12] AN, Y10719–17623, papers of the *commissaires du Châtelet*.

[13] AN, Y13388, 6 October 1762; BA, ms 12025, f. 70, 82; AN, Y11337, 17 October 1758; and AN, Y13388, 24 November 1762.

Table 1   Parterre Spectators by Social Category and Theater, 1717–68

Category	CF	CI	OP	NP	Total
Military officers	6	10	8	—	24
Service class	20	28	8	1	57
Merchants, master artisans	16	18	5	4	43
Soldiers	6	2	1	—	9
Clerks, domestics	9	7	1	3	20
Apprentices	11	9	—	—	20
Students, young men	17	1	—	1	19
Provincials	2	5	—	1	8
Unemployed, other	3	2	1	1	7
Total	90	82	24	11	207

CF = Comédie-Française; CI = Comédie-Italienne; OP = Opera; NP = nonprivileged theaters.
Note: See Appendix for category explanations.
Source: Bibliothéque de l'Arsenal, Archives de la Bastille; Archives Nationales, "Y" series, papers of the Paris *commissaires*.

the variety of individual spectators who all paid for admission to the pit. It is equally difficult to distinguish a popular public in the parterre. Even if we remove the military officers, members of the service classes, and merchants and master artisans (categories of potential wealth and social status), important divisions between the remaining categories still exist. Students and law clerks often came from comfortable or even wealthy families; they aspired to positions of power and prestige and were generally quite literate. Although they were occasionally arrested in numbers proportionate to apprentices and shop assistants, we should not imagine that the former categories responded to spectacle in the same fashion as the latter.

Thus, this sample permits us to build on suggestions about the social composition of the parterre. The presence of financiers, officers, apprentices, students, and others affirms the social heterogeneity of the pit, but this very heterogeneity refutes the distinction between a rich public and a popular public. By and large, the notion of a Sunday public holds, although it should be qualified to accommodate the evidence of a student presence in the parterre at the Comédie-Française on all days of the week. When considering evidence from the police archives, however, we should keep several caveats in mind. Spectators had a variety of reasons for not disclosing their true identities. Those arrested as troublemakers often wished to conceal their detention from employers or family, while those whose pockets were picked might exaggerate their social station to impress the commissioner.

Several examples of this social misdirection exist in the archives. Jean Dejean, Sieur de Hauteterre, was arrested in the parterre of the Comédie-Française on Saturday, 13 January 1748, for crying out, "Paix là! (Quiet over there!)" during the intermission.[14] At first, he told the police agent that he was a military officer, but on his way to prison he revised his story by saying that he was about to purchase a military position. In a postscript, the same police agent noted that Hauteterre had at other times claimed to be a collector of the *gabelles* in Auvergne and to be on the brink of purchasing a position as tax farmer. More straightforward was the case of Pierre Dufresne, a lackey arrested on 25 July 1736 for trying to enter the parterre of the Comédie-Italienne in violation of the King's ordinance that forbade the presence of men of his station in the theater.[15] Dufresne, the domestic of Madame de la Galizière, had accompanied his mistress to the theater in his lackey's attire, then changed into bourgeois clothing that he had hidden in the trunk of her carriage. And equally intriguing was the case of Marc Antoine Monginet, an abbot arrested at the Comédie-Française on 24 October 1737 for having gained admission to the third loges dressed as a woman. Monginet, of course, cross-dressed to circumvent church rules prohibiting ecclesiastics from theater attendance. He was apparently an avid theatergoer, because the police agent noted in his report, "[T]his is not even the first time he has made himself into a woman, having false breasts which appeared to me to be very dirty."[16] Together, these three examples suggest the malleability of social categories in the charged theatrical environment of the public playhouse.

The parterre prosopography afforded by police records confirms hypotheses about the diversity of the audiences that came together to pass judgment on theater, and implicitly on the political issues of the day. It also suggests that the responses of parterre spectators to each other, to other spectators, and to the performance onstage cannot be analyzed solely in terms of socioeconomic standing. Although class is an important analytical tool for any inquiry into the reception of dramatic performance in the eighteenth century, we must also be attentive to fissures within the parterre that did not

[14] BA, ms 11650, f. 31–33.
[15] BA, ms 11319, f. 143–44.
[16] BA, ms 11366, f. 242–43. Lagrave briefly mentions this case in his discussion of priests at the theater. (Lagrave, *Le Théâtre et le public*, 222–25.) He also provides details on the celebrated case of M. de Montempuys, a Jansenist priest arrested for attending the Comédie-Française in drag in 1727 at the height of the convulsionary controversies. See BA, ms 10847, f. 135–44, in addition to the sources listed by Lagrave. Campardon, *Les Spectacles de la Foire*, 2:334–36, recounts the case of an English Benedictine monk in drag at a St-Germain fair spectacle in February 1754. In general on this topic, see John McManners, *Abbés and Actresses: The Church and the Theatrical Profession in Eighteenth-Century France* (Oxford, 1986).

follow class lines, and motivations that did not derive from economic standing. The spectators standing in the pit were not consumers of cultural products in the sense that theatergoers are today; they did not necessarily focus their undivided attention on the activity on the stage for three hours to render a verdict determined by their socioeconomic worldview, as both Lagrave and John Lough have asserted in their studies of Old Regime theater audiences.[17] Instead, it appears that they milled about the parterre, interacting with each other and with spectators in other parts of the hall, all the while keeping track of the onstage performance. The performers, in turn, did not require or assume the silent, rapt attention of the spectators. To understand the cultural context in which these spectators passed judgment on the privileged troupes, we should look beyond the social composition of the parterre to the daily practices of its occupants. We need to reinsert the theatergoing experience into the everyday world of the capital.

Outside the Playhouse

Unlike their London counterparts, the Parisian public theaters at the start of the eighteenth century remained open year-round.[18] Except for the royally mandated three-week break at Easter, the Comédie-Française had played seven nights a week since its establishment in August 1680.[19] On most evenings in the eighteenth century, furthermore, Parisian theater enthusiasts had more than one spectacle from which to choose. When the new Comédie-Italienne troupe began its operations in 1716 after the death of Louis XIV, it also scheduled performances every evening.[20] The Opera staged productions four nights a week in the winter and spring, on Tuesdays, Thursdays, Fridays, and Sundays; during the summer and early fall, it dropped the Sunday performance. And the fair theaters operated every

---

[17] Lough, *Paris Theatre Audiences*, organizes his discussion of both centuries into considerations of the aristocratic, bourgeois, and plebeian elements in the theater audience. Lagrave ends by confirming the idea that "la tragédie [est] faite pour les grandes, la comédie pour les bourgeois, et la farce pour le peuple." (Lagrave, *Le Théâtre et le public*, 251.) In addition, he displays an unfortunate contempt for the spectating practices of these audiences, dismissing them as childish people incapable of appreciating the "sublime nature" of high theater. (Ibid., 445.)

[18] On London, see Emmett L. Avery, *The London Stage, 1700–1729* (Carbondale and Edwardsville, 1968), liv.

[19] But see Lancaster, *The Comédie-Française, 1701–1774*, 595, for exceptional closings.

[20] Brenner, *Théâtre Italien*, 65, 75, and 97, however, suggests that in the first half of the eighteenth century the Italian troupe, which was smaller than the French troupe, occasionally closed its Parisian theater for a month or two at a time when it went to court.

night during the February to April duration of the St-Germain fair and the late July through September run of the St-Laurent fair.

Performances began at all three privileged theaters throughout the century at approximately five in the afternoon. This curtain time accommodated the daily schedule of a variety of Parisians. The city's wealthy and idle residents of both sexes often did not rise until two-thirty or three in the afternoon after the previous evening's lengthy festivities. The *grande audience* of the *Parlement de Paris,* the city's most important law court, ended at four in the afternoon during the winter months, and at five in the summer, thereby allowing judges, advocates, and others associated with the court to attend all or most of the performance. Classes at the University of Paris, near the Comédie-Française, ended at four in the eighteenth century, although many students who frequented the theaters may have had spotty class-attendance records. Others, engaged in commerce or "the King's affairs," worked from the morning until two or three in the afternoon, when they would sit down to their *dîner,* the main meal of the Parisian's day. They would then eat a second, lighter meal, the *souper,* after the theater around ten or eleven. Most *salonnières* invited their guests for *dîner* and conversation, which ended by curtain time.[21]

Once they had finished the day's business and consumed their main meal, parterre spectators might set off through the crowded streets of Paris on their way to the playhouse. As these spectators went about their rounds earlier in the day, they might have consulted the color-coded posters plastered in any of almost two hundred locations, mostly in the more exclusive quarters of town, by the Crown's official bill-posters.[22] Starting in 1777, they might also have consulted the daily listings in the *Journal de Paris,* much as we consult printed movie times in our papers today. Their destinations did not change location for much of the century; until 1770, the Comédie-Française played in a building constructed on the Left Bank in 1689, not far from the Latin Quarter and the law courts on the Ile de la Cité. The Opera performed for most of the century in the same space it had occupied since the early 1670s, the *salle* of the Palais-Royal originally con-

[21] On the elites, see Lagrave, *Le Théâtre et le public,* 499–501; on the law courts, *Almanach Royal* (Paris, 1751), 159; on university students, L. W. B. Brockliss, *French Higher Education in the Seventeenth and Eighteenth Centuries* (Oxford, 1987), 58; on merchants and bureaucrats, Alfred Franklin, ed., *La Vie privée d'autrefois* (Paris, 1891), series 1, vol. 8, *Variétés gastronomiques,* 114–21; on the salons, Marguerite Glotz and Madeleine Maire, *Salons du XVIIIe siècle* (Paris, 1949), 132, 143, 264.
[22] François de Dainville, "Les Lieux d'affichage des comédiens à Paris en 1753," *Revue d'histoire du théâtre* 3 (1951): 248–60.

structed by Richelieu; and the Comédie-Italienne performed in the oldest Parisian theater of the day, the Hôtel de Bourgogne, just north of the city's main marketplace. All three troupes received new homes in a brief three-year span at the beginning of the 1780s; this flurry of building altered the capital's theatrical topography by relocating the Opera further north to the Porte St-Martin, the Comédie-Italienne to the Boulevard along the north-west border of the city, and the Comédie-Française a few blocks south to the newly created place de l'Odéon (see Frontispiece).

Eighteenth-century parterre spectators had two transportation options for their trips to the playhouse: they might choose to approach the theater on foot, or they might travel via carriage. Pedestrians had to brave the mud and waste of the city's streets, which sloped downward from either side of the street, as they had since the Middle Ages, toward a central ditch that collected filth and debris to be washed away. The first Parisian sidewalks were constructed to line the main street leading to the new Comédie-Française building in 1782. Travelers on foot also needed to be attentive to human waste discarded from the windows that lined the streets above them, as numerous "chamber pot" complaints in the judicial archives attest.[23] Theatergoers who wished to avoid these unpleasantries, and those who desired to advertise their distinction from the common people in the street, might rent one of the many *cochers de place*, or carriages for hire, which rumbled through the streets of the capital in search of passengers.

Carriages first appeared in Paris in the early seventeenth century; by the early years of the reign of Louis XIV, the demand for them had grown so great that the saddle-makers guild successfully petitioned the King for the privilege to oversee their manufacture. At first carriage makers sold their wares to the wealthy and aristocratic elites of the capital, but in the second half of the seventeenth century a thriving carriage rental business arose to complement the use of private carriages. Drivers charged twenty-four *sous* for the first hour and twenty *sous* for each successive hour by the mid-eighteenth century. The *Encyclopédie* estimates that fifteen thousand carriages were in use in Paris by the 1750s; undoubtedly their preponderance

---

[23] Alain Corbin, *The Foul and the Fragrant: Odor and the French Social Imagination* (Cambridge, MA, 1986); Alfred Franklin, *La Vie privée d'autrefois*, series 1, vol. 7, *L'Hygiène* (1890), 148–223, offers a vivid, documented account of the streets, sidewalks, sewers, and smells of eighteenth-century Paris; ibid., 169, discusses the sidewalks outside the Comédie-Française in 1782. On chamber pots, see Arlette Farge, *Vivre dans la rue à Paris au XVIIIe siècle* (Paris, 1979), 36 and plate 8.

facilitated the task of traveling long distances through the city to the privileged playhouses, thereby increasing the potential audience for the public theater.[24] The abundance of carriages, however, also created problems for theatergoers as they reached the neighborhoods in which the playhouses were situated. In these older districts the narrow streets, laid out in previous centuries well before the advent of the carriage, were not designed to handle the large numbers of coaches attracted to the privileged theaters or the heavy foot traffic; bottlenecks were common, as the complaints of Mme d'Argenson, who waited impatiently in her motionless carriage for more than half an hour outside the Comédie-Italienne in 1750, attest.[25] The royal administration had stationed guards in these streets to direct traffic since the reign of Louis XIV, but the problem continued to grow in the eighteenth century in proportion to the number of carriages and the popularity of the theaters. Royal ordinances of December 1736 and January 1745 specifically enjoined coachmen to proceed in an orderly, single-file line as they approached the playhouses, and an internal memo written for the opening of the rebuilt Opera house in 1770 details the duties of sixteen officers and thirty-eight riflemen posted at eight different stations in the streets leading to the theater.[26]

Nevertheless, violations of the King's ordinances regulating coaches and public carriages mounted; by midcentury, infractions were so common that the police prepared a printed form that contained a set narrative of carriage drivers' violations replete with blanks for the name of the offender and the date of the offense.[27] A 1762 petition submitted to the lieutenant general of police by a group of neighborhood merchants pointed out that their businesses suffered when their street, near the Comédie-Italienne, became impassable near curtain time. Another letter, written in the 1780s by the inhabitants of the Porte St-Martin quarter after the government moved the Opera house to their neighborhood, com-

---

[24] *Encyclopédie*, 2:704–5, "carrosse"; 14:934, "sellier"; *Recueil de planches sur les sciences, les arts libéraux, et les arts méchaniques, avec leur explication*, vol. 9, plates accompanying the entry "sellier-carrossier" (unpaginated); Alfred Martin, *Etude historique et statistique sur les moyens de transport dans Paris . . .* (Paris, 1894); and Bernard Causse, *Les Fiacres de Paris aux XVIIe et XVIIIe siècles* (Paris, 1972).

[25] BA, ms 11728, f. 120–21.

[26] Campardon, *Les Comédiens du roi de la troupe française*, 317; "Ordonnance du roi pour l'arrangement des carosses aux entrées et sorties des spectacles à Paris du 18 janvier 1745"; AN, O^1 89, f. 21; "Garde de l'Opéra au Palais Royale," SHAT, Y^a 272, dossier "théâtre," chemise "nottes et ordres concernant l'ouverture de la salle de l'Opéra au Palais Royal, 1770."

[27] See the example at BA, ms 11741, f. 76.

plained of the massive traffic jams occasioned by the convergence of carriages dropping passengers at the Opera and wagons bringing provisions into the city through the town gate.[28]

Tempers often flared as coachmen, their passengers, pedestrians, and guards got closer to the playhouses' entrances, particularly as passengers often instructed their coachmen to drop them as close as possible to the theater entrance, while guards were under strict orders to keep the carriages circulating and the areas in front of the theater clear. The volatile crowd of domestics, lackeys, and other passersby who gathered behind the police barrier to watch the arrivals outside the entrance to the theaters as five o'clock approached raised these inherent tensions between coachmen and the soldiers assigned to control them. On Saturday, 3 November 1742, as a large crowd arrived at the Comédie-Française for a performance of La Motte's *Inès de Castro,* the coachman of Mme d'Aiguillon, "who was furiously drunk and insolent," stationed his carriage in such a way that spectators could neither enter nor leave the theater through the door to the parterre. When an officer on duty asked him to reposition his carriage, he refused to do so and told the officer "to go fuck himself." When a contingent of the officer's colleagues and soldiers approached the difficult coachman, another carriage driver named le Pierre reportedly attempted to excite the livery gathered at the entrance in his defense. Although Mme d'Aiguillon's coachman got off with a warning, le Pierre was sent to languish for almost a month in the prison at the Grand Châtelet.[29] Sometimes the conflict originated behind the barrier; a decade later, in February 1751, a domestic named Gossot in the service of the Dutch ambassador, apparently on foot, attempted to break through the police restraints. When ordered back by the sentinel on duty, he refused to withdraw and punched a corporal in the stomach before being subdued by the guards. As he was being led from the scene, however, he cried out to other domestics and liveried servants witnessing the proceedings to rally to his cause *("A moi la livrée!"),* at which point there ensued a small battle between the soldiers and the watch, on the one hand, and mounted and unmounted domestics and liveried servants on the other.[30]

Even on evenings when the parade of carriages proceeded without incident, spectators might encounter other provocative street scenes on their

---

[28] AN, Y13388, for the March 1762 petition from merchants on the rue Petit Lyon, near the Comédie-Italienne; SHAT, Yᵃ 272, dossier "théâtre" for the letter from the Porte St-Martin residents. See also AN, AD^VIII 10, 41 (1); and *Journal de Paris,* 7 April 1782, 387.

[29] BA, ms 11515, f. 226–27.

[30] BA, ms. 11748, f. 36–49. BA, ms 11650, f. 437–41; BA, ms 11671, f. 92–104; and BA, ms 11688, f. 119–20, contain accounts of similar conflicts.

way to the box office, many of them related to the government's efforts to instill discipline in the Parisian populace. Theatergoers arriving at the Palais Royal Opera house in December 1729 observed the figure of Scipion Toussaint, a black runner for the Count de Montanzier, locked in an iron collar on the square in front of the theater on three consecutive performance nights. Toussaint reportedly had shouted "vivid" insults at the army troops stationed at the door and then hit one of them repeatedly with a cane; while attached to the iron collar, he wore a sign from his neck that proclaimed that he was a "Domestic Who Violently Attacked the Opera Guard." A generation later, in 1760, several theater pickpockets were exhibited in the iron collar in front of all three privileged playhouses with placards that read "Theater Thieves."[31] By the end of the Old Regime, as if to emphasize their vigilance, the military would stage a parade in the squares in front of each theater an hour before curtain. Louis-Sébastien Mercier reported in his *Tableau de Paris* that the soldiers would perform battlefield maneuvers and load their rifles in full view of the arriving spectators.[32]

Before obtaining a ticket for the evening's performance, spectators destined for the parterre might stop for refreshment and intrigue at one of the cafés that served patrons in the theater districts. Eighteenth-century Parisian coffeehouses sold tea, chocolate, brandy, liqueurs, wine and beer to their customers in addition to the aromatic bean-based beverage. They did so in settings that were often sumptuously decorated with mirrors, tapestries, and glass chandeliers. The social space of the coffeehouses played an important role in the practice of eighteenth-century theatergoing in Paris, because none of the privileged playhouses had foyers large enough for spectators to gather comfortably before the 1770s. Parisian cafés, which did not charge entry fees, provided a space in which theater patrons could gather, away from the tumult of the carriages, domestics, and guards. The first and possibly the most famous Parisian café, the Procope, opened across the street from the Comédie-Française in the late seventeenth century to serve the needs of theater patrons; among the three hundred coffeehouses in the capital by the start of the Regency in 1716 were a significant number of operations in the streets around each of the privileged playhouses.[33] Parterre patrons mingled in the Procope, the Café de l'Opéra, the Café de la Comédie-Italienne, and other

---

[31] On Toussaint, see BA, ms 10295, f. 65–66; BA, ms 11073, f. 337–38; and SHAT, Yᵃ 274, chemise "discipline"; on the 1758 pickpockets, see BA, ms 12025.

[32] Louis-Sébastien Mercier, *Tableau de Paris* (Amsterdam, 1783–89), 6:121–22.

[33] Brennan, *Public Drinking*, 76–134 uses the police archives to contrast the economic and social functions of cafés with those of cabarets and *guinguettes* in eighteenth-century Paris. See also Franklin, *La Vie privée d'autrefois*, series 1, vol. 13, *Le Café, le thé et le chocolat* (1893), 216–96; François Fosca, *Histoire des cafés de Paris* (Paris, 1934), 17–69; and Jean Moura and Paul Louvet, *Le Café Procope* (Paris, 1929), 42–147.

theater cafés with actors, authors, *gens de lettres,* and the ubiquitous police spies before the curtain; contemporary accounts report that the patrons watched the arrivals at the theaters, disputed the merits of new and old works, and attempted to organize cabals against certain plays and players. The playwright Lesage described a typical café scene in his 1740 novel *La Valise trouvé:*

> Then two playwrights came in, since, as it is said, it rains playwrights in all the coffeehouses of Paris. They began to talk of a new tragedy; one argued that it was excellent, while the other held that it was awful. Each one had his reasons, from which they passed to the most exaggerated insults, following the protocol recently established by men of letters. From insults they moved to the threat of violence, vehemently promising to take up swords against each other, knowing all the while they would be separated before they came to blows.[34]

Although Lesage may have exaggerated his fictional account for comic effect, police reports confirm that the coffeehouses around the theaters were not always tranquil places where theater patrons gathered quietly to discuss literary matters and contemplate the upcoming performance.[35]

Café patrons in need of parterre tickets on popular evenings did not have to look far beyond the confines of the coffeehouse, as a 1748 example attests. Late in the afternoon of 17 February that year, the date of the sixth performance of Jean-François Marmontel's highly successful tragedy, *Denys le tyran,* the police inspector Vierrey approached an unemployed mason in the alley in back of the Café Procope. The young man, named Mercier, asked the incognito inspector how many parterre tickets he needed for the evening's performance. Vierrey inquired how much two tickets would cost; when Mercier replied that the tickets were hard to come by and that the policeman should pay what he judged appropriate, Vierrey took him into custody for scalping theater tickets. He later learned that Mercier's brother, who lived above the Café Procope, had financed the purchase of fifteen parterre tickets for the evening's performance.[36] Vierrey had acted on the complaints of the Comédie-Française troupe and spectators who found regularly priced tickets hard to obtain on nights when admission to the theater was in demand.

---

[34] Franklin, *La Vie privée d'autrefois,* series 1, vol. 13, *Le Café, le thé et le chocolat,* 232.

[35] See, for example, AN, Y12147, complaint of le Sieur Molagne, *secrétaire du roi,* dated 29 May 1744. Roche, *People of Paris,* 253–55, contrasts the popular, boisterous ambiance of the cabaret with the decorum and "comparative silence encouraging intellectuality" of the cafés; but Brennan, *Public Drinking,* provides ample evidence to suggest that this behavioral and class distinction between the two types of spaces is overdrawn.

[36] BA, ms 11653, f. 219–22.

The shadow traffic in illegally resold theater tickets outside the cafés and in the streets approaching the playhouses is difficult to quantify over the course of the century, but anecdotal evidence attests to its presence from the reign of Louis XIV to the Revolution.[37] Police preoccupations may have reached a peak around the time of Charles Palissot's anti-*Encyclopédie* comedy, *Les Philosophes*; on closing night of the 1760–61 season at the Comédie-Française, the police inspector la Janière and the commissioner Chenu set out with a small troupe of men to crack down on the ticket touts in the streets surrounding the theater. These two authorities, noting in their reports that the royal soldiers positioned to oversee the flow of carriage traffic did nothing to discourage scalping, first arrested a wig-maker's assistant selling parterre tickets in an alleyway on the side of the theater. They then proceeded to the end of the street, where they saw the clerk to the lawyer and memorialist Barbier surrounded by a group of individuals who wished to purchase double-price parterre tickets from him. Unfortunately for la Janière, Chenu, and company, their actions drew an even larger crowd of angry domestics and young men in defense of the scalpers. The police were forced to flee with their two suspects across the river to the Petit Chatêlet, where they processed and imprisoned the two ticket touts.[38]

Theatergoers determined to avoid both the box office and scalpers pursued other options to gain access to the theater. The privileged troupes allowed their members to distribute free tickets to friends and patrons, and they also allowed playwrights to offer a small number of free tickets to the opening run of plays that they had written. These tickets proved relatively easy to counterfeit, as several examples from midcentury suggest. In one case, the son of the painter and Academician Aved falsified tickets to a first-run performance of Crébillon *père*'s 1749 tragedy *Catilina*; in another instance the year before, a notary's clerk had confessed to forging actors' signatures for more than a year to get himself and his friends into the Comédie-Française.[39] The practice of distributing *contremarques*, or chits, to theatergoers who exited the building between plays also facilitated illicit entries. Because the stage was empty between performances, many spectators left the theater in search of

[37] Paul Cottin, ed., *Rapports de police de Réné d'Argenson* (Paris, 1891), 323; SHAT, Yª 273, 24 March 1788; and F. W. J. Hemmings, *The Theatre Industry in Nineteenth-Century France* (Cambridge, 1993), 17.

[38] BA, ms 12120, f. 245–54. For arrests of scalpers during the first run of *Les Philosophes*, see BA, ms 12088, f. 239–41; and BA, ms 12092, f. 288–306; for scalping during a 1764 premiere, see AD, 2:225–26.

[39] BA, ms 11689, f. 214–19; BA, ms 11657, f. 313–19; for two other examples of counterfeiting in this period, see BA, ms 11649, f. 331–37; and BA, ms 11671, f. 197–202.

fresh air or a drink at a nearby café; when they did so, ticket takers gave them a *contremarque* that allowed them to reenter the theater for the second play. A 1750 report indicates that young men gathered at the entrance to the Comédie-Française between the plays to request chits from exiting spectators who did not intend to return. Equipped with a *contremarque*, these individuals then had the option of entering the theater themselves or selling the chit to an interested spectator who had been unable, or unwilling, to pay full admission at the start of the evening's performance.[40]

If parterre spectators who made their way to the playhouse did not choose to avail themselves of these "informal" ticket services, they proceeded to the box office to purchase admission to the pit. The price of entry to the parterre at the Comédie-Française and the Comédie-Italienne for most of the eighteenth century was twenty *sous*, or one livre; at the Opera at midcentury, a parterre ticket cost forty *sous*.[41] At the Comédie-Française and the Comédie-Italienne throughout most of the century, customers approaching the front of the playhouse encountered two windows covered with grilles where they could purchase tickets; one served parterre patrons exclusively, thus reflecting their numerical predominance inside the playhouse, while the other offered tickets for the other areas of the playhouse. On nights when attendance at the theaters was modest, the wait at the box office was not overly unpleasant, but on evenings when a new play debuted or a popular play was in the midst of its first run, purchasing a ticket became an ordeal.

Perhaps the height of spectator misery came on 3 September 1760, the premiere of Voltaire's *Tancrède*, when people began to congregate outside the ticket booth at eleven in the morning. A police contingent surveyed this activity to suppress fights and thefts committed by the omnipresent pickpockets. In spite of the officers' best efforts, however, the tumult and the chaos of the crowd waiting to purchase tickets for Voltaire's play was striking: "there was even someone who drew his sword on a domestic; many others had their canes broken, and all those who got tickets obtained them only at the expense of their wig or of torn clothing." The officer also recounted that some wily patrons would grab the hats of those closest to the ticket window and throw them into the street, thus forcing

---

[40] BA, ms 11723, f. 2–6, describes the market in *contremarques*.
[41] Lagrave, *Le Théâtre et le public*, 46–54; Lancaster, *The Comédie-Française, 1701–1774*, 594–95; Brenner, *Théâtre Italien*, 8. As a point of comparison, a Parisian manual laborer earned on average fifteen *sous* a day at the beginning of the century and twenty *sous* at the end. A cup of coffee in a café cost four *sous*; a cup of chocolate, a bottle of beer, or a pitcher of lemonade, five *sous*. (Claude Alasseur, *La Comédie-Française au XVIIIe siècle: étude économique* (Paris, 1967), 57; Brennan, *Public Drinking*, 111–12.)

the frustrated, hatless ticket seeker to choose between a place in line and the headgear now lying in the road.[42]

As spectators proceeded from the ticket window to the entrance, they might have paused to read or listen to the reading of the placards posted on the front of the privileged theaters. In effect, the playhouse façade was one of the many "empty pages" of the capital on which official and illicit bill-posters pasted their texts and images throughout the eighteenth century.[43] Some of the posters on view outside the theater served as justification for the absolutist tutelage of the public theaters, such as the "King's Ordinances concerning the Theaters," reissued regularly throughout the century and always on view at the entrance to the theaters; they were occasionally complemented by legal judgments that explained the public punishments administered to the convicted individuals in the spaces in front of the theaters. Other posters, illegally posted and quickly removed, publicized moral and political issues that neighborhood residents and the royal government sought to stifle. In late summer 1758, anonymous individuals posted printed placards on the Comédie-Italienne and in the surrounding neighborhood that alluded to the supposed sexual promiscuity of one of the theater's actresses, also an inhabitant of the quarter.[44]

One morning a decade later, a royal bill-poster found a handwritten placard on the same theater demanding the suppression of the public theaters "in the name of God and the Prophet"; the unknown author predicted future "woe" *(malheur)* for the royal family if the playhouses remained open.[45] Although these posters were quickly removed, even official posters led a transient existence on the theater façades. At the Comédie-Française in February 1749, the young son of M de Matignon, already characterized by the theater guards as a troublemaker, tried to gain admission to the theater for one of his domestics. When the guard posted at the entrance pointed out the passage in the King's ordinance that forbade domestics entrance to the royal theater, Matignon ripped the offending section off the wall and told the guard, "This is what I make of your ordinance!"[46]

[42] BA, ms 10295, f. 95–96. See a suggested plan to reform the distribution of tickets at the theaters in *Journal de Paris*, 27 December 1777, 3–4.
[43] On the phenomenon of the legible city in eighteenth-century Paris, see Roche, *People of Paris*, 224–33; and Roger Chartier, *The Cultural Uses of Print in Early Modern France*, trans. Lydia G. Cochrane (Princeton, 1987), 230–31.
[44] Campardon, *Les Comédiens du roi de la troupe italienne*, 183–84.
[45] AN, Y13394, 27 April 1767.
[46] BA, ms 11663, f. 66.

Once furnished with tickets, whatever their provenance, theater spectators presented themselves at one of the entrances to the theater, where they handed over their tickets to a ticket taker. In exchange, they received a *contremarque* labeled with the area of the playhouse for which they had purchased admission. An *Encyclopédie* engraving of the floor plan of the Comédie-Française playhouse from 1689 to 1770 permits us to follow the parterre spectators as they make their way into the theater (figure 1). All spectators entered the theater through the doors marked with an R, but those destined for the first loges or the stage proceeded to the two staircases marked P, where another controller permitted them access to the upper levels of the theater in exchange for their chit, from which they would proceed to the loges, amphitheater, or the stage. These spectators, who had all paid at least the twenty *sous* required for admission to the parterre, might also remain in the pit to watch the performance. Parterre ticket-holders, in principle prohibited from the upper floors, had the option of circulating in the passages marked L or passing time in the ground-floor café inside the theater. From at least 1758 onward, a bookseller named Pierre Vente enjoyed the exclusive privilege of running a bookshop within the theater; while records do not specify the location of his stall within the theater, it almost certainly would have been on this ground-floor level where parterre spectators would have had access to it.[47] Finally, when the parterre patron was ready, he made his way up the short staircases to one of the two doors leading into the pit, marked G.

It is instructive to compare the enclosed space of the parterre level of this theater with its counterpart in the Palais Royal theater used by the Opera from 1770 to 1781; the multiple staircases and passageways there provided for greater circulation between the parterre and other portions of the theater (figure 2).[48] In this engraving, D marks the entrances to the theater; F, the grand vestibule; and G, the grand staircase. Spectators thus encountered several paths by which they might ascend to the amphitheater or the boxes before arriving at the entrances to the parterre (H); ticket takers found it impossible in this architectural design to exclude those who purchased parterre tickets from the rest of the auditorium. Opera administrators bemoaned the loss of receipts caused by this openness, because spectators might claim to be a guest of an annual box-holder and then head

---

[47] AN, O¹ 611, f. 358–59.
[48] The theater was rebuilt after a fire had destroyed the previous Palais Royal Opera on the same site in 1763. This second Palais Royal Opera house also burned down in 1781, after which the theater was moved to the Porte St-Martin.

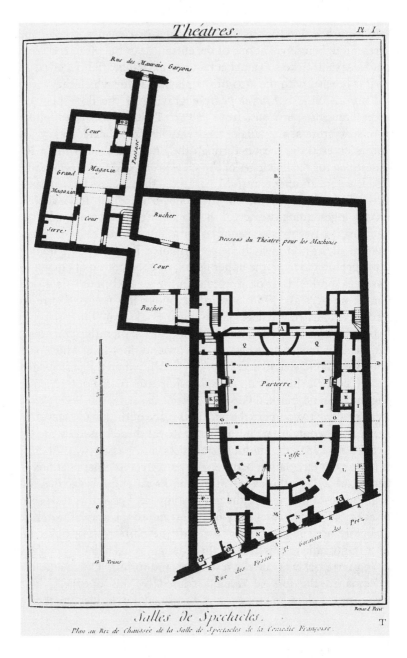

Fig. 1. Overhead view of the Comédie-Française playhouse, 1689–1770, from *Recueil de planches sur les sciences, les arts libéraux, et les arts méchaniques, avec leur explication*, vol. 9 (Paris, 1772). Plates to the *Encyclopédie* of Diderot and d'Alembert. (Courtesy of the Institute Archives and Special Collections, Massachusetts Institute of Technology.)

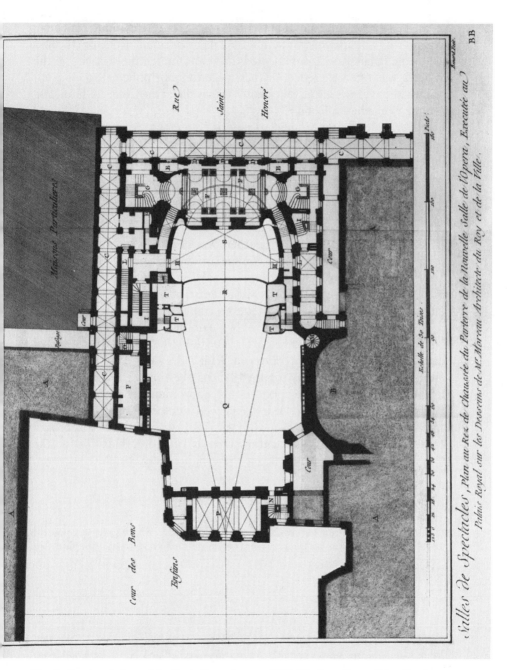

Fig. 2. Overhead view of the Paris Opera house, 1770–81, from *Recueil de planches sur les sciences, les arts libéraux, et les arts méchaniques, avec leur explication,* vol. 9 (Paris, 1772). Plates to the *Encyclopédie* of Diderot and d'Alembert. (Collection of Edward Binney III, Harvard Theater Collection, Houghton Library.)

to the parterre.[49] But the architectural openness of this floor plan may explain why one administrator, in a 1762 memo written just before the first fire at the Palais Royal, commented that even though the capacity of the parterre was often exceeded, neither spectators nor policing agents complained about crowding as vehemently as they did at the Comédie-Française and the Comédie-Italienne.[50]

A lateral view of the Comédie-Française playhouse from 1689 to 1770 helps visualize the physical size of the parterre in that theater (figure 3). In this engraving, also from the *Encyclopédie*, the parterre is the surface that slopes gently downward from left to right below the center of the three balconies; the amphitheater, slightly raised and equipped with benches, is to the left; and the orchestra pit and the stage are to the right. The parterre in this theater occupied a space that was approximately 1,060 square feet; the pits in the other two theaters were comparable in size.[51] It is impossible to know the maximum capacity of these spaces, but the commonsense calculation that each individual required a little more than one square foot of space when standing would indicate that the total number of parterre spectators could never have exceeded one thousand. A pencil drawing by P. A. Wille of the Comédie-Italienne playhouse in the 1760s shows the parterre of the Hôtel de Bourgogne filled to capacity; the sea of spectators in Wille's drawing emphasized their multiplicity and anonymity (figure 4). Official estimates placed the maximum number of parterre spectators at approximately 600 in the two nonlyric theaters, but the largest recorded number of paying parterre spectators at the Comédie-Française was 773, registered on 19 February 1690, and police records mention crowds of more than 700 at the Comédie-Italienne as well.[52] Even these figures may be low, however,

---

[49] AN, O¹620, f. 481.

[50] Campardon, *Les Comédiens du roi de la troupe italienne*, 284.

[51] These figures are all from Lagrave, *Le Théâtre et le public*, 76–89. Lagrave has converted the Old Regime *toises* and *pieds* into modern metric measurements, which I have then converted into feet and inches.

[52] Ibid., 79, 90 fn. 51.

Fig. 3. ➤ Lateral view of the Comédie-Française playhouse, 1689–1770, from *Recueil de planches sur les sciences, les arts libéraux, et les arts méchaniques, avec leur explication*, vol. 9 (Paris, 1772). Plates to the *Encyclopédie* of Diderot and d'Alembert. (Courtesy of the Institute Archives and Special Collections, Massachusetts Institute of Technology.)

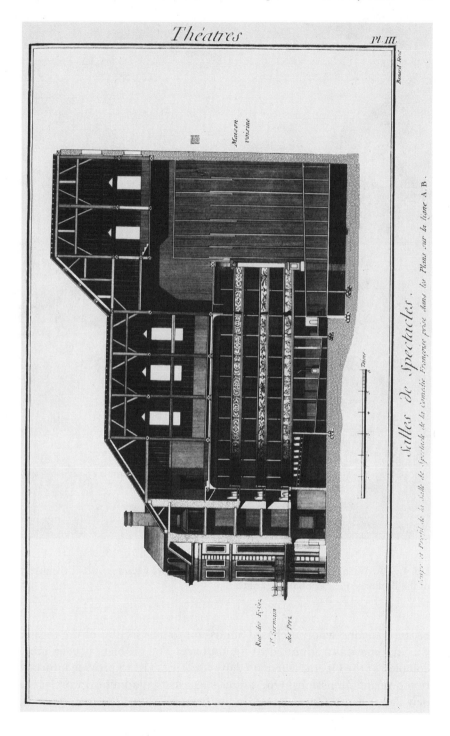

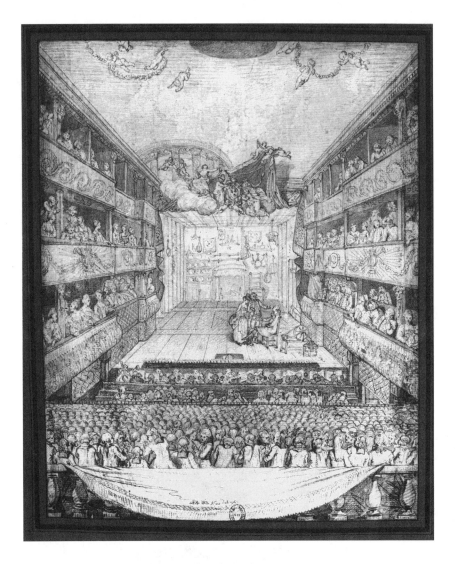

Fig. 4. P. A. Wille, *Drawing of a Playhouse with Actors Onstage*, 1767. (Courtesy of the Bibliothèque nationale de France.)

because anyone who purchased admission to any section of the theater was automatically admitted to the parterre. The problem is even more complex at the Opera, where no daily registers exist to provide information on paid admissions. One source suggests that administrators at the new Palais Royal Opera house, in use from 1770 to 1781 (see figure 2), capped parterre ticket sales at an even one thousand, while another recommended a limit of eight hundred parterre admissions.[53]

In the 1740s, Lieutenant General of Police Marville and Minister of State Maurepas, alarmed by events at the privileged theaters, attempted to take matters into their own hands by imposing a limited number of parterre ticket sales on a recalcitrant Comédie-Française. These officials hoped this measure would limit disturbances in the parterre that were increasingly beyond the control of the overburdened policing agents. They had a difficult time enforcing the policy, however, because the actors were reluctant to give up a portion of their ticket sales on evenings of great interest to the parterre.[54] The Comédie-Italienne was no less guilty in the eyes of the officials. In 1747, the Italians' disobedience prompted an angry outburst on the part of Maurepas, who instructed Marville to summon four of the Italian actors to his office. At this meeting he was to tell the players that if the order limiting parterre ticket sales was not followed, the police would put a controller in the ticket booth, at the actors' expense, with explicit instructions to close the ticket booth when 550 parterre tickets had been sold.[55] It is not known whether Marville carried out this threat, but it seems that the actors followed this policy for a period at the end of the decade. One guard, reporting in February 1749 on an arrest at the Comédie-Italienne, commented that his job was rendered easier by a relatively uncrowded parterre, which he easily penetrated to make an arrest.[56] At the end of the same year, in anticipation of large disturbances surrounding the début of Mme Favart at the Comédie-Italienne, the police successfully limited the number of parterre tickets sold to four hundred.[57] But these strictures proved difficult to enforce over the long haul; by 1761, Lieutenant General of Police Sartine was once again renewing official determination to fix the number of spectators allowed into the parterre of the Comédie-Italienne.[58] A memo written the following year on the occasion of the merger of the Comédie-Italienne with the Opéra-Comique again suggested a parterre head-count of 550 as the optimal limit.[59]

---

[53] Johnson, *Listening in Paris*, 17; AN, AD VIII[10], 29 March 1776.

[54] Arthur Michel de Boislisle, *Lettres de M de Marville Lieutenant Général de Police au Ministre Maurepas, 1742–1747* (Paris, 1896), 2:178–79.

[55] Ibid., 3:174.

[56] BA, ms 11663, f. 66.

[57] Thomas-Simon Gueullette, *Notes et souvenirs sur le Théâtre-Italien au XVIIIe siècle* (Paris, 1938), 49–53.

[58] BA, ms 12117, f. 2.

[59] Campardon, *Les Comédiens du roi de la troupe italienne*, 284.

The Curtain Rises

In 1726, the Academic painter and playwright Charles-Antoine Coypel published a set of five engravings based on his paintings of scenes from the plays of Molière.[60] The first of these engravings, however, represented a scene inside an unspecified theater before the raising of the curtain (figure 5). An address by the artist, printed on the lowered curtain, begs the indulgence of the public for the engravings that follow; presumably the artist himself peers timidly from behind the curtain at the assembled audience that will pass commercial and aesthetic judgment on his versions of scenes from Molière.[61] The scene in the engraving should not be interpreted as a literal rendering of audiences in any of the three privileged playhouses; instead it is likely that Coypel invoked the theater audience as a way to represent the physically disbursed public of engraving collectors whose favor he sought and yet whose criticism, and commercial indifference, he feared.[62] Nevertheless, this visual representation of a lively, self-absorbed group of theater spectators serves as a useful introduction to parterre behavior in the Parisian playhouse of the eighteenth century. In Coypel's construction, unlike Wille's later drawing (see figure 4), we see individual parterre spectators, in the picture's foreground, engaged in a variety of pursuits. The three men grouped under the right chandelier, for example, appear to be engaged in a heated conversation while a fourth, bemused spectator looks on just to their right. A little further to their right, two other spectators share a confidence with each other before the start of the play. Other parterre denizens on the left of the engraving exchange knowing glances with women in the loges on either side of the theater. Meanwhile, on the left-hand side of the stage behind the curtain, a man seated on the stage peers out at the parterre spectators crowded into the pit with an amused look of superiority. Although this image of a vibrant, distracted theater audience originated in Coypel's imagination, firsthand accounts throughout the century suggest that it also bore more than a passing resemblance to the nightly gatherings in the privileged playhouses. Let us raise the curtain on the parterre practices of these eighteenth-century spectators.

---

[60] On the commercial considerations behind Coypel's speculation, see Candace Clements, "Noble Liberality and Speculative Industry in Early Eighteenth-Century Paris: Charles Coypel," *ECS* 29 (Winter 1995–96): 213–18.

[61] The address is reprinted in I. Jamieson, *Charles-Antoine Coypel. Premier peintre de Louis XV et auteur dramatique (1694–1752)* (Paris, 1930), 9 n. 2.

[62] The artist has drawn a theater possessed of only two tiers of loges, rather than the three levels found in all of the privileged Parisian playhouses at this time.

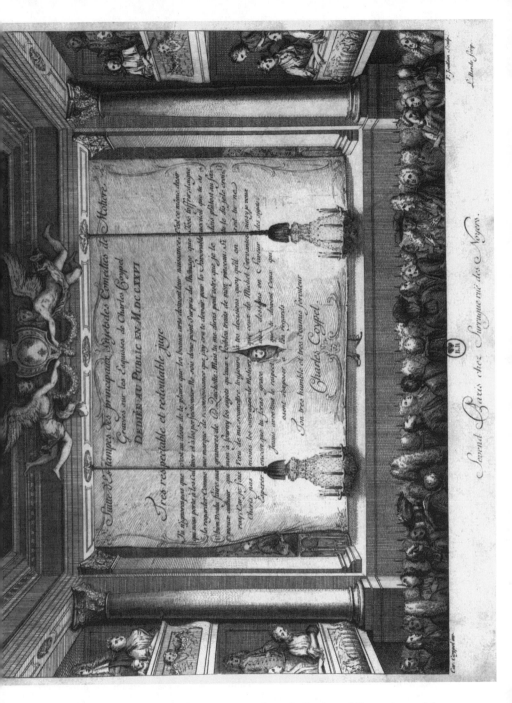

Fig. 5. Charles-Antoine Coypel, *Frontispiece for a Collection of Engravings of the Principle Subjects from the Plays of Molière*, 1726. (Courtesy of the Bibliothèque nationale de France.)

Theater troupes relied on audial cues to indicate the start of a performance, because crude illumination techniques prevented the dimming of lights before curtain.[63] Around five each afternoon, therefore, a stagehand rapped the floor three times with a baton, announcing to both audience members and performers the beginning of the day's performance. The curtain then rose, and the play began. Some parterre spectators undoubtedly stopped bustling about, fell silent, and concentrated entirely on the performance. Others, however, continued to jostle for position, interact with other parterre members, or eye the spectators in the loges who remained entirely visible. The bodily constraints of the parterre conditioned a spectator's perceptions of the play as much as his class status, literary tastes, political views, or religious sympathies. The battle to find one's way through the streets of Paris and into the theater, it turns out, was only the prelude to the physical experience of parterre spectating.

Regardless of title or wealth, every parterre spectator was subject to pushing, shoving, physical fatigue, and unrelenting cries. The immediate bodily experience of standing in the parterre militated against the exercise of dispassionate reason in the playhouse. An example of this disconcerting corporeal intrusion into the critical realm occurred at the Comédie-Italienne on Sunday, 3 November 1748.[64] Fifteen minutes before curtain time, according to a police observer, a group of clerks and shop boys raised such a ruckus that more than forty persons left the theater asking for their money back. According to the evocative, if phonetic, rendering of the commentator, these spectators claimed that the parterre "*s'étoit un nanfer* (It was hellish)."

A parterre spectator's infernal encounter often began with the rise of the curtain. In spite of police efforts to limit the sale of parterre tickets, the commercially motivated troupes jammed as many bodies as possible into the pit. One police agent in 1736 described a parterre so crowded that he could not enter to arrest troublemakers, relying instead on spies planted in the pit to identify victims at the end of the performance.[65] Under these difficult circumstances, spectators would try to shove their way to good vantage points; less aggressive theatergoers would be forced to the extremities of the hall. A nineteen year old from Marseille, detained by the police in December 1742 for allegedly causing disorder in the parterre, explained that the police mistakenly arrested him because he had the misfortune to enter the parterre "at the moment before the play began when people in the parterre pushed each

---

[63] See Rougemont, *Vie théâtrale*, 161, on lighting, which suggests that some improvements occurred toward the end of the century.
[64] BA, ms 11642, f. 8–9.
[65] BA, ms 11317, f. 182.

other in order, most probably, to obtain more advantageous spots."[66] The young man added to his plea, perhaps disingenuously, that he had just come from his flute lesson and that he did not want to enter into the middle of this crowd for fear that his flute, hidden under his clothing, might be broken.

Both spectators and police referred to the waves of people that ebbed and flowed in an effort to see the stage better as the *flux et reflux*. One officer stationed at the Comédie-Italienne noted in March 1747 that the shoving was particularly violent: "between the two plays, some young men in the parterre decided to begin pushing *(faire le flux)* to make more room in the center." Another police agent complained in a February 1749 account that the crowd, not recognizing who he was, had started a *flux* against him.[67] The force expended in these struggles could be prodigious. During the same February 1749 event, the police asked one unidentified individual to leave the theater when he was seen turning his back to the parterre crowd so that he could gain more leverage by pushing with his legs.[68] One parterre occupant, in a letter to the *Journal de Paris* in 1777, complained of elbows in the chest, lashes on the legs, clashing swords, greasy wigs, and pushing that transported him from one end of the pit to the other.[69]

Occasionally, conflicts centered on a spectator's height. At the Comédie-Française on 11 March 1747, a young man standing behind a lawyer's clerk named Louzeau in the parterre initiated some sort of altercation with the latter. As Louzeau recounted it in his plea for release from prison:

> [The young man] pretended that the supplicant, being much larger than him, prevented him from seeing. He tugged on his sleeve, the supplicant tried to pull away, but in spite of this, the unknown man grabbed the supplicant by the ear along with his wig to make him move more promptly. Such an action meant that almost immediately when turning around the supplicant struck the unknown spectator; this caused a great deal of commotion.[70]

Because it was Louzeau, and not the smaller man behind him, who was arrested, we will never know whether Louzeau's blow was as innocent as recounted in his plea. But given what we do know about parterre conditions, it is not surprising to find descriptions of physical confrontation in

[66] BA, ms 11514, f. 216.

[67] BA, ms 11607, f. 228–29; BA, ms 11684, f. 248.

[68] BA, ms 11684, f. 248; for other examples, see BA, ms 11757, f. 260–69; and BA, ms 11778, f. 175–81, for a 1752 example.

[69] *Journal de Paris*, 20 May 1777, 3–4; and a response, Ibid., 28 May 1777, 2–3.

[70] BA, ms 11620, f. 90.

the cramped quarters of the pit. In his fictionalized memoir, *A Sentimental Journey through France and Italy*, the English writer Laurence Sterne transformed this typical confrontation into a comical encounter between a hefty German and a dwarf stuck behind him in the parterre. After a series of threats by the dwarf and comical maneuverings to try to see the stage, Sterne "recorded" that a police officer supposedly placed the midget in front of the German so that he could see the show.[71]

On days when the parterre was less crowded, dancing sometimes replaced the collective waves of the *flux et reflux*. During the break between Voltaire's *Oedipe* and a one-act comedy at the Comédie-Française on 30 November 1733, a group of young men formed a circle and began to dance. The police officer wrote that he "pierced the center of the circle and made the dancing and the tumult stop." The police recorded a similar incident in the parterre of the same privileged theater ten years later.[72] Even on days when the parterre was almost empty, the behavior of those standing there hardly resembled that of the attentive spectator we might have expected. On a Tuesday early in October 1743, according to one account, "There were very few people in the theater, and hardly forty spectators in the parterre, where upon entering before they lit the candles I found five or six officers and soldiers amusing themselves by making one of those huge dogs that follows the carriages bark and race about."[73]

Material discomfort, overcrowding, and excessive drinking of spirits on crowded days in the pit could quickly turn to verbal altercation, as happened on Sunday, 26 April 1750, in the parterre at the Comédie-Française. An apothecary's shop boy named Fleurant joined his friends at the theater after apparently having had too much wine. While he was talking to one of his colleagues during the course of the performance, a third party in the parterre asked him to be quiet. Fleurant told the newcomer that he was talking to a friend and that it was none of his business. When the interruption persisted, Fleurant responded by using the word *foutre*. The use of the same word in response to the policing agent who asked him to quiet down resulted in Fleurant's arrest and imprisonment.[74] In his memoirs, the Marquis de Mirabeau, father of the revolutionary political leader, recounted an altercation from his student days in the 1730s.[75] Although normally a parterre troublemaker of some repute, one night Mirabeau had

[71] Laurence Sterne, *A Sentimental Journey Through France and Italy* (New York, 1968), 58–61.
[72] BA, ms 11218, f. 388–89; BA, ms 11534, f. 231.
[73] BA, ms 11537, f. 124–25.
[74] BA, ms 11708, f. 8–15.
[75] "Journal de la jeunesse du Marquis de Mirabeau," *Revue rétrospective* 4 (1834): 367.

bought second balcony seats with a friend. A young musketeer spotted him in the balcony and cried out, "Down with the noisy Knight! (*A bas le chevalier tapageur!*)" Mirabeau quickly descended to the parterre, exclaimed that he would cut off the nose of his accuser, and threw himself at the musketeer. Once the two had tangled long enough for both to save face, friends intervened. Mirabeau concluded his account by noting that the two men separated friends. Other confrontations, however, had more deep-seated causes. In the parterre of the Comédie-Italienne in November 1760, a painter of the Academy of St-Luke accosted a doctor from his neighborhood. Subsequent police investigation discovered a long-standing dispute between the two men over the former's efforts to cover up a love affair with his wife's maidservant.[76]

Stuffiness and overheating contributed to the general edginess of the crowd. The familiar cry of *ouvrez les loges* (open the boxes), a request to open the doors to the boxes to allow some circulation of air in the hall, rang out in the theater on days when the parterre was crowded. At times, theater employees complied with these requests, but they often did so against the wishes of the loge occupants, particularly in the winter; one exasperated police officer in January 1749 responded to these parterre cries with the following reprimand: "Sirs . . . you must not imagine that the loge doors should always be open; in fact, quite the opposite, since the women seated there are under no obligation to contract a cold in order to satisfy you!"[77]

The stoves that heated the theater halls and foyers in the winter also caused the poorly ventilated buildings to become stiflingly hot during the warmer months. Theatrical architects only remedied this state of affairs at the end of the century in the new theaters when they included extra openings behind the third balconies and multiplied vents within the buildings to facilitate the circulation of air.[78] These designers, however, never entirely eliminated the mortal threat posed by fire to eighteenth-century theatergoers. The Opera house in the Palais Royal burned to the ground twice, in 1763 and 1781, the latter conflagration killing eleven individuals; after the second fire, authorities decided to move the Opera house away from the center of the city to its northern boundaries. Although none of the buildings used by the Comédie-Française and the Comédie-Italienne caught fire in the eighteenth century, spectators wedged into the parterre with difficult

---

[76] BA, ms 12093, f. 159–74; AN, Y15457, 4 December 1759; and AN, Y15458, 13 April 1760.
[77] BA, ms 11681, f. 282–93; other examples of the cry "ouvrez les loges" include BA, ms 11394, f. 15–18; BA, ms 11481, f. 269–79; BA, ms 11514, f. 214–18; BA, ms 11683, f. 23–34; BA, ms 11818, f. 69–72; BA, ms 12117, f. 2–15.
[78] See Rougemont, *Vie théâtrale*, 155–72, on eighteenth-century French theater architecture.

access to exits were skittish. To assuage these fears, the lieutenant general of police supervised a fire drill at the Comédie-Italienne, situated in a more densely populated quarter than the other two privileged troupes, shortly after the second Opera fire in June 1781. According to one observer, the simulation, "which succeeded in directing water into all corners of the theater as well as drenching the exterior of the building within less than a minute," was a success.[79] The following year, a stagehand at the Comédie-Française accidentally set off a fire alarm; before the error was recognized, nervous firemen had inundated the stage, halting the performance.[80]

Parterre spectators also faced more mundane threats posed by the pickpockets and other thieves who circulated in eighteenth-century playhouses. During a performance at the Comédie-Italienne in 1770, a band of thieves played on spectators' fear of flames by falsely shouting that a fire had broken out; in the ensuing panic, they profited from the confusion to such an extent that three dozen declarations of theft were allegedly filed with the police the following day.[81] Policing agents did their best to counteract the omnipresent *filoux*, many of whom they suspected of gaining access to the theater by purchasing chits from exiting spectators during performance intermissions.[82] In most cases, their efforts were for naught, but in late 1758 they managed to break up a ring of organized theater pickpockets and recover many items that had been pilfered in the parterre.[83] The perpetrators, a gang consisting of a woodworker, a pastry maker, a fair merchant, and a horse trader, had for several months made off with gold watches, ornately decorated snuffboxes, and other valuable pocket items from the three privileged playhouses and other public spectacles. The ensuing investigations, which uncovered a fencing network that extended as far as Lyons and Rouen, resulted in the arrest and conviction of the thieves, who were publically exhibited in the iron collar in front of the privileged spectacles, whipped, branded, and sent off to serve as forced laborers in the King's galleys.[84] Among their victims who filed declarations with the police were theater aficionados such as the underground chronicler Louis Petit de Bachaumont (a stolen gold watch at the Opera),

[79] MS, 17:227, 229. On fire prevention see also Fayçal el Ghoul, *La Police parisienne dans la seconde moitié du XVIIIe siècle (1760–1785)* (Tunis, 1995), 293–95; and Lagrave, *Le Théâtre et le public*, 107 and figure 13.

[80] CS, 13:115.

[81] Victor Fournel, *Curiosités théâtrales, anciennes et modernes, françaises et étrangères. Nouvelle édition, revue, corrigée, et très-augmentée* (Paris, 1878), 163; AD, 1:256.

[82] BA, ms 11723, f. 2–3.

[83] BA, ms 12025, f. 1–237; AN, Y10872–73 and Y11337.

[84] See the printed *Arret* of 11 March 1760 in AN, Y11337.

and Voltaire's long-time friend and correspondent the Comte d'Argental (also a stolen watch at the Opera).[85]

Accounts of the thefts by victims recreated the distracting discomforts of the parterre; Joseph de Villières, who lost a green silk purse with twenty *louis* inside, remembered noting a man next to him in the Opera parterre who was "cinq pieds, six pouces" tall with a pale and pockmarked face and a gray cloak; he had eyed the man suspiciously during the play.[86] The Comte de Morges, also relieved of a silken money purse, notified the police while the performance was still in progress that a small, wigged, pock-marked man had feigned an exit from the parterre owing to the press of spectators; at de Morges request, the guard followed the man for a while but then lost sight of him.[87] Two other unfortunates reported the theft of their snuffboxes during the interlude when they had left their seats in other parts of the Opera house to mingle momentarily in the pit.[88]

Within the crowded, overheated, theft-prone pit, the steadily advancing threshold of bodily shame, studied in Early Modern Europe by Norbert Elias, frequently retreated. Excessive consumption of food and beverage and the open display of bodily functions countered the civilizing process. Eating and drinking were common activities in the parterre; in addition to the cafés and taverns surrounding the theaters, each of the privileged theaters had a *limonadier* operating a café under the amphitheater that sold food and drink to theater patrons.[89] At the Comédie-Française, it also appears that the Café Procope, across the street from the theater, provided refreshments for spectators in the playhouse.[90] The ready availability of drink led to disturbances in the parterre, as on 4 October 1739, when a drunken former assistant to a tax collector *(cy-devant sous-brigadier des fermes)* hit another spectator with his cane, threatened to hit the guards who eventually arrested him, and swore violently at his captors. When asked his name by the police agents, the inebriated and uncooperative tax collector replied that he was called "va te f[aire] f[outre]."[91]

[85] On Bachaumont, see BA, ms 12025, f. 44, 68; and AN, Y11337. On the Comte d'Argental, see AN, Y10872, *déclaration du 20 novembre 1758*, and *information du 12 décembre 1758*.

[86] BA, ms 12025, f. 72, 83; AN, Y11337.

[87] AN, Y13377.

[88] BA, ms 12025, f. 91, 98; AN, Y11337, *déclaration et information d' Henri Joseph LeDran*; AN, Y10872, *déclaration de M. Saulnier de la Garenne*.

[89] Lagrave, *Le Théâtre et le public*, 423; William L. Wiley, *The Early Public Theater in France* (Cambridge, MA, 1960), 224.

[90] BA, ms 10789, f. 4–5.

[91] BA, ms 11432, f. 2.

Bodily excretions as well as bodily intake were frequent in the over-crowded parterres. When the police attempted to outlaw whistling in the spectacles, inventive audiences learned to express their displeasure via coordinated choruses of coughing, spitting, and sneezing.[92] It is probable that they included another long-standing tactic, that of breaking wind, in their eighteenth-century repertory. One police officer noted in an August 1751 report that the cry "Paix là!" (Quiet over there!) was heard "these days during every scene and from every corner of the parterre."[93] But the spelling found in a plea for the release of an arrested apprentice to a jewelry merchant that same year suggests that the cry may have been a scatological pun. Louis Bellanger, writing on behalf of his apprentice, noted that the latter was arrested *pour avoir dit 'pet là' à la Comédie* (for having said "fart over there" at the theater). Word play on the verb *péter* (to fart) may explain the frequent recurrence of this cry in police reports.[94]

No product of the "material bodily lower stratum" was excluded from the parterre.[95] On Monday, 13 January 1777, the Comédie-Française disappointed its audience, which included the Duchess of Bourbon, when it was unable to perform the advertised play, *Les Horaces*, owing to the lead actor's unexplained absence. The actors sought to mollify a discontented parterre, but their efforts proved futile, as the *Mémoires secrets* of Bachaumont reported:

> Meanwhile the parterre manifested its humor; in vain the actors tried to calm the spectators with a preparatory dialogue, but the ruckus did not stop until the troupe offered to return the price of admission to the upset patrons. One audience member pushed these indecencies so far as to defecate in the middle of the assembly, while escorted and supported by a few other depraved individuals like himself.[96]

The creation of this fecal deposit signified the audience's unwillingness to follow the normal rules of exchange governing the spectator-spectacle relationship. This transgressive act might be interpreted as a protest against any of a number of contemporary power dynamics being replicated in the parterre. Significantly, the author of the *Mémoires secrets* continued his recounting of the incident by noting, "The Duchess of Bourbon stayed, but did not want to be the judge between the Public and the actors, as the lat-

---

[92] Lagrave, *Le Théâtre et le public*, 438–40.
[93] BA, ms 11738, f. 2–3.
[94] BA, ms 11745, f. 51; see also BA, ms 11301, f. 275–82; BA, ms 11650, f. 31–33; BA, ms 11728, f. 120–27.
[95] The phrase comes from Mikhail Bakhtin, *Rabelais and His World*, trans. Hélène Iswolsky (Bloomington, 1968).
[96] MS, 10:11–12.

ter group desired, or rather she told the players that they would have to submit to the desires of the Public."[97] The text did not specify whether the duchess stayed in spite of the excremental performance in the parterre or in spite of the substitute performance onstage. Her unwillingness to contradict the wishes of the parterre, however, indicated her acknowledgment of the pit's response to the actors' abrupt and inconsiderate change in program. Some parterre spectators had resorted to the semiotics of the marketplace to show their displeasure, and the actors, the duchess, and the author of the account could not fail to mistake a protest couched in a language far from that of rational discourse.

The open display of bodily functions in a public space such as the parterre could also disrupt many standard assumptions of social rank and practice. On 18 August 1751, the police arrested the tax farmer Berthe, an extremely wealthy venal officeholder, for allegedly urinating in the parterre of the Comédie-Française.[98] Berthe already experienced intermittent paralysis in his left arm and leg, a condition that had prompted him to visit the "wine country" *(pays de vin)* to soak his leg in *marc de vin*.[99] The sergent who arrested Berthe wrote that he had taken action against the tax farmer "for having pissed in the parterre without any precaution and for making insulting remarks to the guard."[100] It is unclear what the absence of "any precaution" might mean, but in his plea for release to the lieutenant general of police, Berthe stated that he had been "falsely accused of having pissed against the orchestra while seated on a small bench [in the parterre]."[101] Perhaps Berthe, swayed by the giddy liminality of the pit, participated in a Rabelaisian moment of bodily renewal, but by the time he had sobered up to find himself in prison, he denied the carnivalesque social equality of the parterre. His defense against the accusation was one of social station: "I beseech Your Greatness to please note that an honest man knows how to act decently and is not capable of that which I am accused, and that it is quite sad for an established man and for a [illegible] known for his honesty to find himself led off to prison."[102]

In other words, given Berthe's wealth and high social status, he argued that it was simply impossible for him to have transgressed the boundaries of his civilized station by openly urinating in the public space of the parterre.

---

[97] Ibid.
[98] Berthe's official title was *payeur des rentes de l'hôtel de ville*, a venal office with revenues of anywhere between 150,000 to 600,000 livres per year, according to Marcel Marion, *Dictionnaire des institutions de la France aux XVIIe et XVIIIe siècles* (Paris, 1923), 435–36.
[99] BA, ms 11671, f. 100–101.
[100] BA, ms 11737, f. 303.
[101] Ibid., f. 307.
[102] Ibid., f. 307.

The authors of the police reports are strangely complicit in this argument, for after initially stating that Berthe had *pissé* in the parterre, they resort to euphemisms in subsequent accounts. Thus, Delavault, a brigadier of the watch, wrote that Berthe was arrested for *indécens expliqués dans mon raport* (indecencies explained in my report); and the order for Berthe's release from prison the next day stated that he was imprisoned *pour s'y être mal comporté* (for having behaved badly).[103] In the documentary traces left of the incident, then, the civilizing process had already begun to efface any traces of Berthe's inappropriate behavior. On paper, order and social hierarchy vanquished the festive chaos of the parterre.

Male bodies in the parterre thus ate, drank, broke wind, defecated, and urinated; they also experienced sexual desire, if we can believe even a fraction of the accounts left behind in journals, novels, and other sources.[104] The exclusion of women from the pit partly determined (and was in turn determined by) expressions of parterre sexuality. Tradition, rather than law, prohibited women entry to the parterre, because none of the King's ordinances issued in the seventeenth or eighteenth centuries specifically barred women from the floor area. Fears of parterre violence may initially have accounted for this exclusion, but in the eighteenth century women were not banned from other potentially violent urban spaces such as taverns, marketplaces, and the street itself. More likely, concerns about prostitution and the disruption of male, and possibly homosocial, sociability in the pit combined to prohibit a female presence in this area of the playhouse.

Nevertheless, exceptions existed. In 1778, when a bust of Voltaire was triumphantly crowned at the Comédie-Française during a performance of *Irène*, his final play, one observer reported that women crowded into the parterre of the packed Tuilleries theater.[105] Although it is possible that women may have wedged into the pit on other tumultuous occasions, such as free performances or opening and closing nights, other sources suggest that women might have been present in the parterre on many other evenings as well. In February 1763, the censor Marin sent a memo to Chrétien Guillaume de Lamoignon de Malesherbes, the director of the book trade, in which he recounted an interview with Mme de Beaumer, the newly appointed editor of the *Journal des Dames*. Marin derisively notes that Beaumer appeared in his bureau in pants and a large hat, with a sword at her side. When the censor asked her why she had dressed as a man, she

[103] Ibid., f. 305, 309.
[104] Lagrave, *Le Théâtre et le public*, 510–40, provides numerous excerpts from literary sources that evoke this theme.
[105] CL, 12:70.

responded that she planned to attend the theater that evening to review the new play for her paper, and that she wished to save money by purchasing a parterre ticket. Furthermore, she asserted that cross-dressing was her usual practice when she went to the theater.[106]

The nineteenth-century novelist George Sand, writing in her autobiography, remembers her mother saying that she and Sand's aunt wore male attire to accompany their husbands to the theater during the Revolutionary and Napoleonic periods, also allegedly to purchase cheaper parterre tickets.[107] Noneconomic factors motivated female transvestism in preindustrial Europe as well, such as the need for safety when appearing in public or traveling, the empowerment provided by a male identity, and the cultural difficulties presented by a female same-sex relationship. It is conceivable that Mme de Beaumer, Sand's mother and aunt, and other eighteenth-century female theatergoers were also prompted by some or all of these reasons to don male garb and head for the parterre.[108]

Given that some "men" in the pit may have been women and therefore deviated from the standards of male heterosexual desire, it would not be surprising to learn that other parterre spectators who met the biological criteria of masculinity were interested in nonheterosexual experiences. Although the crowded, milling, semi-anonymous nature of the pit would appear to facilitate male homosexual activity, evidence is difficult to locate. One interesting passage occurs in the memoirs of the father of the revolutionary Mirabeau, who narrated an encounter in the parterre of the Comédie-Italienne in the 1730s.[109] As he stood watching a performance one night, he felt a hand running along his belt. At first he suspected the intrusive appendage belonged to a thief, but since he was not dressed sumptuously and had only twenty-four *sous* in his pocket, he did nothing. The hand stopped at the opening to his pocket, but pulled away when Mirabeau shuffled his feet slightly. The young Marquis, turning to his side, saw a man "who seemed to look agitatedly up and down." Mirabeau, curious to see what would happen, allowed the man to approach him again; as soon as he did, Mirabeau looked directly at him and said "something which the man pretended not to hear." He did, how-

---

[106] BN, ms. fr. 22135, pièce 90, ff. 164–64v. This incident, and Mme de Beaumer's tenure as editor of the *Journal des Dames*, are analyzed in Nina R. Gelbart, *Feminine and Opposition Journalism in Old Regime France: Le Journal des Dames* (Berkeley, 1987), 95–132.

[107] George Sand, *Histoire de ma vie* (Paris, 1928), 4:81.

[108] On female transvestism in Early Modern Europe, see Judith C. Brown, *Immodest Acts: The Life of a Lesbian Nun in Renaissance Italy* (Oxford, 1986); and Rudolf M. Dekker and Lotte C. van Pol, *The Tradition of Female Transvestism in Early Modern Europe* (New York, 1989).

[109] Mirabeau, "Journal de la jeunesse," 4:368.

ever, pull away his hand once again. As a final test of the unidentified man's intentions, Mirabeau put his hand in the pocket of his vest and pulled at the opening; the man began to pull the vest up by its corner. In his memoir, Mirabeau confesses to a certain amount of embarrassment and indecisiveness at this moment. He considered attacking the individual, but then he would have been bundled off to prison while his solicitor went free. Eventually, he decided to rid himself of the man by announcing to a group of youths standing nearby that if they indulged in the "new fad," the "dandy" nearby had been pestering him for an hour. ("Si quelqu'un de vous était dans le nouveau goût, voilà une perruque qui me persécute depuis une heure.") On which, according to Mirabeau, the man slipped away into the crowd. Although the incident is interesting in part due to the author's combination of bravura and unease, which reveals something about the provisional nature of his own sexual identity, it is also intriguing because it suggests that this exchange was not an isolated event. Did the standing parterres of the Parisian playhouses provide an opportunity for men such as Mirabeau's nervous accoster to cruise in search of homosexual encounters?[110]

The threat of female transvestism and male homosexual activity in the parterre may have exaggerated the already aggressively heterosexual behavior displayed by many of the men who stood in the pit. These actions began outside the parterre. One 1724 police report described the scene at the entrance to the Comédie-Française, where a number of young men, drunk and armed with swords, gathered to comment on the women as they entered the playhouse: "These young men . . . said out loud, 'Oh, this one here is ugly, that one has good legs, that one has a great ass, the one getting out of her carriage dressed in yellow has bigger tits than the other.'"[111] The assumptions that sanctioned this behavior continued inside the playhouse, as men in the parterre scanned the balconies in search of women. A 1782 engraving of the interior of the Bordeaux theater offers visual evidence of this playhouse pastime: three men in different areas of the pit hold spyglasses to their eyes as they ogle the women on display in the balconies (figure 6). Casanova recounted such an experience in his *memoires* when he stated that soon after his arrival in Paris he was at the Comédie-Italienne "in the pit, gazing at the ladies in the boxes."[112] The writer Bridard de la Garde, in his 1740 *Lettres de Thérèse*, had one female loge occupant comment to a girl new from the provinces,

[110] On male homosexuality in eighteenth-century France, see the essays by Bryant T. Ragan and Jeffrey Merrick in *Homosexuality in Modern France*, ed. Ragan and Merrick (Oxford, 1996).

[111] BA, ms 10856, f. 44–45.

[112] Casanova, *Memoirs of Jacques Casanova*, ed. Leonard Louis Levonson (New York, 1958), 127.

Vue perspective de l'intérieur de la Salle qui fait voir la partie du Théatre.

Fig. 6. *Perspective View of the Interior of the Playhouse Facing the Stage*, from Victor Louis, *Salle de spectacle de Bordeaux* (Paris, 1782). (By permission of the Houghton Library, Harvard University.)

You would be quite naive to believe that it is a taste for theater that brings men here; the theater is only a pretext, an occasion which would never draw them out of their homes if the parterre that you see below was filled with blind men. But this formidable body is an Argus whose vagabond gaze constantly sweeps the playhouse. Among all the eyes that compose this gaze, what a shame it would be for us if we did not cause some of them to stop as they passed over us![113]

Women may not have had similar conversations in the boxes at the Comédie-Française, but the male novelist's fictionalized report speaks to masculine intentions in the pit. Male aggression frequently manifested itself through cries of *place aux dames*! On a Sunday in 1750, the police arrested a legal clerk and a boutique owner's assistant in an attempt to quiet parterre spectators who were yelling, "Make room for the ladies, make room in the second balcony, make room for the *demoiselle* with the handkerchief!"[114] Apparently, the presence of several men in a loge situated in front of the woman with the handkerchief triggered these cries. Women in the loges often willingly indulged the visual inspections of parterre spectators, as the Bordeaux engraving (see figure 6) suggests; one male occupant of a second-tier box at the Comédie-Française in 1743 found himself displaced from his front-row spot before the curtain rose when he yielded to a woman from the next box over who sought, along with two female companions, to escape the oblivion of the back bench.[115] At the Comédie-Italienne one afternoon in 1749, the police themselves attempted to satisfy wandering parterre eyes by requesting before the performance that men seated in front of women in the second and third balconies cede their places to the female spectators.[116] Another frequently heard cry from the parterre, "Haut les mains M. l'abbé," also gave vent to sexual frustrations on the part of parterre spectators. The cry supposed that a cleric's hands were straying, particularly when seated next to a female spectator. In *A Sentimental Voyage*, Sterne recounted his surprise on learning the significance of this cry:

And can it be supposed, said I, that an ecclesiastic would pick the grissets' pockets? The old French officer smiled, and whispering in my ear, opened a door of knowledge which I had no idea of—Good God! said I, turning

---

[113] Quoted in Lagrave, *Le Théâtre et le public*, 521.
[114] BA, ms 11700, f. 230; see BA, ms 11024, f. 140–42; BA, ms 11230, f. 297–99; and BA, ms 11326, f. 11–13, for similar examples.
[115] Cornell University, Carl A. Kroch Library, Rare and Manuscript Collections, Maurepas Collection, 2.083.
[116] BA, ms. 11684, f. 248.

pale with astonishment—is it possible, that a people so smit with sentiment should at the same time be so unclean, and so unlike themselves—*Quelle grossierté!* added I."[117]

Sterne's innocence served his comic purposes well, but parterre regulars knew that *grossierté* of this sort was common in the loges as well as the pit. In a particularly extreme case in 1701, a young man from Nemours, characterized by the police as a "libertine," was arrested at the Comédie-Française when he used force to try to gain access to the loge of two women he had seen from the pit.[118] The assumptions of many parterre spectators were reinforced by the variety of amorous (and at times commercial) encounters that occurred in the amphitheater, the second and third balconies, and backstage in the wings and the players' dressing rooms.[119] Indeed, speculation about the sexual activities of actresses was rampant in the pit, as a 1733 clash between three parterre spectators attests. One of the men, discussing the merits of various actresses during an intermission, opined that Mlle Dangeville acted with wit, but had none outside the theater, at which point another leaped to her defense. Tensions escalated until the two men left the pit to draw swords at the entrance to the playhouse; before they engaged in combat, however, they were separated and arrested.[120] At approximately the same time, the Count of Clermont, Abbot of St-Germain-des-Prés, carried his obsession with his mistress, the celebrated Opera dancer Camargo, to even greater extremes: from 1734 through 1740, he forced her to abandon the stage, allegedly because of "his jealousy of the public with which he shared the pleasure of viewing her."[121] After midcentury, a few actresses, singers, and aristocratic women in the loges viewed or performed in erotic sketches staged in private Parisian homes, although the number of women and the frequency of performances in these events is susceptible to exaggeration. Nevertheless, through the circulation of clandestine newsletters, popular songs, and pornographic literature, many parterre spectators suspected that some of the women performing in the *drames bourgeois* in the public theaters also exhibited themselves before the aristocracy in libertine spectacles.[122]

---

[117] Sterne, *Sentimental Journey*, 62; for another example of this cry, see BA, ms 11326, f. 467–70.

[118] Cottin, ed., *Rapports de police de René d'Argenson*, 75.

[119] Lagrave, *Le Théâtre et le public*, 529–40; Erica-Marie Benabou, *La Prostitution et la police des moeurs au XVIIIe siècle* (Paris, 1987), 362–83; Lenard Berlanstein, "Women and Power in Eighteenth Century France: Actresses at the Comédie-Française," *Feminist Studies* 20 (1994): 475–506.

[120] BA, ms. 11229, f. 119–22.

[121] Campardon, *L'Académie royale de musique*, 1:87 n. 4.

[122] Karl Toepfer, *Theatre, Aristocracy, and Pornocracy: The Orgy Calculus* (New York, 1991), 59–80; but see also the reservations in Rougemont, *Vie théâtrale*, 307.

Sexual desire did not motivate all the interactions of parterre spectators with individuals in other areas of the theater. For instance, one police officer commented that "troublemakers" in the pit often sought refuge in the third tier of the loges, where they believed they would escape the policing efforts of the King's men; apparently men in the pit would then shout at their acquaintances stationed in the top loges, as we have already seen with the Marquis de Mirabeau in the 1730s. At the Comédie-Italienne in February 1750, a secretary to a royal Master of Requests, seated in the third balcony, was accused of shouting "Paix là-bas" between the first and second acts of the main play, an action which drew a prolonged and vocal response from many men in the pit. The police agent in charge of the evening's performance deemed it necessary, to restore order to the theater, to place the young man under arrest. In his plea for release, the alleged troublemaker, a twenty-five year old named Noel Vautrin, asserted that he and a friend had only resorted to the third balcony when they were unable to obtain parterre tickets at the box office; furthermore, he claimed that his cry had been inspired by a genuine desire to hear the musical interlude performed between the two acts.[123] Two years earlier, a domestic situated in the third balcony at the Comédie-Française was also incarcerated for crying "Place aux dames!" before the play started; the police report suggests that his shouts irritated many parterre spectators, but a plea on his behalf claims that he was only echoing a sentiment that began in the pit itself.[124]

In addition to the women who adorned the balconies and these sallies between the parterre and the *paradis*, the wealthy and flamboyant spectators who sat on the stage itself before 1760 also commanded the attention of individuals in the parterre. Coypel's image of a stage curtain bursting from behind with spectators, discussed earlier (see figure 5), may often have corresponded to the preperformance scene within the privileged theaters. One night at the Comédie-Italienne in December 1743, just before the start of the play, an astonished group of parterre spectators watched the stagehand charged with lighting the chandeliers at the foot of the stage go flying into the orchestra. The police arrested one Chevalier de Monaco, who explained in his letter of apology that he had been peering out through a hole in the curtain when a friend had shoved him from behind, causing him in turn to send the stagehand tumbling into the orchestra.[125] Hijinks by onstage spectators, and the responses they drew from individuals in the

123 BA, ms 11728, f. 120–27.
124 BA, ms 11644, f. 165–67.
125 BA, ms 11537, f. 124–31.

pit, became legendary as the century progressed. The three-volume 1775 compilation of French theatrical lore, the *Anecdotes dramatiques*, recorded many telling stories, including a supposed incident involving a cleric seated on the stage of the Comédie-Française during the performance of an obscure tragedy in 1729. Parterre spectators, spying him onstage, began to cry "A bas M l'Abbé," in the belief that he should join them in the pit. The cleric, however, told the noisemakers that "since my gold watch was stolen while I stood amongst you, I prefer to pay for a seat onstage rather than risk the loss of my snuff box as well!" The derisive cries of the parterre spectators reportedly turned to applause with this witticism, and the man remained onstage.[126]

These entertaining anecdotes compiled throughout the century appear plausible when compared to incidents recorded in the police archives. Just before the elimination of stage seating in March 1759, a spectator appeared onstage during the well-attended second performance of Colardeau's *Astarbé* with a huge bouquet of flowers that he displayed to the assembled audience in between acts; in response, parterre spectators rhythmically clapped their hands and chanted "Bouquet! Bouquet!" until the police intervened by arresting the tallest man in the pit and quieting the remainder.[127]

Perhaps the most provocative confrontation of the century, one that symbolized the potential animosity between those seated onstage and those who stood in the pit, occurred at the Opera house on 24 March 1787, just two years before the Revolution. That day, the Marquis de Gouy d'Arsy, a nobleman in his thirties and a colonel in the King's armies, purchased a ticket that entitled him to sit in one of the boxes on the stage of the Opera, which had by then moved to its Porte St-Martin location.[128] At some point during the second act, he decided to place his chair on the stage itself in such a way that it blocked the view of a large number of parterre spectators. According to the commanding officer who reported the incident, de Gouy had knowingly stationed himself to block sight lines to the stage; when parterre spectators began to yell at him to move, he willfully ignored their request, looking disdainfully at them through his eyeglasses. While pit occupants continued to yell at him, other spectators seated in the stage boxes also requested that he reposition himself so that the tumult would cease. Rather than ceding to the wishes of audience members on the stage and in the pit, he borrowed a

---

[126] AD, 1:2.

[127] BA, ms 12031, f. 335–42.

[128] SHAT, Yᵃ 274, chemise "délits par des particuliers contre les gardes françaises"; and Jean Chagniot, *Paris et l'armée au XVIIIe siècle. Etude politique et sociale* (Paris, 1985), 181.

lorgnette from another spectator so that he could show even greater defiance toward the parterre spectators, who had begun to pelt him with oranges. At this juncture, the Opera guard finally approached him, requesting that he retire from the stage. According to the sergeant's report, he did so only after "many difficulties." The senior-ranking military presence in attendance at the Opera that night, the Maréchal de Noailles, observed the incidents from his box above the stage; he quickly made his displeasure with de Gouy's antics known and suggested that it was necessary "to content the parterre."

Participating in the Performance

Neighborhood quarrels, provocative nobles onstage, pickpockets, libertines, and disorderly youths—a spectator in the parterre might encounter all of these and much more. These examples suggest that eighteenth-century parterre practices resulted in a theatergoing experience vastly different from the quietly contemplative aesthetic event with which we are familiar today. Some eighteenth-century observers, however, implied that the chaos of the pit only heightened the intellectual and emotional intensity of the theatergoing experience. Before we rush to condemn the eighteenth-century public theater as unruly and its audiences as unappreciative, we might do well to listen to the comments of two contemporaries, the philosophes Condillac and Diderot, on the experience of attending the public theaters in their day.

In his 1746 essay on epistemology, *Essai sur l'origine des connaissances humaines*, the Abbé de Condillac used a theatrical example to help illuminate the workings of memory. Condillac questioned why the human mind did not retain sensory perceptions previously present in the consciousness. In response, he called on the idea of "attention" to explain how perception passed to memory. Attention, according to Condillac, was the principle that made some perceptions more vivid to the human mind than others. The experience of theatergoing illustrated this principle:

[E]veryone has had the occasion to remark that one is never more apt to believe oneself the only witness of an interesting scene, than when the theater is filled to capacity. This is perhaps because the number, the variety, and the magnificence of the objects stir up the senses, heat up and lift the imagination, and thereby make us more susceptible to the impressions the poet wants to arouse. Perhaps, too, the spectators mutually prompt each other, through the examples they give each other, to fix their gaze on the stage.[129]

For Condillac, the crowded, tumultuous experience of the theater paradoxically served to heighten one's attention, focusing it on oneself as the receptor of the events onstage. The mental effort necessary to block out parterre disturbances and process the impressions generated by the playwright and actors facilitated the theatrical illusion, rather than destroying it. The energy expended by one's neighbor, whether in the pit or the loges, only served to reinforce the sense of isolation in the midst of the crowd. Although Condillac sought to elaborate a sensationalist epistemology, his resort to the example of the public theater underlines the importance granted to the playhouse experience by his contemporaries.

Condillac's philosophical colleague, Denis Diderot, wrote much more extensively and systematically on the dramatic arts, yet his most insightful moment may have come during the course of a 1758 epistolary response to the playwright and novelist Mme Riccoboni:

> Fifteen years ago our theaters were tumultuous places. The coolest heads got overheated on entering and reasonable men more or less shared the transports of the mad. . . . People became agitated, moved about, pushed one another, spirits went wild. What mood could be more favorable to a poet? The play commenced with difficulty and was interrupted often, but when a good part was reached . . . The enthusiasm went from the parterre to the loges, and from the loges to the boxes. The people had arrived flushed with excitement; they left the theater intoxicated. . . . It was like a storm that would dissipate far in the distance, a storm whose rumbling would last long after it had moved on. That was pleasure.[130]

Diderot's tempest-laden imagery underlines what he perceives to be the positive impact of playhouse unruliness. The agitations, the *flux et reflux*, the easily aroused passions of the spectators, especially those standing in the parterre, all served to maximize the dramatic impact of the play rather than dissipate

---

[129] Abbé de Condillac, *Essai sur l'origine des connaissances humaines* (Paris, 1924), 18; English translation from Suzanne Gearhart, *The Open Boundary of History and Fiction: A Critical Approach to the French Enlightenment* (Princeton, 1984), 174.

[130] Denis Diderot, "Réponse à la lettre de Madame Riccoboni," quoted in Marie-Hélène Huet, *Rehearsing the Revolution: The Staging of Marat's Death*, trans. Robert Hurley (Berkeley, 1982), 31–32.

and diminish it. The Habermasian-inspired vision of the enlightened public sphere has prepared us to find critical activity only in the serene encounter of the reader and the printed object. But the example of the eighteenth-century public theater demonstrates that reasoned critique was not incompatible with a lack of civility, or with carnivalesque behavior. In fact, as Condillac and Diderot each appreciated, the physical stimulus of the parterre might serve to heighten a spectator's critical acuity, thereby prompting him to intervene in the performance. Rather than preserving the critical sense of detachment that we value when we attend the theater today, eighteenth-century parterre patrons insisted on collaborating within the playhouse in physically demonstrable and emotional ways. Their modes of participating in and evaluating spectacle were inseparably linked to the practices, inside the playhouse and without, which we have examined so far.

Nevertheless, these practices were disquieting to authors and performers forced to collaborate with interventionist spectators. Throughout the century, they fought back in print and on stage; one of their most potent weapons was the accusation that an audience's response had been unfairly manipulated by a cabal, or group of spectators instructed beforehand to respond to the play in a certain fashion, regardless of the performance's merits. Cabals certainly existed in the eighteenth-century playhouse; the magistrate Hénault described one of the most vivid ones, organized against Voltaire's medieval tragedy *Adélaïde de Guesclin* in 1734, in a letter to an acquaintance.[131] But the cabal often proved to be a mirage imagined by shunned authors and spurned performers.

The response to the Abbé Nadal's 1725 tragedy, *Mariamne*, demonstrates the fate of authors who resorted too readily to blaming the cabal. Nadal premiered his play two months before the Comédie-Française staged a successful rewrite of the same topic by Voltaire.[132] When Nadal's play closed after four disastrous performances, he published his text with an explanatory preface that blamed its failure on Nicolas Thieriot, a friend of Voltaire, who had supposedly organized a cabal in the parterre against his work. His bitter accusations backfired, however, when a letter dated 20 March 1725 circulated in response to this preface. The missive was signed "Thieriot," but most scholars have suggested that it was the work of Voltaire.[133] In a viciously witty performance, Voltaire pointed out that the final resource of all bad

[131] Lagrave, *Le Théâtre et le public*, 472–73.
[132] See Jeffrey S. Ravel "*La Reine boit!* Print, Performance, and Theater Publics in France, 1724–1725," *ECS* 29 (Summer 1996): 391–411; and chapter 3.
[133] For example, Theodore Besterman, ed., *Voltaire's Correspondence* (Geneva, 1953–64), 1:297–301.

poets and playwrights was to complain of the cabal. He agreed with the abbé that there was a cabal that evening in the parterre; it had been organized by Nadal, who had given out free tickets to his friends, but his partisans were so bored by the performance that they had returned the tickets, saying they preferred to pay their money and hiss the play along with everyone else. Furthermore, those in the audience who remembered that Nadal had authored plays on other biblical subjects said that he had redone the Bible in burlesque verse. The letter contained dozens more insults and barbs aimed at Nadal, all of which rendered the abbé's accusations petty and pointless.

The devastating response occasioned by Nadal's preface demonstrated the perils of preface polemics. Far from achieving a closure that would have allowed for a more favorable reception of his tragedy, he provided a forum in which further abuse was heaped on both himself and his dramatic effort. Nadal's successors ignored his example, however; and their accusations continued to cast suspicion on the independent judgment and practices of parterre spectators down to the Revolution. The playwright and philosophe Marmontel attempted to combat this facile reflex on the part of authors, which he thought unfairly characterized playhouse audiences, in an article labeled *Cabale*, published in a 1776 supplement to the *Encyclopédie*.[134] In this essay, Marmontel wrote that one could measure the degree to which a century was enlightened "by the amount of influence the cabal exerts over public opinion, and by the amount of time it props up bad plays, or supresses good ones." He reassured young authors considering the stage that "in a century where taste has been formed," a good work had never succumbed to the cabal, and that bad plays had never managed to maintain their place on the stage. In other words, he remained supremely confident that the cabal, while posing a momentary threat to works of merit, would never triumph over a "public opinion which was just, and which marked each work with the proper degree of admiration, esteem, or scorn." For Marmontel in the final quarter of the century, the much-vaunted tribunal of public opinion was alive in the parterres and the loges, easily able to vanquish the prejudices and inconsistencies of the cabal.

Writing just four years earlier, however, Voltaire himself was not nearly so sanguine on the subject. Nearing the end of his life, the patriarch claimed that "it was principally in the parterre at the Comédie-Française, on opening nights, when cabals burst forth with the greatest passion. . . . [They] disgusted men of genius, and have contributed no small amount to the discrediting of the theater which had for so long been the glory of the

---

[134] *Supplément à l'Encyclopédie* (Amsterdam, 1776), 2:88–89.

nation."[135] Voltaire, of course, had reason to decry the cabal; *Artémire, Hérode et Mariamne, Mahomet, Sémiramis,* and many other works in the Voltairean canon had suffered the slings and arrows of outrageous parterre factions on their premiere. But contemporaries also suspected him of distributing parterre tickets to his friends and admirers on opening nights of his plays and of plotting the downfall of plays written by his dramaturgical opponents. The *théâtre de société* playwright Charles Collé gave voice to some of these widespread suspicions in his journal entry recording the premiere of Voltaire's 1750 tragedy *Oreste*:

> The entire auditorium hissed the dénouement except the parterre, which was more modest, having been paid to behave that way. Despite itself, however, the pit could not help but emit, from time to time, several marks of its disapproval. . . . The co-opted parterre did its duty, and tried to earn its keep, so that aided by fanatics and sustained by cabals and his stratagems, I have no doubt that Voltaire will succeed in prolonging his run for eight or ten performances, and perhaps even make himself a little unmerited fortune, much as he procured for himself with *Sémiramis* (by paying for it, of course).[136]

Collé's final remark referred to the accusations that Voltaire had bought out the parterre and distributed the tickets to his friends and admirers, thereby ensuring the play's success. It must be noted, however, that in spite of the rumors that consistently swirled around the controversial poet and man of letters, no hard evidence exists attributing any cabal directly to the actions of Voltaire. An inquiry into the ledgers of the Comédie-Française during the opening run of *Sémiramis,* for instance, does not show that Voltaire purchased an extraordinary amount of parterre tickets to redistribute to the cabal.[137]

Beyond the formal, organized characteristics of the cabal, always a threat to playwrights and actors, were the more or less spontaneous interventions of parterre spectators in the onstage proceedings. Through these actions, audience members continually served notice that they expected to

[135] Voltaire, *Les Cabaleurs* (1772), reprinted in *Oeuvres de Voltaire,* ed. M. Beuchot (Paris, 1833), 14:255–68; quote in note on 256–57.
[136] Charles Collé. *Journal et mémoires sur les hommes de lettres, les ouvrages dramatiques et les événements les plus mémorables du règne de Louis XV (1748–1772),* ed., H. Bonhomme (Paris, 1868), 1:121, 123.
[137] Lagrave, *Le Théâtre et le public,* 488–89. See ibid., 465–98, for a useful discussion of the "myths and realities" of the cabal in the eighteenth century.

participate in the performative aspects of the public theater. Mirabeau *père* recounts an episode from the early 1730s that demonstrates the audience's presumptive collaboratory rights.[138] One day in the pit during intermission, after he and his colleagues had silenced the orchestra to sing the provincial songs "that the Parisians love," someone sent him word to request that the actors play *Tartuffe* within the next few days. When the troupe's spokesman addressed the audience at the end of the evening to announce the next several days' performances, Mirabeau made his request, to which the spokesman consented. The next day however, the posters plastered on the walls of Paris made no mention of a performance of Molière's masterpiece in the next few days.

Mirabeau sent word to a man named Ducré, "a leader of youths," to meet him at the Procope at four that afternoon with as many young men as possible. According to Mirabeau's estimates, Ducré arrived at the rendezvous with four hundred followers in tow. They plotted their revenge on the actors, distributed parterre tickets to the youths, and descended on the playhouse. In spite of an increased guard, Mirabeau and his allies refused the actors permission to begin *Britannicus*, the scheduled tragedy. A police officer, sword drawn and accompanied by twenty-five soldiers armed with rifles and bayonettes, entered the parterre in search of the instigators. But the density of the crowd in the pit forced the soldiers to hold their rifles up in the air, and the spectators pushed them from behind and the sides, crowding in on them so that they could not lower their weapons to fire. Eventually, Mirabeau claimed, the soldiers quit the parterre, murmuring under their breath, an event that amused some of the other spectators on hand in the theater. At this point, a prominent but unnamed duchess arrived, and the actors, encouraged by her presence and the support of the men seated onstage, began the Racinian tragedy again. Sensing that the moment might be lost, Mirabeau cried out, "All right, my friends, all or nothing!" In his own words, "all hell broke loose in the pit." He reports that some young men tried to climb onstage to attack the actresses, who were quickly pulled offstage, while others began to scale the walls of the parterre toward the loges.

At this point, anarchy threatened to envelope the theater. The police had failed to contain the youths, and the actors had been unable to quiet the group long enough to continue the performance. The duchess chose to mediate between the troupe and Mirabeau's gang at this moment. She sent a page to Mirabeau and Ducré in the pit, asking them to come to her

---

[138] Mirabeau, "Journal de la jeunesse," 4:368–72.

box. After some hesitation, out of fear that they would be attacked by the guard if they left the parterre, they climbed the stairs to her loge, where she requested that they listen to the actors' reasons for why they had failed to perform *Tartuffe*. They did so in the actors' green room, then returned to the duchess's box, and granted her request to allow the troupe to finish the performance without further disturbance. These remarkable incidents attest to the willfulness of parterre spectators. Mirabeau did not organize a cabal for or against a specific playwright or player; rather, he presented his struggle as an effort to "save his honor" in the face of an insult from the actors. Class issues in part influenced the outbreak and the resolution of the affair. Mirabeau could not suffer disobedience from the lowly actors, who were forbidden the sacraments by the church and many civil privileges by the state. Likewise, only the duchess, a high-ranking courtier, could resolve the dispute in such a way that the actors could continue the performance and Mirabeau would not lose face. But the incident also should be interpreted as a power struggle between the performers and parterre spectators over the repertory, a basic issue of the public theater.

The hierarchy of this partnership was manifest in instances in which the parterre would mediate between members of the privileged troupes; in these cases, the parterre transformed backstage quarrels between actors into onstage dramas that superseded performance of the dramatic text. On 19 February 1757 at the Comédie-Italienne, the actors Rochard and Chaville began to argue with each other backstage.[139] The latter actor had taken the former's place onstage for almost a month because of Rochard's illness, but Rochard had finally returned to the stage. Rochard, displeased by the latter's success in his roles, chose the night in question to criticize Chaville backstage. Rochard's criticisms, according to witnesses, were spoken so loudly that they could be heard by the parterre. By the time the guard intervened, the two men had come to blows and were preparing to draw their swords on each other. Chaville was taken off to prison, but Rochard managed to flee the theater before the guards caught up with him.

Two nights later, both actors were playing a scene from the same play, *Ninette à la cour*, which had occasioned Rochard's outburst. In the play, Rochard played the Prince; Chaville, Ninette's lover Colas; and Mme Favart,

---

[139] Gueullette, *Notes et souvenirs*, 53–55; BA, ms 11957, f. 134–42. Gueullette was an attorney who had penned plays for the Comédie-Italienne in the 1720s and who had personally known many of the troupe's leading actors throughout the first half of the eighteenth century.

Ninette. During a scene between the Prince, Colas, and Ninette, the actress sang the following lines to the Prince/Rochard:

You will cause our disgrace Colas,
Don't say a word,
It's a Lord, Colas.
Oh, my Lord,
I am at your service,
Ninette at your heart,
It is a great honor for us.

Then, in a singing aside not intended for the Prince/Rochard's ears, she sang the following four lines to demonstrate her loyalty to Colas/Chaville:

Go to the devil,
This event overwhelms me,
Go to the devil,
You lying rascal.[140]

The parterre, aware of the actors' dispute that had led to Chaville's imprisonment, began to applaud the double entendre vigorously. Rochard, incensed and personally offended, broke character and addressed the following words to the parterre: "Since I perceive, Sirs, that my efforts do not please you, I quit, and I retire from the stage this very moment." The offended actor then left the stage, thereby disrupting the performance. Chaville and Mme Favart left as well in pursuit of their colleague, while the spectators seated onstage also cleared out to view the performance of Rochard's displeasure as it evolved backstage.

No sooner did Rochard reach his dressing room than the police appeared to arrest him for disobedience. Before being incarcerated, however, the actor was given the choice of returning to the stage to finish the performance or going off to prison. He apparently hesitated backstage while a number of the actors advised him to return to the performance. Meanwhile, the parterre responded to Rochard's exit by crying the actor's name repeatedly in an effort to woo him back onstage. His colleagues finally persuaded Rochard that his penalty would be less severe if he played out the performance. Returning to the stage, he made a sweeping bow and said, by way of apology, "Your favor is so dear to me, Sirs, that it obliges

---

[140] Gueullette, *Notes et souvenirs,* 54.

me to seek you out." At these words the parterre burst into great applause, which continued throughout the remainder of the performance.

A week later, with Chaville released from prison, the same trio of players found themselves onstage at the end of a play called *La Bohémienne*. The play's resolution occurred when Mme Favart, playing an old wife, told her equally aged husband (Rochard), to embrace his brother-in-law (played by Chaville). The two men, acting out their own personal drama as well as that of the text, embraced each other a number of times. They did so, according to Gueullette, because the parterre requested the repeated gesture of reconciliation. Parterre spectators thus collectively wrote the performance they wanted to see, and the actors obliged. The incident provided the perfect moment of eighteenth-century theatergoing; the lines between text and subtext were blurred as reality and theater converged. The author of the account concluded his story by writing: "This theatrical reconciliation was heartily applauded. Rochard obtained his liberty."[141]

At times, however, the parterre did not wait until the actors disrupted the performance before intervening. On 22 November 1749, expecting disturbances in the pit because of the troupe's rejection of a certain actress dear to the Paris public, the Italian actors were ordered to sell only four hundred parterre tickets.[142] This total was approximately two-thirds of the parterre's capacity at the Hôtel de Bourgogne, where the Italians played. No limit, however, was placed on the number of stage tickets the troupe might sell. When the curtain rose, the stage was so full of spectators that the actors "barely had three feet of space" in which to perform. When the players attempted to begin the second act, the parterre prevented the performance by yelling "Clear the stage!" *(Place au théâtre!)* The troupe's Harlequin tried to start the act, but the parterre then demanded that the actors lower the curtain and refund their money. Harlequin replied that once the play began, the actors never returned the price of admission; he continued to play the scene.

The parterre soon discovered that it had room to accommodate several hundred more people. When they cried out to their colleagues onstage to join them, however, Harlequin and Scapin thought the audience wanted them to continue the performance in the parterre. Although the spectators onstage would not let the actors off the set, the players evaded the onstage audience by passing through a trapdoor to the pit area, where they continued the performance. As they played in the empty space on

141 Ibid., 55.
142 Ibid., 49–53.

the floor of the parterre, the two actors reached a moment in the script where Harlequin sought protection against an angry Scapin by crying out, "A moi, camarades!" At this cry, the parterre spectators engulfed the two actors and tossed them about in a surge of bodies *(flux et reflux)*. The actors barely escaped to the foyer, and police agents needed an hour to restore order in the pit. In this instance, not only did the pit claim the final word over the placement of spectators in the playhouse, but it drew the performers into its midst and then physically intervened in the performance itself.

The Curtain Falls

Around eight or eight-thirty on most evenings, before the curtain fell at the end of the evening's performance, a member of the troupe would step to the front of the stage to announce the troupe's offerings for the next several nights, a form of publicity intended to complement the billboards posted throughout the city.[143] This final address of the evening also allowed spectators one more opportunity to comment on the production they had just witnessed. In 1716, parterre spectators seized on this occasion to express their displeasure with changes the actors had made to La Grange-Chancel's version of *Sophonisbe*; according to one account, the troupe's spokesperson was silenced by the angry crowd.[144] At the end of the unsuccessful premiere performance of Saint-Foix's *La Colonie* at the Comédie-Française in October 1749, the guard reported that the announcement of the play's next performance, scheduled for the following Monday, was met with whistles and cries of disapproval. The next day, the lieutenant general of police, informed of the "murmuring in the parterre" occasioned by the play, suspended its performance; the troupe did not stage the work again until 1761.[145]

Although the performance onstage ended with the announcement of each troupe's upcoming offerings, the nightly comedy in the hall continued as theatergoers made their way out of the doors into the Parisian evening. Parterre spectators who had eyed the women in the loges during the play

---

[143] For the origins of the practice, see William S. Brooks, "*Harangue* or Dialogue? The Publicity of the French Stage, 1634–1673," *Seventeenth-Century French Studies* 8 (1986): 166–76; and "Chappuzeau and the *orateur*—A Question of Accuracy," *Modern Language Notes* 81 (April 1986): 305–17.

[144] AD, 2:472.

[145] BA, ms 11671, f. 96–97; Lagrave, *Le Théâtre et le public*, 591.

scrambled to continue their inspections as the women left the theater, a practice described in La Morlière's 1746 novel, *Angola*:

> After the curtain, Aménis and her friends waited awhile in their loge while the crowds exiting the theater thinned out, then proceeded to the staircase. There they were examined and evaluated by men, crowding the passage, who practically shoved their lorgnettes under the ladies' noses.[146]

Spectators fortunate enough to own carriages made their way to the front entrance, where special criers hired by the theaters announced their presence to the coachmen waiting on the adjoining streets. Even these privileged individuals, however, briefly encountered the crowds of lackeys, servants, and pickpockets who milled around the spectacles at their conclusion, just as they did before the curtain. The Marquis de Marana, for example, writing to the police on behalf of one of his servants arrested after a 1768 Comédie-Italienne performance, described a conflict between a group of domestics who crowded toward the entrance and the sentinels who pummeled them with their rifles. When the master of the servants in question scolded the sergeant for allowing his troops to beat the men, Marana's servant apparently cried out that the soldiers deserved a hundred lashes for their actions, a sentiment that resulted in his prompt arrest.[147]

The torches used to illuminate the night created problems unique to the end of an evening at the theater. In addition to the fire hazards they posed, they might also be used as weapons by disgruntled individuals, as a police officer named Chevery discovered in front of the Comédie-Française in November 1724.[148] Exiting the playhouse after the performance, he came on a tall man, dressed in bourgeois attire and holding two wax torches, who was burning the King's ordinance plastered on the front of the playhouse. When Chevery asked the man, later discovered to be a domestic who had illegally shed his livery, to cease his activities, the man swore at him and then waved his torch in Chevery's face. Although the latter quickly recoiled, his wig caught on fire; the servant escaped into the crowd in the resulting tumult.

Later in the century, a 1762 memo from the lieutenant general of police noted that individuals carrying torches were offering their services at the entrances of the privileged theaters to patrons who needed to find their way home through the darkened streets. So many of these individuals gathered

---

[146] La Morlière, *Angola* (Paris, 1746), 30; quoted in Lagrave, *Le Théâtre et le public*, 418.
[147] BA, ms 12332, f. 24–25.
[148] AN, Y13297, 30 November 1724.

just outside the entrances, however, that "the public has difficulty leaving the building, and their flames have often caused accidents." The soldiers were therefore instructed to move these torchbearers further away from the entrances, and also to encourage those carrying lanterns, a safer form of illumination, to place themselves closer to the exiting spectators.[149]

In 1770, guards stationed in passageways around the Palais Royale were ordered to ensure that these passages stayed well lit from sundown through the departure of spectators at the end of the performance. In addition, they were instructed to prevent Opera patrons from making noise, quarreling, and "leaving their filth" in the outdoor corridors.[150] In spite of these precautions, individuals were never entirely safe once beyond the threshold of the theater. A young female singer named Jeanne-Eléanore Thibert filed a complaint with the police in September 1737 against two men who cornered her in the arcades of the Palais Royal after a performance as she was returning home. The two men, addressing her facetiously as *notre petite reine*, apparently tried to force her to take tobacco, then struck her face and arms viciously when she attempted to escape their grasp, and called her a thief and "insults even more atrocious that modesty does not permit [the police agent] to record."[151]

Conclusions

Male spectators who chose to view a play from the pit two to three centuries ago experienced a social space and a set of cultural practices that were *sui generis*. The parterre audience did not resemble the crowd of rural riots or the urban marketplace, nor did it match the organized, disciplined polity of the modern, Western democracy. Rather, the parterre lay somewhere between early modern notions of crowd activity and modern representative political practices; like the eighteenth-century French regime that supported and policed it, the public theater drew on its Renaissance predecessors and anticipated its modern, commercial successors. In the eighteenth century, then, parterre spectators had more control over the spectacles staged before them than at any other moment before or since. For this reason, the parterre is important not only for the history of French

---

[149] AN, Y13388, 22 December 1762.
[150] SHAT, Yª 272, chemise "Gardes françaises," dossier "théâtre," document labeled "consignes des postes," p. 6.
[151] Campardon, *L'Académie royale de musique*, 2:318–19.

aesthetics and high culture, but also for the history of the transition from absolutist rule to modern democracy. In the chapters that follow, I turn to a diachronic treatment of parterre spectators in which I trace their rising autonomy from the reign of Louis XIV to the Revolution, and in which I also study efforts by the government and others to stifle, or channel, this sense of independence.

2

Origins of the Contested Parterre, 1630–80

It is not a hundred years ago, since dramatic poetry began to flourish in France, since which time, the French have not only been remarkably united, but have advanced their conquests so fast, that they have almost doubled their Empire. Cardinal Richelieu was the person who at the same time laid the foundation of the greatness of their Theatre, and their Empire. And it is a surprizing thing to consider that the spirit of dramatic poetry leaving them just before the beginning of the last war [1689] by Molière and Corneille's death and by Racine's age, they have since that time lost almost half their conquests.

—John Dennis, *The Usefulness of the Stage*, 1698

Politics, Theater, and Gardens in the Age of Richelieu and Louis XIV

The English and the Spanish first established public theater companies that performed on a regular basis before paying patrons in the late 1570s, more than half a century before their French counterparts. It was not until the 1630s, a generation after Shakespeare, that a critical mass of educated Parisian theatregoers capable of supporting two nonambulatory troupes emerged in the capital.[1] The companies performed plays by a group of college-trained playwrights, the best known of whom today is Pierre Corneille. These troupes, one of which adopted the name of the King's Players *(les comédiens du roi)*, received assistance and protection from both Louis XIII and his first minister, the Cardinal Richelieu. During the next half-century, the works of Corneille, Racine, and Molière brought the French stage prominence throughout Europe. Indeed, John Dennis, an English critic writing in 1698, noted the parallels between the seventeenth-century fortunes of the French stage and the French monarchy. Although he did not outline a cause and effect relationship between the decline of the French stage after its great seventeenth-century triumvirate and the

---

[1] Walter Cohen, *Drama of a Nation: Public Theater in Renaissance England and Spain* (Ithaca, 1985), 136–85; Colette Scherer, *Comédie et société sous Louis XIII* (Paris, 1983).

67

wartime failures of Louis XIV's reign after 1689, his testimony does convey the international esteem achieved by the French stage in its classical age under Richelieu and Louis XIV.

The subsequent canonization of Corneille, Racine, and Molière, a process already well under way during the eighteenth century, guaranteed that the story of their poetical and dramaturgical brilliance would often be told.[2] A less familiar tale connected to the theater history of the Grand Siècle is that of the various social and political uses of theater in the Parisian playhouses and at court. Kings and ministers, players and spectators, playwrights and readers, all pursued their own agendas during this formative period of the French stage. While institutional and aesthetic innovations fixed the social geography of the public theaters in this period, Richelieu and Louis XIV acted to capitalize on the symbolic politics of theatrical ritual at court and in the city. And while the crown explored the political possibilities of the stage, Parisians of many different occupations grew accustomed to standing in the parterre to watch the plays of the classical period. At first the French did not think of the spectators in this area as a coherent group with critical interests. But by the end of the century, writers, actors, and spectators alike had begun to forge an identity for the parterre.

The word *parterre* acquired new meaning in the gardens of seventeenth-century France, as well as in its theaters.[3] The parallel is instructive, because both royal pleasure gardens and public playhouses were shaped by a Bourbon dynasty seeking cultural forms of legitimation. Rémy Saisselin, a literary and cultural historian of the Old Regime, has remarked that "the French garden [of the seventeenth and eighteenth centuries] is a stage setting; it is the exterior version of the palace interior which is also a court stage set for a perpetual opera . . . representing nobility, royalty, kingship, majesty and grandeur."[4] Thus, it is not surprising to find formal gardening labels, such as *amphitheater* and *parterre*, applied to specific areas of the French theater. By the beginning of the seventeenth century, "parterre" in its gardening sense meant a meticulously designed arrange-

[2] Prominent examples in this century are Henry Carrington Lancaster, *A History of French Drama in the Seventeenth Century*, 9 vols. (Baltimore, 1929–42); Antoine Adam, *Histoire de la littérature française au XVIIe siècle* (Paris, 1948), 5 vols.; and Jacques Scherer, *La Dramaturgie classique en France* (Paris, 1950).

[3] On French pleasure gardens, see Denise Le Dantec and Jean-Pierre Le Dantec, *Reading the French Garden: Story and History*, trans. Jessica Levine (Cambridge, MA, 1990); and Kenneth Woodbridge, *Princely Gardens: The Origins and Development of the French Formal Style* (London, 1986).

[4] Rémy G. Saisselin, "The French Garden in the Eighteenth Century: from *belle nature* to the Landscape of Time," *Journal of Garden History* 5 (1985): 286.

ment of low-lying boxwood or closely cut turf set against a background of colored earth or flowering beds; writers frequently called the entire unit a *parterre en broderie.* These ornamental creations, which required a great deal of labor to maintain, demonstrated the wealth and power of the house's occupant.[5] Unlike the unstable semiotic and political functions of the theatrical parterre, the meaning of the "garden variety" parterre by the end of the century had been permanently fixed in the gardens created by Louis XIV's prized landscape architect Le Nôtre at Vaux-le-Vicomte, at Versailles, and at other aristocratic country residences.

Antoine-Joseph Dézaillier d'Argenville, a contemporary of Le Nôtre's, codified the French formal garden style as perfected under Louis XIV in a 1709 treatise, *La Théorie et la pratique du jardinage.* This text, republished several times in subsequent decades, became the standard reference for eighteenth-century European gardeners instructed by their masters to emulate Versailles. In this work, d'Argenville succinctly characterized the relationship between the *parterre en broderie* and the building it ornamented:

A parterre is the first thing that must present itself to view. It should occupy the position closest to the building, either directly opposite or on the sides, as much for the discovery of the building as for its own beauty and richness, which is endlessly present to the eyes, and which can be seen from every window of the house.[6]

D'Argenville was fully aware of the reciprocal relation between parterre and building. Not only was the view of the garden from the house an important consideration for the gardener as he laid out the parterre; the house could only be fully appreciated from the vantage point of the parterre. Independently, the significance of either was diminished. This passage also suggests that both chateau and garden could be used to stage the spectacle of power favored by the elites of seventeenth-century France, and that either space was appropriate for viewing this spectacle.

In seventeenth-century France, efforts to "trim" the social spaces of pleasure gardens and public theaters belonged to the same cultural moment. First under Richelieu, then under Louis XIV, the Crown recognized an opportunity to stage its own spectacle of power in both arenas. In each instance, the parterre harbored the audience for these royal dramas. The absolute subjugation of nature in the gardens of the powerful corre-

---

[5] Woodbridge, *Princely Gardens,* 143.
[6] Antoine-Josephe Dézaillier d'Argenville, *La Théorie et la pratique du jardinage* (Paris, 1709), 20.

sponded to the perspectival restructuring of French theatrical aesthetics; attention to "parterres," whether they adorned a chateau or flanked the stage, became crucial to the cultural elaboration of absolutist power.

Social Geography of the Public Playhouse

While the Crown experimented with strategies for staging its power in the seventeenth century, the French theater's other significant "patron," the paying Parisian public, began to appear. In the decade of the 1630s, the Paris theatrical scene gained a legal and economic stability comparable to its London and Madrid counterparts; aesthetic changes accompanied this institutional growth. Before 1630, stage designers assumed an essential unity of place between the spectator and spectacle. Royal entries and the medieval mystery plays served as the models for this relationship. Both examples exhibited, as T. E. Lawrenson has suggested, a "larger unity of place, [a] sense of oneness between stage and auditorium" that was not present in the pre-1630 Paris public theater.[7] Set designers replicated this effect of oneness by creating two-dimensional backdrops that they placed relatively close to the front of the stage. Typically, these backdrops represented four or five different spaces. Actors indicated location by speaking their first few lines in front of the locale where the scene took place. They would then drop downstage to the candles at the foot of the stage to play the remainder of the scene. Stages themselves were usually platforms erected at one end of rectangular tennis courts.

Starting in the 1630s, designers, influenced generally by Renaissance ideas of perspective and specifically by the examples of Italian indoor theaters, began to redefine the spatial relationships of audience and spectacle in the indoor theater. The appearance of prosceniums and curtains served notice that set designers intended to "frame" the dramatic portrait, thereby articulating a distinction between the space of performance onstage and that occupied by the audience. Equally significant, however, were the changes that took place in the scenic backdrops found onstage. Sometimes through a carefully painted backdrop restricted to one cloth, sometimes through a series of staggered backdrops placed to achieve the desired effect, set designers sought to give the impression of unlimited space extending beyond the back wall of the stage. Lawrenson has labeled

---

[7] T. E. Lawrenson, *The French Stage in the Seventeenth Century: A Study in the Advent of the Italian Order* (Manchester, 1957), 29–47.

this new set the "theater of pictorial illusion."[8] The contrast with its predecessor was striking; whereas pre-1630 theatrical space emphasized the unity of spectator and spectacle at the expense of unity of place on stage, post-1630 design rigidly separated the viewer from the theatrical tableau while insisting on the unity of the fictional theatrical space.

These innovations seemingly called for a seating arrangement in the public theaters that would have placed the greatest possible number of spectators in a position to appreciate the vanishing-point perspective. The capital's theatrical proprietors, however, failed to follow this cue. Instead, they adapted the rectangular spaces of the former tennis courts *(jeux de paume)* in ways that conformed to the demands of the social hierarchy. The result was an audience configuration that appears contradictory and inefficient to the twentieth-century theatergoer accustomed to searching for the best seat from which to watch the performance. In the seventeenth century, however, public theater patrons used different criteria to identify preferential seating. These criteria offer an insight into the ways in which the Parisian spectator's needs differed from those of the monarchy.

The tennis court audiences in these early French playhouses settled into three spatially distinct areas. The first space for spectators consisted of the five or six rows of seats found on either side of the stage itself. This seating area was known as the banquettes, or the *théâtre*.[9] These were normally the most expensive seats in the house, priced at three livres, twelve *sous*, toward the end of the reign of Louis XIV.[10] John Lough has argued convincingly that the spectators who chose to purchase these seats were in all likelihood the wealthier and more aristocratic elements of the audience.[11] They were also, with few exceptions, all male. Although the practice of seating spectators on the stage apparently began before the premiere of Corneille's *Le Cid* in 1637, the overwhelming popularity of the playwright's controversial work prompted the tragedians of the Hôtel du Marais to place rows of chairs on the stage and charge extra for the privilege of using them.[12] Throughout most of the seventeenth century, no barrier existed on the stage to separate the playing area from the seating area. Spectators moved freely from one side of the stage to the other, shouting at

[8] Ibid., 49.
[9] The word *théâtre* referred to the stage in the seventeenth century; a playhouse was usually called a *salle*.
[10] Lough, *Paris Theatre Audiences*, 108.
[11] Ibid., 115–17.
[12] Barbara Mittman, *Spectators on the Paris Stage in the Seventeenth and Eighteenth Centuries* (Ann Arbor, 1984), 1–10.

their counterparts across the way or engaging in banter with spectators sitting or standing in other parts of the theater.[13] Only with the opening of the Comédie-Française's new building in 1689 did the actors erect balustrades on either side of the stage to confine the banquette patrons.[14]

The presence of spectators on the stage at the end of the seventeenth century appears to be a surprising development in light of the century's concern with theatrical *vraisemblance*. The image of the nobles seated on the stage, moving around and behaving uproariously, hardly added to the illusion of reality urged by dramatic theoreticians of the day. Furthermore, it is difficult to imagine that the effects of perspectival set design retained their impact when superimposed against the crowd seated in the banquettes. The presence of an elite audience on the stage suggests that the aesthetic imperatives of perspective design were not yet as important as the spectacle of social display that took place in the banquettes every evening.[15]

Examination of the adjacent seating area, the loges, reinforces the notion that seventeenth-century theatergoers experienced performance differently than we do today. The origins of the loges can also be traced to the first decades of the seventeenth century. As traveling theater groups began to appear in the borrowed Parisian tennis courts with greater frequency, they attracted a more literate, elite audience, distinguished in part by an increasing female presence. It would have been improper for these female spectators to stand on the ground with the common people, so the tennis-court proprietors installed balconies. Throughout the century, the balconies gradually evolved into distinct boxes rented and furnished by the elite for entire theatrical seasons.

Most of the early public playhouses boasted two tiers of loges; of these two levels, boxes in the first row commanded higher prices.[16] It was here that the women of Parisian society would sit, entertaining male and female friends as though enjoying their own mini-salon. Spectators of both sexes would slip in and out of various boxes to visit friends and pursue various combinations of social intercourse. Men seated in the banquettes also visited the loges to participate in the social scene enacted in the balconies. For

---

[13] Ibid., see the Campistron quote, 10; and the passage from Molière's *Les Fâcheux*, quoted in Lough, *Paris Theater Audiences*, 115–16.

[14] Barbara G. Mittman, "Cinq documents portant sur l'enceinte de la balustrade de l'Ancienne Comédie," *Revue d'histoire du théâtre* 33 (1983): 174–89, and Mittman, *Spectators on the Paris Stage*, 59–66.

[15] The banquettes lasted on the stage of the Comédie-Française until 1759; see Mittman, *Spectators on the Paris Stage*, 77–96.

[16] Lough, *Paris Theatre Audiences*, 108.

some of these spectators, little difference existed between the private spaces of their homes and the semipublic space of the loge; Bussy-Rabutin's correspondence recounts the behavior of three aristocratic women in the 1670s who relieved themselves in a chamber pot in their loge and then emptied it onto the heads of unsuspecting parterre members, just as the chambermaids in their Parisian *hôtels* would have dumped the contents out the window onto the street.[17] Although the balconies carried a certain prestige in the public theater hierarchy, they also followed the rectangular space of the audience hall to the extent of interfering with the viewing angle of their occupants. One had to turn almost a full ninety degrees to see the play from the loges on either side of the hall. Although the sight lines to the stage were poor, loge patrons enjoyed a prime view of those seated in the loge across the way. The physical situation of the balconies reinforced the elite, insular world inhabited by their occupants.

As with the banquettes, it would appear that loge seating was not designed to take full advantage of the critical perspective offered by theoretical and material developments in the French theater in these decades. In part this reflects the construction of spectator space predominant at court spectacles. The King's courtiers surrounded the monarch and the spectacle on all sides; their attention was drawn as much to the reaction of the monarch as to the activity of the performers. Jean-Marie Apostolidès has written of the *public du cercle*, the single, unitary circle formed by the elite spectators seated in the first row of loges and in the banquettes. He stresses the sense of identification these *comédiens de la cour* felt with the professional actors onstage; the actors of the Comédie-Française, in representing the princes and tragic figures of the French classical stage, acted out a ritual that confirmed the superiority of those seated in the *cercle d'élite*. According to Apostolidès, the spectators standing in the parterre, those of a social level below the audience seated onstage and in the boxes, bore witness to the sense of superiority enjoyed by spectators in the "better" seats.[18]

Apostolidès, however, underestimates the significance of the parterre in these early public theaters. Although social elites insisted on a definition of space within the public theater that would allow them to maintain their spatial hierarchy with respect to the parterre, they also abandoned the vanishing point, the focus of critical perspective. In their absence, that "privi-

---

[17] Ibid., quoted, 114.
[18] Jean-Marie Apostolidès, *Le Prince sacrifié. Théâtre et politique au temps de Louis XIV* (Paris, 1985), 41–43; and Jean-Marie Apostolidès, "La Scène comme lieu du sacrifice (imaginaire) du roi," *Stanford French Review* 9 (Spring 1985): 5–16.

leged" perspective position was filled by the spectators who crowded into the pit. After the benches on the stage and the balconies, the parterre was the third space occupied by spectators in the converted tennis courts of the early seventeenth century. This area remained unraked until the latter half of the century in most of the theaters. At the Hôtel de Bourgogne, estimates have placed the total floor space of the parterre at more than two thousand square feet, thus leading to speculation that the pit of the ancient theater could accommodate up to a thousand men. Venders circulated in the parterre, selling bread, cookies, and alcoholic refreshments in the first part of the century; after 1650, they added seasonal refreshments such as lemonades, strawberries, currants, and Chinese oranges.[19] The Comédie-Française's playhouse, built in 1689, had large stoves on either side of the parterre to warm the standing spectators, but it is unknown whether this was a common feature in public theaters before 1680 (see figure 3).

The parterre, although exclusively male, was the most socially heterogeneous sector of the public theater throughout the seventeenth and eighteenth centuries. Admission in most instances in the seventeenth century cost fifteen *sous*, but this did not necessarily exclude the poorest elements of the population, as there were many ways to sneak into the playhouses for free. The composition of the parterre included students from nearby Sorbonne, magistrates, clerks, and other administrative figures from the courts and governmental bureaus, merchants dealing in luxury items from the rue St-Denis, and figures from the literary and cultural world of the Parisian salons.[20] The parterre remained a rowdy and boisterous sector of the theater throughout the seventeenth century, to be sure, but it also underwent a continual refinement in terms of its capacity to evaluate a theatrical performance. By the establishment of the Comédie-Française in 1680, both actors and playwrights had begun to seek the favor of the parterre.

It is unclear exactly when and how Parisians first used the word "parterre" in connection with public playhouses. A 1588 religious diatribe against spectacles performed in the Hôtel de Bourgogne railed against the sinful activities that took place in the *salle basse* of the theater.[21] To my knowledge, the earliest mention of a parterre in the world of the Paris theater occurred in a lease agreement between the Confraternity of the Passion

---

[19] Information on the size of the parterre and the libations sold therein can be found in Wiley, *Early Public Theater*, 211, 225.

[20] Lough, *Paris Theater Audiences*, 55–99; Erich Auerbach, "La Cour et la Ville," in *Scenes from the Drama of European Literature* (New York, 1959), 154–55.

[21] Rolland du Plessis, *Remonstrances très humbles au Roy de France* (Paris, 1588), quoted in Lough, *Paris Theatre Audiences*, 79 n. 1.

and a troupe of ambulatory Italian actors in October 1621, eight years before the establishment of the first permanent acting company in the capital. The lease specified that the actors were not to interfere with the commerce of a Widow Dollin, who sold "macaroons, bread, wine and other things" in the parterre of the Hôtel de Bourgogne.[22] A little more than three years later, in January 1625, the word appeared again in a key clause in the confraternity's standard lease contract. Whereas in previous contracts visiting troupes had agreed to rent the main hall, the loges, and the stage of the Hôtel, this agreement also specified that the players would rent the "par terre" of the theater.[23] Thus, the earliest mention of the word confines its use to designating a physical location within the theater.

By the end of the pivotal decade of the 1630s, however, writers began to use the word in a metonymic sense to refer to the group of spectators who stood in the parterre. Furthermore, they characterized this composite image of the *peuple* in decidedly unflattering terms. La Mesnardière, an important mid–seventeenth-century dramatic theorist, discussed the common classes who attended the theater in the preface to his 1639 treatise *La Poétique*. Declaring that these spectators were unable to derive either pleasure or instruction from the theater, he wrote: "the crude multitude cannot find any pleasure in a serious, grave, chaste and truly tragic discourse, and . . . this many-headed monster is unable to appreciate anything more than theatrical ornaments."[24] In the same year, the playwright Georges de Scudéry also used pejorative animal imagery in an explicit evaluation of the parterre. Claiming in his *Apologie du théâtre* that the lowest class of theater spectators, the "ignorant ones," could be divided into loge ignoramuses and parterre ignoramuses, he characterized the latter in the following passage: "But it is time, finally, to descend from the loges to the parterre and to say a word in passing about that animal of many heads and many opinions that is called the people."[25] After drawing appropriate references to the theatrical rabble of classical antiquity, Scudéry excoriated the ignorance and stupidity of this audience, finishing by calling them centaurs, or, following Guarini, an earlier Italian writer, "half man, half goat, and all beast."

It is not surprising that these 1639 texts use bestial metaphors when discussing the parterre; the sign of a many-headed creature representing the lower ranks of the Third Estate was common in seventeenth-century polit-

---

[22] The lease is reprinted in Wilma Deierkauf-Holsboer, *Le Théâtre de l'Hôtel de Bourgogne, 1548–1635* (Paris, 1968), 199.
[23] Ibid., 202.
[24] Quoted in Lough, *Paris Theatre Audiences*, 70.
[25] Ibid., quoted, 65.

ical rhetoric. Most often it took the form of a monstrous hydra representing the democratic tendencies of the period that threatened monarchical
government. Furetière, for example, included the following definition of
"Hydra" in his 1690 dictionary: "Hydra is used figuratively in moral
issues, when speaking of popular seditions, and other things which pullu-
late and which multiply themselves the faster one tries to destroy them . . .
the people is a hundred-headed hydra."[26] Thus, in an attempt to condense the
many voices of the parterre spectator into a coherent whole, writers by the
end of the 1630s had recourse to disturbing political imagery that con-
jured up visions of the popular insurrections that plagued France in the
first half of the seventeenth century.[27]

Not all seventeenth-century writers were hostile to the parterre, however.
Molière, in the midst of the early-1660s quarrel occasioned by his comedy
The School for Wives, appealed favorably to the parterre spectators. In the
act of responding to his critics, he created a new dramatic genre, the one-
act *critique,* which revealed the possibilities inherent in a public appeal to
parterre sympathies.[28] *The School for Wives*, which Molière's troupe first
played in December 1662, came under heavy criticism for its supposed
indelicate language and indecent references to cuckolded husbands. Many
of the critics were actors or playwrights jealous of the newcomer Molière's
success at court. When several pamphlets appeared attacking both play and
playwright, Molière wrote *The Critique of the School for Wives*, a one-act,
staged response to his assailants.

The Critique occurred in the private space of a lavish home belonging to
Uranie, an occupant of *le monde* in Paris, several hours after the end of the
first performance of *The School for Wives*. Two female socialites were
joined by an older woman, a frivolous and uncritical marquis, a chevalier
who served as mouthpiece for Molière's views, and a pretentious poet. In

---

[26] Quoted in Pierre Ronzeaud, *Peuple et représentations sous le règne de Louis XIV. Les
Représentations du peuple dans la littérature politique en France sous le règne de Louis XIV*
(Aix-en-Provence, 1988), 222. See Ronzeaud, 221–22, in general for a discussion of Hydra
imagery. For the sixteenth- and seventeenth-century English case, see Christopher Hill, "The
Many-Headed Monster," in *Change and Continuity in Seventeenth-Century England* (Cam-
bridge, 1975), 181–204.

[27] The earlier debate on seventeenth-century uprisings between Boris Porchnev and Roland
Mousnier has been continued in Yves-Marie Bercé, *Histoire des croquants: Etudes des soulève-
ments populaires au XVIIe siècle dans le sud-ouest de la France*, 2 vols. (Geneva, 1974); and
Rene Pillorget, *Les Mouvements insurrectionels en Provence, 1596–1715* (Paris, 1975).

[28] I have counted approximately fifty *Critique* plays between 1663 and 1750, when the genre
died out. Lough, *Paris Theater Audiences*, 104–6, discusses the *Critique* plays of Molière and
Regnard.

the play, conflict quickly surfaces over the merits of Molière's work. The Marquis, a decidedly inarticulate buffoon, is unable to carry his criticism of the play further than the assertion that "it is detestable because it is detestable."[29] When the Chevalier, Dorante, attacks his tautological reasoning, the Marquis responds that the play must be worthless because it incites the parterre to continuous gales of laughter. Dorante responds by deriding the Marquis and others like him who sneer at a play simply because it is appreciated by those who view it from the cheaper areas of the theater. "Good sense has no fixed spot in the playhouse,"[30] he advises the Marquis, and then concludes his defense of the parterre's claim to critical legitimacy by saying: "[I]n general, I rely a good deal on the approbation of the parterre, for the reason that among those who stand there, there are many who are capable of judging a play by the rules, and others who pass judgement according to the proper way to judge, which is to let oneself be struck by things, and to have no blind preventatives, nor any affected complaisance, nor any ridiculous scruples."[31]

Instead of a many-headed monster, Dorante's parterre now possessed a solid capacity to evaluate theatrical representation. How did Molière construct this parterre, which responded to plays according to *le bon sens*? He based it on an opposition between the masculine space of the parterre, forbidden to women spectators, and the feminine space of seventeenth-century salons. In the passage cited above, Molière has Dorante say that some of the parterre spectators judge plays according to "the proper way to judge," which is to "let oneself be struck by things," phrases that fail to clarify the author's meaning. But then Dorante specifies that one must not "have . . . blind preventatives, nor any affected complaisance, nor any ridiculous scruples." In effect, Molière shifts his attack from the ignorant marquis to the pretentious salon women who attacked the propriety of *The School for Wives*. The author of the *Les Précieuses ridicules* sought to construct a critical space outside the salons of the period; in this passage, he relied heavily on a parterre emptied of any feminine, *précieuse* presence.

Molière mistrusted the judgment of the salons; at times he was extremely reluctant to publish his theatrical texts, as Abby Zanger has shown.[32] In *The Critique of the School for Wives*, Molière wanted to fashion a literary

---

[29] Molière, *La Critique*, scene 5, line 23.
[30] Ibid., scene 5, lines 47–48.
[31] Ibid., scene 5, lines 51–56.
[32] Abby Zanger, "Paralyzing Performance: Sacrificing Theater on the Altar of Publication," *Stanford French Review* 12 (Fall-Winter 1988): 169–85.

public sphere, in the words of Habermas, where authors and actors might call on nonprecious reasoning to judge a performance. In this passage, Molière was still far from the fraternal and democratic sociability of clubs, academies, and the periodical press of the eighteenth century that would give birth to a politically sovereign public sphere. But he had embarked on that path, and he had done so distinctly in opposition to the feminine preciousness of the first salons.[33]

Uses of Theater at Court

The self-display of Parisian society in the converted tennis courts of the capital and the tensions that arose between various sections of the theater, between players and spectators and between playwrights and their multiple and overlapping publics, form an important segment of the emerging story of French theater publics in this first half-century of the Parisian public theater. For a number of reasons, however, the narrative is incomplete if one does not consider the uses of dramatic spectacle at court in the same period. First, Louis XIII, Louis XIV, and their courtiers were frequently in attendance in the public theaters; they, along with the playwrights and performers of the period, carried the memory of public performances in the urban spaces of the Parisian theaters back to the more select world of court ritual. Second, the repertory of the public playhouses and the court theaters overlapped, in the sense that plays that premiered at court often found their way into the public theaters and works that proved initially successful at the Hôtel de Bourgogne or the Hôtel du Marais might subsequently be staged before the court at the King's request. Because court productions of dramatic works often incorporated more elaborate musical and balletic interludes than Parisian stagings, and on occasion folded the presentation of these plays into several consecutive days of entertainment for the court, the repertory overlap is not exact. Yet thanks to the government's efforts to publicize its activities to the kingdom and to its foreign rivals, public theater audience members excluded from attending the festivities at Versailles nevertheless knew of the uses made of theater at court, or at least knew of those uses that the government wished to publicize.[34]

---

[33] On Molière and preciosity, see Landes, *Women and the Public Sphere*, 30; and Domna Stanton, "The Fiction of *Préciosité* and the Fear of Women," *Yale French Studies* 62 (Fall 1981): 107–34.

[34] See, for example, André Félibien, *Relation de la fête de Versailles du 18 juillet 1668* . . . (Paris, 1679); or Félibien, *Les Divertissements de Versailles* . . . (Paris, 1676).

Most significant, however, the performance moment in the capital's playhouses cannot fully be appreciated without examining the role played by the staging of dramatic poetry at court in what Peter Burke has called the "fabrication" of the King. Burke's study is only the most recent in a long line of efforts to analyze the "work" done by royal texts, images, and performances to legitimize the seventeenth-century Bourbon monarchs.[35] By far the lion's share of attention in this literature has been devoted to the study of Versailles and the cultural "system" of Louis XIV's government; Louis, his ministers, and his image makers, however, drew liberally on the precedents established at his father's court, the Spanish court in the seventeenth century, and the courts of the Italian Renaissance states.[36] For our purposes, it is important to consider Richelieu's approach to the staging of drama at court before moving on to the uses of the theater during the early reign of the Sun King.

Although Louis XIII is known to have attended the theater as early as age six, he was not an active patron of the theater and did not actively encourage the performance of dramatic poetry at court. It appears that the father of the Sun King preferred ballet, in which he frequently performed throughout his reign.[37] His chief minister, however, moved to seize on the political possibilities of the theater throughout the crucial decade of the 1630s; the most famous example of Richelieu's theatrical intervention in this period, of course, is the *Querelle du Cid*, in which Richelieu stage-managed the efforts of his newly established Académie Française to rewrite Corneille's hugely popular play according to rules articulated for dramatic poetry by Aristotle.[38] But Richelieu's initiatives can best be appreciated in connection with events that took place in 1641, a year before his death. In December of that year, Richelieu celebrated the inauguration of his own private playhouse, built in the Palais Royal, where he resided, by commissioning a new work by the playwright Desmarets entitled *Mirame*.[39] The evening of festivities

---

[35] In addition to Burke, *The Fabrication of Louis XIV* (New Haven, 1992), the following discussion relies on Robert Isherwood, *Music in the Service of the King: France in the Seventeenth Century* (Ithaca, 1973); Louis Marin, *Portrait of the King*, trans. Martha M. Houle (Minneapolis, 1988); and two works by Jean-Marie Apostolidès, *Le Roi-Machine: Spectacle et politique au temps de Louis XIV* (Paris, 1981) and *Le Prince sacrifié*. See also Abby E. Zanger, *Scenes from the Marriage of Louis XIV: Nuptial Fictions and the Making of Absolutist Power* (Stanford, 1997).

[36] See Burke, *Fabrication*, 179–98.

[37] See Mark Franko, *Dance as Text: Ideologies of the Baroque Body* (Cambridge, 1993), 63–107.

[38] Armand Gasté, *La Querelle du Cid. Pièces et pamphlets publiés d'après les originaux avec une introduction* (Paris, 1898); and the analysis in Merlin, *Public et littérature*, 153–93.

[39] My account of Richelieu's theater is indebted to Timothy C. Murray, "Richelieu's Theatre: The Mirror of a Prince," *Renaissance Drama*, n.s. 8 (1977): 275–98.

carefully orchestrated by Richelieu at the opening of his theater represented a paradigm of theatrical patronage that linked the developing ideology of French absolutism to the drama in ways that foreshadowed the uses of spectacle during the famous *divertissements* at Versailles under Louis XIV.

Although the "machine" play commissioned for the evening violated principles of *vraisemblance* and the unity of action, these deformities served Richelieu's purpose.[40] In effect, the most important spectacle occurred not on the stage, but in the audience; Richelieu's theater operated to focus the attention of the spectators on the Cardinal himself. The perspectival set design for *Mirame* suggested that only one seat in the audience offered a perfect vantage point to its occupant (figure 7).[41] Richelieu situated himself so that he would occupy this seat along with his guests, the King and the Queen. Only in the persons of Richelieu and the royal couple, seated on the dais at the point of perfect perspective in the hall, did the unity of action portrayed on the stage come together. Only the sovereigns and their First Minister, the latter of whom had revised the script of *Mirame* and possibly penned the entire drama himself, were able to overcome the script's lack of *vraisemblance* to understand the story. And only they enjoyed the perfect perspective suggested by the elaborate scenic backdrop. The remainder of the courtiers in attendance, suffering from various degrees of flawed perspective, were obliged to turn to Richelieu and the royal couple to ascertain their reaction to the spectacle.[42] In the generation before the great spectacles staged by Louis XIV at Versailles, then, Richelieu exploited the political possibilities that arose from the new theatrical aesthetic developed in France in the first half of the seventeenth century. Like the aristocratic chateau and pleasure garden, the Cardinal's stage and his parterre served equally well for the staging of spectacles of power.

Two decades later, when Louis XIV came into his majority, he proclaimed his intention to rule without the aid of a chief minister in the mold of Richelieu. He did, however, appoint a nonclerical, nonnoble administrator, Jean-Baptiste Colbert, to his Council of State in 1661; three years later, Colbert also became superintendent of the King's works. From these two posts, Colbert directed Louis's efforts in a variety of domains, one of which we might call today the management and manipulation of the King's image at home and abroad. The institutional structure of these efforts is fairly clear in retrospect. Colbert and the King identified certain literary and artis-

---

[40] Ibid., 283–88.
[41] Ibid., 290.
[42] Ibid., for a discussion of figure 7, 278–81.

Fig. 7. Michel Van Lochon, *Le Soir*, early 1640s. (Courtesy of the Bibliothèque nationale de France.)

tic figures who would best advise them on writers, artists, and musicians, in France and abroad, who were qualified to serve the King.

Gradually, during the course of the 1660s, these various advisory functions evolved into permanent academies along the lines of Richelieu's Académie Française and the Royal Academy of Painting and Sculpture, which was founded in 1648. Academies devoted to music, architecture, science, and dance, as well as a French Academy in Rome to train artists, had appeared by the beginning of the Dutch War in 1672. In each case, these new institutions were assigned the task of creating works to celebrate the glory of the monarch. Passing final judgment on all their efforts was a shadow institution founded in 1663, known by the label Petite Academy, which was more of a standing committee than an academy. Composed of five men, it attempted to create a single-volume collection of the many compositions in various media intended to glorify the actions of the King. Although they never succeeded in publishing this emblematic history of the reign, they did become the focal point of the government's efforts to propagate the King's image. They rewrote texts, edited plans for royal fêtes, commented on designs for medals and other plastic arts, and wrote inscriptions for monuments and tapestries; Colbert reserved the right of last review over the Petite Academy's work.[43]

The goal of this sizable "arts bureaucracy" was to glorify the King in the eyes of his subjects and foreign observers, at court and abroad. What role did the theater play in the activity of royal image-making? The first item to note is the absence of a Royal Academy of Theater by the end of the key decade of the 1660s; in fact it would take more than another century before the Bourbon monarchy, in its waning days, would create such an academy.[44] Several reasons might plausibly be advanced to explain this absence. The marginal social and ecclesiastical status of players prevented the Crown from granting them the status of royal academicians. Income from box-office receipts may have made it less imperative for actors to seek royal patronage under the restrictive terms that painters, scientists, and architects accepted in the 1660s. And unlike buildings, medals, and paintings, the ephemeral nature of the theater arts made it difficult for the Crown to reap lasting benefits from tutelage of the theater, and in any event, the dramatic poetry produced by playwrights already fell within the domain of the Académie Française. Although all of these reasons may have contributed to the absence of an academy for theater arts, another

[43] Apostolidès, *Roi-Machine*, 29–34; Burke, *Fabrication*, 49–59.
[44] See Isherwood, *Music in the Service*, 201–2, for a failed effort to establish an "Academy of Spectacles" in the 1670s.

factor may well have been crucial. No matter how efficacious the Petite Academy might have been in vetting play scripts and acting styles, it could not control the reception of performance at court or in the public theaters of Paris. In the heat of performance, audience members and players might come up with interpretations that would subvert the intentions of the image makers. Although paintings, medals, and buildings also have a reception history that is potentially subversive, their reception and inter-pretation is less immediate, more textually based, and therefore more manageable than the response accorded to a theatrical performance.

In spite of the potential instability inherent in theatrical performance, plays helped to fashion the King's image at court. The King regularly called the public theater troupes to entertain his court in the Louvre or in the chateaux located throughout the Parisian basin. In addition, in each of the three major festive cycles staged at court in the first fifteen years of Louis's personal reign, the drama featured prominently in the court's amusements. These fêtes, which the King's entertainment bureaucrats spread out over days, or even weeks, incorporated masques, fireworks, simulated military combat, dance, and elaborate allegorical displays staged against the back-drop of the royal chateau and its gardens.

Engravings from these events can give us an introduction to court per-formances of plays that were also staged in the public theaters. Jean Le Pautre's 1676 engraving of the performance of Molière's *Malade imagi-naire* in 1674, for example, recalls the principles of royal spectatorship articulated by Richelieu at the Palais Royal twenty years earlier (figure 8). The King sits at the center of the foreground of the composition with his back to the viewer of the engraving. As with Richelieu and the royal cou-ple in 1641, the King is perched at the perfect point for appreciating the vanishing-point perspective of the staging and decor. Unlike the earlier image, however, the artist does not feel compelled to represent the face of the King turned back toward the viewer; the King, positioned at the point of perfect perspective, needs no further identification. The engraving, in fact, shows the majority of the spectators seated in chairs that force them to face the King rather than the stage; their orientation toward the monarch rather than toward the stage, is more prominently displayed than in the image of Richelieu's theater. In this engraving, Le Pautre under-lines even more forcefully than his predecessor the function of court spec-tacle in the legitimation of the King before his courtiers.

In general, the scale of Louis XIV's dramatic patronage was much greater than that of Richelieu in the earlier period; the dimensions of the outdoor stage required five chandeliers to illuminate the proceedings, compared to three in the Cardinal's palace. The Versailles stage was also larger to

Fig. 8. Jean Le Pautre, *Third Day*, from André Félibien, *Les Divertissements de Versailles donnez par le Roy à toute sa Cour au retour de la conqueste de la Franche-Comté en l'année M.DC.LXXIV* (Paris, 1676). (Courtesy of the Harvard Theatre Collection, Houghton Library.)

accommodate the balletic interludes between acts of the comedy. The King could host more courtiers than Richelieu twenty years earlier. While Richelieu followed the performance of *Mirame* with a ball, the performance of *Le Malade imaginaire* was one of many events taking place over six days; while Richelieu himself supervised the writing of his machine play, the King entrusted oversight of the fête to Colbert and the Petite Academy. Finally, on completion of the fêtes, the Crown financed the publication of elaborate volumes that memorialized the festivities in words and images.[45]

Yet, even if the staging of dramatic spectacle at Versailles appeared to play its role in the larger project of royal propaganda so energetically undertaken in the 1660s and 1670s, the messages conveyed during these performances might not have coincided with the wishes of the royal *metteur-en-scène*. Molière tells us that the King suggested a character for his play *Les Fâcheux* in 1661, as well as the theme for the 1670 court entertainment *Les Amants magnifiques*.[46] Yet, some critics have suggested that the flow of advice moved both ways when Molière staged his comedies at court. Marc Fumaroli, for example, has argued that Molière provided the King with a lesson in humanistic governance in the *Impromptu de Versailles*, and Abby Zanger has suggested that in *Les Amants magnifiques* Molière took the King's scenario and created a plot that instructed the monarch in the power of theatricality.[47]

Finally, if we return to the performance of Molière's *George Dandin* during the festivities of 1668, we are reminded that plays performed at court also had an independent presentation in the theaters of the capital, and that their meanings, as well as their performance conditions, might differ radically from one venue to the other.[48] At court, the performers intermingled a pastoral tale in dance and song with the five acts of Molière's comedy to the extent that viewers were not sure whether the courtiers perceived the spectacle as a comedy with musical interludes or as a musical and balletic composition interrupted by the five acts of the comedy. Furthermore, the

---

[45] In addition to the works in note 34, see Molière, et al., *Les Plaisirs de l'Isle enchantée* (Paris, 1664).

[46] Evidence also indicates that the King may have chosen the theme from Tasso used for the *Plaisirs de l'Isle enchantée*; Burke, *Fabrication*, 69.

[47] Marc Fumaroli, "Microcosme comique et macrocosme solaire: Molière, Louis XIV et *L'Impromptu de Versailles*," *Revue des sciences humaines*, 37 (January–March 1972): 95–114; and Abby Zanger, "The Spectacular Gift: Rewriting the Royal Scenario in Molière's *Les Amants magnifiques*," *Romanic Review* 81 (March 1990): 173–88. See also Matthew Wikander, *Princes to Act: Royal Audience and Royal Performance, 1578–1792* (Baltimore, 1993), 148–205.

[48] This paragraph summarizes the argument of Roger Chartier, "From Court Festivity to City Spectators," in *Forms and Meanings: Texts, Performances, and Audiences from Codex to Computer* (Philadelphia, 1995), 43–82.

aristocratic audience at Versailles responded to the story of the rich peasant cuckolded by his young aristocratic wife and her courtier-lover in a way quite different from that of the socially heterogeneous audiences that viewed the play in Paris at the Palais Royal. This response was in part conditioned by the anxiety that surrounded the royal decrees defining nobility that Louis XIV issued during the 1660s. In Paris, theatergoers saw *George Dandin* performed without the courtly pastoral that had been woven into the performance at court; stripped of the courtly magnificence that surrounded it spatially and temporally at Versailles, the play's humor relied on a different register, one that emphasized the social inequality of husband and wife and reminded the largely nonnoble, urban audience of the social disparities encountered in the daily life of the city. At court, the King's image makers could tailor the message of Molière's text through the frames with which they surrounded it, although disgruntled courtiers and anxious newly ennobled aristocrats might not have viewed the play and its interludes exactly according to royal dictates. In town, however, Molière's text took on a very different set of meanings in the eyes of spectators whose daily concerns were often far removed from those of the court.

The discrepancies between the 1668 performances of *George Dandin* at court and in the city underline the difficulties faced by the government of Louis XIV as it contemplated the Parisian public theaters. The challenge to control the meanings of dramatic performance at court was already great, in spite of the precedents set during the time of Richelieu and the elaboration of these techniques during the first decades of the Sun King's personal rule. When these productions moved from the court to the urban theaters, the authority of the Crown continued to be at stake; the King's Players performed a text originally created by a pensioner of the King to divert the court; should the capital's spectators jeer the production, or should the performance be interrupted by disorderly spectators, the "work" of the play at court threatened to come undone. How was the Crown to respond to the multiplicity of interpretations that a socially heterogeneous public theater audience might generate on any given night in the capital? Louis XIV and his policing agents turned their attention to these questions during the 1660s and early 1670s.

Beginnings of Theater Policing, 1661–74

Although it appears that neither Parisian nor royal authorities carefully policed the capital's theaters before the 1660s, surviving records indicate that the government chose during this period to intervene on the behalf of spectators in their conflicts with the players; this tendency is consistent with recent characterizations of the paternal aspects of the pre-1660s police.[49] Nevertheless, violent disturbances were commonplace in the capital's playhouses before the reign of Louis XIV. In his *Pratique du théâtre*, published in 1657 but possibly written around 1640 at the urging of Richelieu, the Abbé d'Aubignac had suggested the establishment of a troupe of soldiers to police the theaters, because performances were "endlessly troubled by young debauched men who only attended the theater to display their insolence, who cause fear throughout the theater, and who often commit murders there."[50] Although there is some suggestion that Aubignac may have exaggerated the dangers of theatergoing, a 1658 poster advertising a performance at the Hôtel de Bourgogne mentions that it is forbidden to soldiers to enter the playhouse "upon pain of death," and the recorded testimony of many playhouse doorkeepers in the 1660s, some of whom were mortally wounded by swords or pistols in the course of performing their duties, suggests that Aubignac did not exaggerate the level of disorder that occasionally disrupted public performances.[51] In the absence of governmental policing initiatives, the doorkeepers and ticket takers often constituted the only line of defense against theater "hooligans." A formal complaint filed with the police in 1661 by the porters in the pay of Molière's troupe indicates that it was the responsibility of the porters to curb violence in the theaters.[52]

As this complaint suggests, issues of theater violence became a question for governmental concern at the outset of Louis XIV's personal reign in 1661. One particularly vivid example of this type of violence occurred at the entrance to the Palais Royal on Tuesday, 8 November 1661, during a performance by Molière's troupe.[53] That day, an individual named Le Sueur, also known by the name of Champagne, clad in gray and likely drunk, claimed the right to enter the theater without paying. When Gilles Pegou, the troupe's porter at the street-level entrance to the loges, disputed Le Sueur's claims, the latter protested loudly, "swearing many times in the

---

[49] Paolo Piasenza, "Juges, Lieutenants de Police, et Bourgeois à Paris aux XVIIe et XVIIIe siècles," *Annales ESC* 45 (September–October 1990): 1189–1215.

[50] Quoted in Wilma Deierkauf-Holsboer, *L'Histoire de la mise-en-scène dans le théâtre français de 1600 à 1657* (Paris, 1933), 261.

[51] Pierre Mélèse, *Le Théâtre et le public à Paris sous Louis XIV, 1659–1715* (Paris, 1934), 237; Fournel, *Curiosités théâtrales*, 157–61; Madeleine Jurgens and Elizabeth Maxfield-Miller, *Cent ans de recherches sur Molière, sur sa famille et sur les comédiens de sa troupe* (Paris, 1963), 362 n. 4.

[52] Jurgens and Maxfield-Miller, *Cent ans de recherches*, 364.

[53] Ibid., 362–65.

saintly name of God." He raised such a ruckus that the doorkeeper granted him entry to the theater so that he would not disturb the performance. Once he had ascended to the loges, however, he was not content with the box where Pegou attempted to place him and yelled at the embattled *portier:* "Goddammit, I don't want this place, I want another." When the porter suggested that he should see "Monsieur de Molière," Le Sueur replied, "Why don't you and Monsieur de Molière go fuck yourselves!" At this point, the various relations of the encounter are unclear; some suggest that Le Sueur left the theater in search of weapons. All witnesses agree, however, that the confrontation escalated. The porter Pegou and his colleague Germain Diot, doorkeeper at the entrance to the parterre, claimed in their sworn testimony that Le Sueur returned with a sword and some pistols and that several friends seconded him. According to the porters, an armed skirmish ensued between themselves and Le Sueur's group. In the complaint filed by Molière's troupe and their porters, Le Sueur and his companions were accused of threatening other audience members. One witness claimed that Le Sueur tried to kick down the door to the loge he wished to enter, then kicked Pegou, who fell several steps down the staircase leading to the loges. The same witness swore that the altercation ended when Molière and actor Charles Varlet de La Grange managed to convince Le Sueur to leave the theater.

Although the exact narrative of events is unclear from these documents, the appeal to the Crown for assistance in suppressing disorder is evident throughout the various complaints and sworn testimony collected by the authorities. The complaint filed by the troupe and the porters on 11 November, for example, argues that such actions are not only "prejudicial" to the players and their employees, the porters, but also "hinder the liberty of the *bourgeois*" who attend the theater. The lieutenant *criminel* of Paris (the immediate predecessor of the lieutenant general of police established in 1667) was asked to investigate the matter because it concerned the interests not only of the actors but of the "*bourgeois*, who are not secure in the presence of such persons." In their sworn testimony the next day, the porters (or more likely the acting troupe and its legal representatives) stated that they had an interest in "making the justice of their actions known," and that they wished the lieutenant *criminel* to give the King's prosecutor permission to investigate the case further. It is clear from these statements that the players wanted the government to assume the responsibility of maintaining order in the public theaters of the capital. Although the documents refer to the troupe's royal patronage as one reason why the Crown should police the theaters, the major argument put forth is that the persons of the *bourgeois* of Paris in attendance at the theater must be made to feel secure. The actors reasoned that the role of government in this instance was the protection of individual life in the public spaces of the capital; if these state activities facilitated the undisturbed presentation of spectacles also performed before the King and his court, so much the better.

Although the next eleven years were repeatedly marred by similar acts of violence in the public theaters, the government's newly formed Parisian police bureaucracy did not respond meaningfully to the players' requests until 1671.[54] In March of that year, soldiers from the King's household and other Parisian servants and lackeys had stormed the door of the Opera house when the King, in response to a request from Opera administrators, had denied them free entry to that spectacle.[55] Two months later, the King issued an order commanding his procureur to identify the troublemakers and bring them to justice to ensure "public security" *(la seureté publique)*. Furthermore, the order called for the Parisian commissioners to be prepared to escort troublemakers to prison with the assistance of any "officers of justice" they required, and it forbade Parisian citizens living in the neighborhood to assist any miscreants. In spite of the King's wishes, violence continued to plague the entrance to the Opera. In March of the following year, the King issued *lettres patentes* to the Florentine composer Jean-Baptiste Lulli, granting him control of the Royal Academy of Music founded three years earlier.[56] Although the authors of this document devoted much of their attention to the various privileges accorded Lulli, they also encouraged him to hire guards to be stationed at the entrance to the Opera house. These guards would forcefully prevent customers from entering the auditorium without paying. It is unclear whether the King intended for Lulli to pay the salary of these men out of the academy's proceeds; in addition, no authorization for armed intervention in disputes that might arise once spectators had entered the Opera house existed. So by the start of the 1672–73 theatrical season, the Crown had authorized policing measures at the door to the Opera but had not committed its own resources to the task. Furthermore, policing measures were not yet sanctioned in any of the other public theaters of Paris.

Then, in the four-month period from October 1672 to January 1673, a series of disturbances in three of the four public theaters of the day prompted the evolving police bureaucracy of Paris to articulate rudimentary procedures for policing the theaters. The first of the incidents occurred on Sunday, 9 October 1672, at the Palais Royal when Molière's troupe

[54] Ibid., see in particular, 370–75, 430.
[55] BN, ms 21625, 23 May 1671.
[56] Mélèse, *Le Théâtre et le public*, 415–17; Isherwood, *Music in the Service*, 170–203.

performed *La Comtesse d'Escarbagnas* and *L'Amour médecin.*[57] Several of the witnesses interviewed by the police afterward recalled that the performance itself had been interrupted when someone in the parterre had thrown an object, described by two observers as "the large end of a pipe for smoking," at the actors. In spite of this interruption, the actors finished the performance. No sooner had the plays ended, however, than spectators on the stage and in the amphitheater noticed that a group of pages in the pit surrounded a colleague who was beating a young man with his baton; the victim was crying out for help. Several of the witnesses recognized that some of the young men wore the livery of the Duc de Gramont, a leading figure amongst the *noblesse d'épée*, or the old-line French military nobility.[58] They also noticed that the pages seemed to be led by a young man dressed in a black cape, wearing a sword and a hat with a white feather; this individual spoke to the pages in an animated fashion. Because the Crown did not yet provide policing agents to contain violence in the theater, the ranking official of the French judiciary present in the auditorium, the Procureur du Roi, felt compelled to step to the edge of the stage in his judicial robes to address the riotous pages. All the recorded accounts stress that he addressed the pages "with sweetness and moderation": "Sirs, it is not decent *(honnête)* to cause such a scene in a place of respect such as the Palais Royal. Put down your batons." When the youths ignored this plea, the *robain* repeated his appeal, telling them that he would inform the Duc de Gramont of their behavior. They continued to spurn his advice. Some of them apparently waved their arms at him in a mocking fashion.

At this point, according to the recorded accounts, another royal official seated on the stage stepped forward to warn the miscreants that they found themselves before "Monsieur le Procureur du roi, who is your judge."[59] This intervention quickly drew the following seditious retort from one, or possibly many, of the pages gathered in the parterre: "We have no judges, we mock our judges!" The Procureur du Roi and his supporters, in light of this threatening response, hastily left the theater. One of the witnesses, who

---

[57] Jurgens and Maxfield-Miller, *Cent ans de recherches*, 532–37.

[58] Ibid., 534, notes that the Duc de Gramont at this time was Antoine III (1604–1678), "Maréchal de France, duc et pair, colonel des gardes françaises," and that Molière's troupe had performed privately for him in 1660, 1662, and 1663.

[59] According to the testimony of a thirty-eight-year-old engineer in the King's army, the individual who stepped forward after the procureur was Pierre Boileau de Puymorin, *trésorier des menus plaisirs de Sa Majesté*, and also the godfather of Molière's child. (Jurgens and Maxfield-Miller, *Cent ans de recherches*, 535.)

exited the theater in the company of the King's procureur, reported that the black-caped youth and several of the pages tried to accost the procureur outside the theater, but they were hindered by other spectators leaving the theater who told them, "What are you trying to do? Let him go." Two other witnesses remarked in their sworn testimony that the actions of the pages and the departure of the Procureur du Roi, the symbol of the King's justice, left the youths "masters of the parterre."

These actions, taken within the confines of a royal palace on the eve of the Dutch War, transgressed hierarchies of royal authority in a number of ways. First, as the procureur remarked, they showed a lack of respect for the King's palace, which he opened to the Parisian theatergoing public. The procureur's remark may also have referred to the lack of respect shown for the King's troupe of actors. Second, the disrespect of Gramont's men for the royal authority with which the procureur spoke raised the question of latent *frondeur* tendencies within the military nobility, now resurgent with the renewal of the King's bellicose policies in the Low Countries. Their disregard for the legal authority of the procureur also highlighted the tensions in the nobility between the magistrates and the warriors. Finally, the sense among two of the witnesses, one of them a twenty-seven-year-old "bourgeois de Paris," the other a twenty-year-old royal musician, that the violent youths had become "masters of the parterre" indicated that the public space of the pit was a prize to be won, perhaps by military combat if not by judicial reason. As the actors of Molière's troupe stated in their initial complaint to the police, "it is not right that these sorts of violence and disorders, which are of great consequence for the public, should be tolerated." What would the police do?

By the end of the year, the King's forces began to organize their response. On 11 December, royal trumpeters and bill posters proclaimed and posted a new decree, issued by the King and his highest aides, regarding the maintenance of order at the Opera.[60] This decree went well beyond the provisions for establishing guards found earlier in the year in Lulli's *lettres patentes*, and it also, for the first time, directed the lieutenant general of police to intervene in theatrical affairs. The proclamation reminded Parisians that the King not only had established order and security in the city of Paris, but also had created institutions such as the Opera so that Parisians could "reap the benefits of the tranquility that they now enjoyed." At the same time that he established the Opera in Paris, he also

---

[60] BN, ms 21625, 11 December 1672. No evidence of a direct royal response to the events of 9 October 1672 survives.

desired that Parisians be able to attend the Opera in safety. Therefore, the intent of this proclamation was "to make it known that the King would take extraordinary action against those who caused tumult and who troubled the spectacles and public divertissements at the Opera, whether inside or outside the Academy." Furthermore, the King expected the obedience of his subjects more out of the respect owed to His Majesty's wishes than out of the fear of punishment. The order then specified, inter alia, that pages and lackeys who caused disturbances at the spectacle would be fined two hundred *livres*, to be payable to the municipal hospital; their masters would be financially responsible for their actions. The order also prohibited vagabonds and soldiers from gathering outside the academy on performance evenings and reiterated that no one was to enter the academy bearing firearms, nor was anyone permitted to draw a sword, quarrel, or create any other disturbance during the performance. Finally, the neighborhood policing officials known as the *commissaires*, or commissioners, were ordered to present themselves at the theater whenever necessary and to interrogate and possibly imprison individuals in violation of the King's will.

On 9 January 1673, a little less than a month later, the government issued a second ordinance, this time in response to a specific disturbance that had taken place "a few days earlier" at the Hôtel de Bourgogne, the theater in which the royal troupe specializing in tragedy performed. The ordinance, typographically similar to its Opera counterpart issued a month earlier, began with a narrative of the recent disorders at this theater:

> [C]ertain persons, without station and carrying swords . . . several days ago forced open the doors of the Hôtel de Bourgogne with great temerity and scandal. They executed this plan with many vagabonds, all of whom assembled in great number, armed with rifles, pistols, and swords, and by force entered the theater during the performance, which they halted, and then committed such violence against all sorts of people that everyone sought to leave the theater by any available exit. The said persons threatened to set the theater on fire, and with a brutality without precedent, abused all sorts of people without regard to rank.[61]

The ordinance then noted that the theater had not opened its doors since these events. The King, not wishing that "such an excess remain unpun-

---

[61] These disturbances may have been prompted by the premiere of Racine's *Mithridate*, although the exact date of the play's first public performance is unknown; it is conceivable that the disorders may have begun as part of an organized cabal against the playwright.

ished," ordered the police to seek out those responsible for the disturbance, as well as those who assisted them. Furthermore, the King ordered his policing force to prohibit such disorders in the future, and "to establish in these places devoted to public amusement, the same safety that one finds established in other places of Paris by the cares and the goodness of His Majesty."

The remainder of the ordinance repeated many of the same injunctions found in the Opera ordinance of a month earlier; its novelty lay in a demand that the *bourgeois* of the town assist the commissioners in the seizure of malefactors and in the insistence that those captured be tried according to the rigor of the King's ordinances. At this point, then, three of the four public theaters had experienced violent disruptions within the previous three months. The King's policing bureaucracy was beginning to take note of the situation, but provisions for establishing "tranquility" in the theaters did not yet provide specific administrative remedies. No plans existed to offer the procureurs, commissioners, and the *bourgeois de Paris* royal manpower to suppress the disorders. The disparity between the government's desire to establish "tranquility" in the public theaters and the continued playhouse violence underlined the shortcomings in early Bourbon attempts to police the theaters.

The reaction of these disruptive elements to the ordinance of 9 January was swift. Four nights later, as Molière and his troupe prepared to perform *Psyché*, an opera-ballet created at court, a group of twenty-five to thirty men armed with swords entered the parterre of the Palais Royal and threatened "by means of their gestures and their words," to interrupt the performance.[62] When the actors learned of their presence, they sent for the local commissioner, without whose presence they refused to perform. The commissioner's report records that once the performance began, the men approached the stage, began to talk amongst themselves, and stomped the ground with their feet. Soon thereafter, when the machine carrying Venus "descended" from the clouds and the chorus sang, "Descend, mother of love," the troublemakers interrupted the performance with shouts, derisive songs, and foot stomping to such an extent that the players halted the performance. The commissioner, situated on the stage, suggested that one of the actors speak to the armed men. This he did, "civilly" asking them the reasons for their disturbances, inquiring as to whether they wished a refund of their money, and threatening to close the theater for the evening if they did not end their noise-making. The men then responded in unison,

[62] Jurgens and Maxfield-Miller, *Cent ans de recherches*, 542–44.

and in a firm voice: "We don't care about the money we gave you, we don't want it! Begin the performance again, we want to be amused for our money!" The report ends at this point, with the commissioner's remark that the performers began the play all over again.

According to the commissioner, this event was linked specifically to the disturbances at the Hôtel de Bourgogne that month, and more generally to the disruptions at the Opera and the Palais Royal at the end of the previous year. The "King's counselor" reported that this "quantity of men with swords . . . plotted disorder and sedition amongst themselves, just as they had previously done at the Hôtel de Bourgogne, against the will of His Majesty, and in scorn of the ordinance of the Lieutenant General of Police dated and posted the ninth of [January]." In the battle for "mastery" of the Parisian public theaters, and particularly for control of the parterre in these playhouses, the Crown's financial and physical resources still were unable to enforce the King's will as expressed in his ordinances. The King, or his ministers, articulated a vision of public theater space where the public of the capital would feel unthreatened. The Crown went no further than expressing a desire for the physical safety of its urban subjects as they amused themselves in the playhouses; the government did not actively seek to promote independent critical activity among theatergoers. But even these limited goals proved challenging when the King's forces found themselves confronted by a well-organized, armed segment of the audience determined to disrupt performances and contest the royal will within the playhouse.

The King renewed his orders regarding the Royal Academy of Music a year later in January 1674, once again threatening to take extraordinary action against those who violated the security and tranquillity of the royal spectacle and forbidding officers of his household, soldiers, pages, lackeys, and others to cause trouble at the door or in the assembly hall.[63] But the ordinances proclaimed and posted in the public spaces of Paris seemed dictated more by the needs of the publicity machine controlled through the Petite Academy than by the actions of the policing bureaucracy of the capital; one of them states:

> [T]he King, having not only wished to give the Royal Academy of Music the means to augment the pleasures of the public since the establishment of this spectacle, but also wanting to increase the comfort and insure the security of those who attend the spectacle by establishing it in one of his Royal households, has deemed it important that the public be informed of his wishes. . . . And after the general prohibitions against troubling spec-

---

[63] BN, 21625, f. 326–29, 782.

tacles and public diversions . . . it seems that no one can doubt the severity of the punishments which will be enforced against those who show a lack of respect, or against those who would commit an act of violence in the place where it has pleased his Majesty to establish this Academy.[64]

The discrepancy between the royal proclamations and the actions of violent spectators was striking. Although the King's officers and bureaucrats sought to impose themselves through the use of the day's most advanced publicity techniques, those in attendance during the violent evenings in 1672 and 1673, described above, had encountered the limits of the state's ability to enforce the King's will in the public spaces of Paris. Perhaps in acknowledgment of these limitations, the King had issued another ordinance three days earlier regarding the Hôtel Guénégaud, the theater where the remnants of Molière's troupe had taken up residence after his death in February 1673.[65] This document repeated the commonplace observation that disorders in the theater "impeded the liberty and interrupted the pleasures of the public." It also reiterated prohibitions against forced entry by those who refused to pay admission at the door. But unlike the preceding ordinances of the 1660s and 1670s, this document also urged the police to maintain a physical presence in the Hôtel Guénégaud: "we command the Lieutenant Criminel of the Short Robe to establish at the door of the theater the squad of guards that he judges necessary for the execution of this ordinance." The ordinance, like Lulli's *lettres patentes*, limited to disturbances at the door, did nothing to curb violence in the auditorium. But it did provide relief for the embattled porters and established a precedent for theater policing on which the government would expand over the next century. In early 1670s, however, the King and his advisors still struggled to overcome the gap between the desired "tranquillity" discussed in royal ordinances and the flagrant violations of public order that repeatedly beset the public theaters. The founding of the Comédie-Française at the start of the next decade did little to resolve the problem.

"Founding" of the Comédie-Française

In the 1670s, therefore, Louis XIV took two steps that shaped the role of the theater in French political culture down to the Revolution. First, as we have just seen, he established the beginnings of a system to police spectators in the

---

[64] Ibid., f. 782.
[65] AN, O¹ 18, f. 8. See also Samuel Chappuzeau, *Le Théâtre François* (Paris, 1674), 156–58.

Parisian playhouses. Second, after a half century of rivalry between French-language theater troupes in the capital, he restructured the theatrical market by combining the existing troupes into a single entity, the Comédie-Française. Although the seventeenth-century "theatrical marketplace" was never entirely free of government intervention, up to 1673 it did continue to expand. The return to Paris of Molière's troupe in 1658, and the permanent arrival of an Italian troupe in 1662, offered Parisian theatergoers a number of options comparable to that enjoyed by their counterparts in London or Madrid. Beginning with the death of Molière in 1673, however, and coinciding with the theater disturbances detailed in preceding sections, the Crown began to narrow the number of troupes and public playhouses in the capital. These events, more than the onstage achievements of Corneille, Racine, and Molière, would determine the contributions of the theater to French politics in the final century of the Old Regime.

The institutional changes in the 1670s were owed in part to the brilliant success of the Opera under the direction of Jean-Baptiste Lulli. Lulli's operas adapted an Italian art form to the extravagant and spectacular tastes of the French court under Louis XIV. One observer in 1709, when Lulli's works still dominated the stage of the Opera, labeled them a "universal spectacle," one in which a dramatic poem was set to music and accompanied by dances, machines, and decorations.[66] Beginning sporadically in 1671, the Royal Academy of Music began to perform operatic spectacles for a paying Parisian audience at the newly established theater on the Rue Mazarine, often called the Hôtel Guénégaud. The academy was initially directed by Pierre Perrin, an opportunistic poet who teamed with various composers to produce musical dramas at court in the 1660s. In 1672, however, Lulli, an adept courtier and an innovative composer, convinced Louis and Colbert to grant him control of the academy. The next year, when Molière died of respiratory failure after the fourth performance of *Le Malade imaginaire*, Lulli laid claim to the desirable Palais Royal, Richelieu's theater, as the Parisian performance venue for the academy. By the end of 1673, only three active theaters and four troupes existed in Paris: the Palais Royal, occupied by the Opera; the Hôtel Guénégaud, used on alternate days by the Italians and the newly created French troupe; and the ancient Hôtel de Bourgogne, where the direct descendants of the 1629 troupe, now known as *la troupe royale*, still performed.

The creation of the Comédie Française in 1680 was the final act in the Crown's efforts to restructure the Parisian theatrical scene. By 1679, tensions between the various remaining troupes had already rendered the

---

[66] Durey de Nionville, quoted in Isherwood, *Music in the Service*, 189.

Parisian theatrical world tumultuous; that year, the Guénégaud troupe had convinced the leading tragedienne at the Hôtel de Bourgogne to join its ranks, and the Italian and the French troupes at the Guénégaud were quarreling about the use of the theater's stage machinery. Most historians of the French stage, however, see the fusion of the two remaining French-language troupes enacted by royal decree in August 1680 as the result of a larger governmental policy designed to control artistic production within the kingdom.[67] The *lettre de cachet* issued in Louis's name in October 1680 supports this thesis: "His Majesty, having decided to unite the two troupes established at the Hôtel de Bourgogne and the rue Guénégaud . . . in order to render the representation of plays more perfect by means of the actors and actresses to whom he gives a place in this troupe . . . orders that in the future the two troupes of French actors be united into one and the same troupe whose composition will be determined by His Majesty."[68]

The same document proclaims that the newly created troupe will also have exclusive rights to the performance of French-language plays in the city and suburbs of Paris "to give them the means to perfect their art to an ever greater degree." Although the government never established a royal academy of drama, through its actions it created a troupe that enjoyed a monopoly over the performance of French-language drama in the capital. This troupe was in some sense similar to the Royal Academy of Music in that the Crown intended the actors to have the exclusive right to exercise their art in the capital and to provide examples of this art for court festivities.

Thus, by the end of 1680, Parisian theatergoers encountered a drastically restructured number of choices. Twenty years before, when Molière's troupe first began to play in the capital, a theatergoer might, within one week's time, see performances by three different French-language troupes, the Italian troupe, and the Spanish troupe. But by the end of a decade of governmental intervention in the theatrical marketplace, spectators had only three choices in any given week: the Comédie-Française, the Comédie-Italienne, and the Opera, which performed three nights a week in the Palais Royal theater. It was true that the new Comédie-Française, with its expanded personnel, was now in a position to offer productions of as many as five or six different plays within a week, whereas the smaller, competing troupes had often offered only one play three times a week. But theater patrons could not "vote" with their money; in principle, the offer-

---

[67] See, for example, Jules Bonnassiès, *La Comédie-Française: histoire administrative (1658–1757)* (Paris, 1874), 52.
[68] AN, O¹ 844 *Lettre de cachet pour l'établissement des Comédiens du Roy*; reprinted in Mélèse, *Le Théâtre et le public*, 421.

ings of the troupe that now performed nightly at the Guénégaud did not have to respond to competition posed by other French-language troupes. The Italian troupe took advantage of this competitive lacuna to begin offering greater portions of its nightly fair in French, a tendency they had begun before 1680; but when the King's wishes became known in 1680, these directions were not evident to the players or the spectators.

The "creation" of the Comédie-Française by royal decree in 1680 is often seen as the founding moment of the French national theater, particularly by those who have wanted to view the institution as part of the underpinnings of an "official French culture" that dates back to the Old Regime; certainly, the institution that exists in Paris today under the name "Comédie-Française" dates its origin to the legislative actions of Louis XIV in that year. Theater historians of the Grand Siècle have tended to understand the events of 1680 as the culmination of a half century of extraordinarily creative French theatrical activity. The Comédie-Française, often referred to as *La Maison de Molière*, has centered its repertory on the works of the playwright-performer and his two contemporaries, Corneille and Racine, since its creation. But as important as the date 1680 is for notions of French national culture and the trajectory of French theatrical history, it is also significant because it marks a turning point in the history of French theater audiences. Before 1673, Parisian theatergoers had several playgoing options; after that date, an audience member had only one choice for French-language theater. This choice was a troupe of actors assembled by the King's ministers and dependent on the royal government for personnel decisions, repertory choices, and an annual pension. Furthermore, the Paris theatergoer knew that on any given night, the troupe's best performers might be called to court to entertain the King and his entourage. Finally, a spectator in the capital was aware that playwrights had to tailor their scripts to the needs of a troupe that had to answer to the government before it had to answer to the paying audience member.

The government's actions of 1673 and 1680 gave the disparate, heterogeneous theater audiences of the capital reasons to unite, reasons they had not known in the previous fifty years: although they continued to pay admission to the theater and support the players who performed before them, they had less economic input than ever in the productions they patronized. At the same time, they gained an awareness of the government and its determination to create an official culture, an awareness that had perhaps been masked before. Over the course of the next fifty years, audience members would respond in an increasingly coherent manner to the plays staged before them. The needs of these spectators would make the first half-century of the Comédie-Française's existence difficult indeed.

3

"The Parterre Becomes an Actor," 1680–1725

Among our parterre spectators are those who have been granted by heaven superior judgement; but their number is so small that they account for no more than a thirtieth of those in the pit. These enlightened judges have no way to bring the ignorant majority around to their views unless a play has a lengthy run; but too often plays fail after a single performance. . . . This is why, for several years now, any stage debut has become a general assault on the playwright and the players.

—L'Abbé Simon-Josèphe Pellegrin,
"Discourse on the Manner in Which One Judges Plays," 1724

When Louis XIV and his ministers established the Comédie-Française in 1680 "to render the representations of the actors more perfect," they could hardly have imagined that a generation later actors and spectators would brawl in the playhouse foyer over a passage from Racine. Yet on the evening of 3 June 1711, during a sparsely attended performance of *Britannicus*, that was precisely what happened. As the actor Beaubourg exited the stage in Roman costume, he found several of his colleagues engaged in a conversation with a spectator named Mathieu Mey.[1] Beaubourg, in the role of Nero, had just recited the lines "You want to present my rival to the army / Already the rumor has spread throughout the camp."[2] Mey, who claimed in a sworn complaint taken by the police to know one of the actors, had approached them to ask where, in the classical sources, Racine had learned of the presence of this army. One of the actors demanded of Mey whether he was "not tired of critiquing Racine with his ridiculous complaints." At that instant, according to another spectator who witnessed the confrontation, Beaubourg, in his Roman costume, told Mey that it did not become him to criticize a writer "as famous as the author of *Britanni-*

---

[1] Emile Campardon, *Les Comédiens du roi de la troupe française pendant les deux derniers siècles* (Paris, 1879), 23–27.
[2] "Vous voulez présenter mon rival à l'armée, / Déjà jusques au camp le bruit en a couru . . .," Jean Racine, *Britannicus*, Act 4, Scene 2.

cus." Mey replied that he thought Beaubourg hardly capable of judging Racine, Molière, and Corneille; Beaubourg threatened to have him barred from the theater. Mey then called the actor a "plaisant juge de Pont-Neuf," associating him with the popular culture of one of the capital's most uproarious urban spaces. The two men attacked each other, throwing punches and pulling at each others' wigs, until they were separated by the actor and playwright Dancourt.

The confrontation between the aggressive spectator and the offended actor typifies transformations in the Parisian public theaters during the first half-century of the Comédie-Française. Three decades after the King had created a privileged space for the presentation of French-language drama also performed at court, a commoner attending this theater thought himself authorized to question a text by one of the most revered writers of the French stage, and to query the performances of the actors who received pensions from the King and entertained his court. Mey's understanding of the role of the spectator, like that encouraged at the fairs at this time, involved critical interactions between audience members and spectators that had not existed at the outset of Louis XIV's reign; apparently, Mey often approached the players with his observations, because one of them complained to him one evening that he "always had the most extraordinary questions" for them.[3]

In addition to demonstrating the ways in which spectators might challenge the cultural authority of the Comédie-Française and its actors, the incident also calls into question this royal institution's ability to serve as a marker of class and prestige. Spectator and actor each attempted to belittle the social standing of the other; both implied that their interlocutors were too lowly to call into question Racine's play, already an artifact of official court culture. Mey in particular associated the Comédie-Française actor with displays of popular culture found in the streets of Paris. This insult provoked the troupe member to violence. The derisive laughter of the streets and the markets hung over this incident in another sense as well; in this period, the fair theater troupes referred to the French troupe as the "Romans," and represented them onstage as ridiculous, toga-clad personifications.[4] The actor in his toga scuffling in the foyer of the theater with a paying spectator only seemed to confirm the fair jibes at the pretensions of the privileged players, as well as the latter's callous disregard for their audience.

[3] Campardon, *Les Comédiens du roi de la troupe française*, 26.
[4] See, for example, Louis Fuzelier, *Le Retour d'Arlequin à la foire* (Paris, 1712), which was performed at the St-Germain fair that year.

The Mey incident indicates that by the beginning of the eighteenth century notions of cultural authority and social hierarchy "staged" at the Comédie-Française differed from the models that Louis XIV had in mind in 1680; the public theater where the royal troupe performed did not reproduce the forms of political and cultural authority generated at Versailles. In part, of course, this shift reflected growing disenchantment with louisquatorzian absolutism at the end of the Sun King's lengthy reign. The diplomatic and religious blunders of the 1680s, epitomized by the Revocation of the Edict of Nantes, had given way to the disastrous War of the League of Augsberg in the 1690s and the humiliating War of the Spanish Succession in the first decade of the eighteenth century. These military debacles were accentuated by the poor harvests, famines, and plagues that marked the second half of Louis's reign, and the increasing social unrest characterized by the revolt of the Camisards in the Cevennes from 1702 to 1705. The administrative reforms of Colbert ossified in the hands of his successors, and the fiscal crises brought on by war and poor harvests caused the Crown to multiply venal offices and increase tax burdens in ways that plagued the monarchy for the remainder of the Old Regime.[5] As Louis's military, diplomatic, and domestic actions encountered opposition, his cultural initiatives also stalled out.

Once the court moved permanently to Versailles in 1682, the spectacles and cycles of entertainment that had dazzled Louis's subjects and foreign ambassadors in the first two decades of his personal reign were folded into the daily ritual of court life in ways that ceased to amaze and inspire the most creative French minds. Similarly, the King lost interest in active patronage of the arts and sciences, with the result that the generation of Molière, Boileau, and Racine was the only one fully supported by the Crown. Advances in natural and moral philosophy by foreigners, such as Newton, Leibniz, and Locke, failed to find an appreciative audience at court or in royal institutions increasingly devoted to dogmatic interpretations. As one twentieth-century French historian has written, "The so-called '*Grand Siècle*,' with the 'Great King' as its patron, was a brilliant firework display which lasted no more than fifteen years."[6]

Thus, the boundaries of political and cultural authority within which Mey and Beaubourg challenged each other in mid-1711 were less evident

[5] Robin Briggs, *Early Modern France, 1560–1715* (Oxford, 1977), 144–65; Pierre Goubert, *Louis XIV and Twenty Million Frenchmen*, trans. Anne Carter (New York, 1970), 149–315; and Lionel Rothkrug, *Opposition to Louis XIV: The Political and Social Origins of the French Enlightenment* (Princeton, 1965).
[6] Goubert, *Louis XIV and Twenty Million Frenchmen*, 294.

than they had been on the founding of the Comédie-Française in 1680. But events internal to the theater had also contributed to the environment in which actor and spectator wrestled each other to the floor of the playhouse. Two themes stand out. The first is the disintegration of textual authority on the stage.[7] Authors and audiences had a variety of stages to which they could turn their attention before 1680; a combination of learned critics, educated amateurs, and seasoned playgoers determined the success of dramatic poetry on the stage and in print. After 1680, the actors of the Comédie-Française and the government's censors became the gatekeepers of dramatic literature; the role of live theater audiences and various literary critics was seemingly diminished. At the same time, however, the Italian players and, after their expulsion in 1697, the fair troupes took to staging spectacles that relied on gesture, song, characterization, physical comedy, and other nontextual means of performance to circumvent the Comédie-Française's monopoly and find favor with audiences.

The second development, that of increasing audience intervention during live performance, is related to this initial tendency. The "mixed-media" performances staged by the Italians and the fairs created a larger role for audience participation in dramatic spectacle; at the fair theaters, audiences were invited to sing along with the players, "to become an actor," in the words of one observer. By the end of the period, potent audience interventions had found their way back to the Comédie-Française, transforming this spectacle as well in ways that the Sun King would not have recognized or condoned when he established a theatrical monopoly in 1680. The first half-century of the Comédie-Française, far from perfecting theatrical representation in the capital, left a legacy of legal and artistic contention that redirected the French stage in the eighteenth century away from the tenets of classicism supposedly embodied in the troupe's seventeenth-century repertory. More important, it was obvious by the mid-1720s that audiences in the capital's public theaters played an increasingly important role in determining questions of taste and repertory in the public theaters.

The Parterre: Definitions and Personification at the End of the Century

In a 1935 article entitled "La Cour et la Ville," the literary historian Erich Auerbach ranged widely over the literature of seventeenth-century France in an effort to understand what contemporaries meant when they used the

---

[7] For an introduction, see Jeffrey S. Ravel, "Language and Authority in the Comedies of Edme Boursault," *Papers on French Seventeenth-Century Literature* 28 (1988): 177–99.

words *le public* and *la cour et la ville*.[8] He concluded that by the end of the century *la cour et la ville* were a "unit" that denoted "a public in the modern sense."[9] This unit was a socioeconomic class composed of a courtly nobility stripped of all military functions and a venal urban bourgeoisie also cut off from its original economic duties. As part of his analysis, Auerbach also investigated the sociological significance attached to the word "parterre." He concluded that "the parterre did not represent the people, not at least in the sense we have come to use the word."[10] Rather, the parterre meant, in the minds of contemporaries, an urban bourgeoisie in pursuit of status rather than wealth. Auerbach was particularly convinced by the evidence he assembled that the luxury merchants of the rue St-Denis were the epitome of this new *bourgeois* spectator.

Subsequent research into the social history of the Old Regime of course makes us wary of the precision that Auerbach claimed for the categories of nobility and bourgeoisie.[11] Close attention to dictionary definitions at the end of the century suggests that the metonymic meaning of the word "parterre" was far from stable in the minds of contemporaries. In the space of ten years, from 1680 to 1690, two major French-language dictionaries, those of Richelet and Furetière, defined the word "parterre."[12] Both dictionaries began by giving the gardening sense of the word, then devoted a paragraph to "parterre" as a space in a playhouse. But both lexicographers also acknowledged a third, metonymic meaning that referred to the group of spectators who stood in the parterre.

Richelet, writing in 1680, captured this meaning in the following manner:

> The spectators who are in the parterre while the play is performed. "The parterre does not dare to contradict." (Molière, *Précieuses,* scene 9). "These men do not want to admit that the parterre exhibits common sense." (Molière, *Critique de l'école des femmes,* scene 5).[13]

Ten years later, Furetière was somewhat more expansive:

> Figuratively said of the people contained in the parterre. Molière made an impertinent Marquis say, "Laugh Parterre, laugh," in order to show con-

---

[8] Auerbach, "La Cour et la Ville," 133–79.

[9] Ibid., 179.

[10] Ibid., 155.

[11] See William Doyle, *Origins of the French Revolution* (New York, 1980), 7–40.

[12] The 1694 inaugural edition of the dictionary edited by the Académie Française did not define the word "parterre."

[13] César-Pierre Richelet, *Dictionnaire françois* (Geneva, 1680), 126.

tempt for the judgment of the people. Still, it is the parterre which provides the most applause in the playhouse.[14]

Richelet's definition lacked social nuance; he labeled the men standing in the parterre as spectators and relied on Molière's authority to establish the word's metonymic usage. Furetière's definition is somewhat more suggestive, because he used the word "people" to refer to those gathered in the parterre. Furthermore, he buttressed Molière's authoritative voice with his own observation that the theatergoers standing in the parterre seemed to be the most important critics in the audience. Furetière's statement in the passage defining "parterre" as an area in the playhouse emphasized the importance of the parterre in his mind: "The parterre would be the best place to watch the play, were it not for the discomforts one finds there, and without the quarrels that often take place there." Thus Furetière was of two minds concerning the parterre; he granted its increasingly important critical functions, yet he also registered the lack of civility that disorderly patrons could still bring to the pit on occasion. His dictionary definition underlined the problems inherent in trying to stabilize the meaning of a word that still proved problematic late in the seventeenth century.

By the end of the century, then, the metonymic use of the word "parterre" was still uncertain. The great dictionaries could only point out the term's fluidity; common usage had two models to rely on, the negative bestiary used to represent the "people," and Molière's masculine vision of a public yet unborn. In other words, the parterre was still contested territory circa 1690. These conflicts received a corporeal incarnation in a play performed at the Comédie-Italienne in 1692 entitled *Les Chinois*.[15] The play's interest lay in the allegorical figure that appeared in the last scene, a character called the *Parterre*. The surviving text of the play, edited by one of the troupe's actors and published in 1700, contained the following stage directions for the Parterre's entrance: "Mezzetin, representing the Parterre, dressed in many fashions, with many heads, a large whistle at his side and many others hanging from his belt."[16]

Playwrights and actors, still attuned to the Hydra imagery used earlier in the century to represent the parterre, appropriated this political symbolism for their own comic purposes. Yet while drawing on this political bestiary, they also attempted to give the figure of the Parterre a weight of

---

[14] Antoine de Furetière, *Dictionnaire universel* (Rotterdam, 1690).
[15] Jean-François Regnard, *Comédies du Théâtre Italien,* ed. Alexandre Calame (Geneva, 1981).
[16] Ibid., 499.

authority comparable to that of the King who supported the Comédie-Française. The result was a comic figure that represented the heterogenous mix of people found in the parterre, both through the use of the Hydra image and through the costume the character wore, a mélange of the many types of fashion undoubtedly found on the backs of parterre spectators. The Italians presented this figure as a comic alternative to the paternal authority of the King and his court.

One sees this intention clearly when considering the role played by the Parterre in the plot of *Les Chinois*. Most of the play relates the travails of an old magistrate named Roquillard, who seeks an appropriate match for his daughter Isabelle. By the end of the play, Roquillard has narrowed his choice to Harlequin, impersonating a Comédie-Française actor, and Octave, a Comédie-Italienne player who is Isabelle's true love. As Roquillard is about to decide, his porter announces that "a fat man who is raising hell to get in" is at the door. "He says his name is Parterre." As the Parterre enters, he throws Roquillard to the ground, crying out, "Down with you, rascal!" In response to Roquillard's wounded observation, "The Parterre has an imperious tone," the Parterre responds, "Who makes you so bold, my friend, as to usurp my jurisdiction? Don't you know that I am the only natural judge, and the last resort of actors and plays?"[17]

Thus, the Parterre's first action on entering the scene, that of throwing Roquillard to the ground, signifies that he will replace Roquillard as the play's male figure of authority, the one who will decide which of the two suitors Isabelle will marry. Owing to the plot's conflation, he is also asked to pass judgment on the two theatrical troupes. The parallels between the position occupied by the King at court and that occupied by the Parterre in *Les Chinois* are intentional on the part of the actors and playwrights. A few moments after the Parterre's entrance, Colombine, the representative of the Comédie-Italienne, praises the Parterre in the following distinctly royal terms: "I only render the hommage due to this sovereign plenipotentiary: he is the spur of authors, the restraint of actors, the controller of the seats onstage, the inspector and the curious examiner of the upper and lower boxes, and of all that goes on therein; in a word, he is an incorruptible judge who, far from taking money to judge, begins by handing it over at the entrance."[18]

Columbine's description of the Parterre immediately recalls the place occupied by the young Louis XIV during dramatic performances at court;

---

[17] Ibid., 499.
[18] Ibid., 500–501.

the all-knowing, all-seeing, divine-right monarch. The Parterre is thus set up as a final figure of authority. He replaces the patriarchal figure of authority represented by Roquillard (indeed, brutally and comically so) and has final right of judgment in all matters pertaining to the theater. This point is underscored by the play's tag line. After the Parterre has pronounced his verdict in favor of Octave/Comédie-Italienne, Harlequin/Comédie-Française cries out that he intends to appeal this judgment to the loges. "My judgments cannot be appealed," replies the Parterre, as the printed text of the play ends.[19]

The figure of the Parterre found in *Les Chinois* was clearly not intended to be a faithful transcription of parterre audiences at the end of the seventeenth century. Rather, through its comic appeal, it suggested an alternative figure of male authority, one that would support the Italians in their commercial and philosophical disputes with the Comédie-Française. The personified parterre was an interesting study in the representation of the parterre at the end of the seventeenth century. Regnard and the actors invested the character with authority in legal, violent, and visual ways. The Parterre, as the tribunal of actors and playwrights, claimed a "mock" legal right to choose between Harlequin and Octave, rival suitors and representatives of the two troupes in the conflated world of the play. By blustering and throwing Roquillard to the ground, he bolstered his legal claims through the use of violence. Finally, the troupe adorned the Parterre with multiple whistles, the visual trappings of sovereignty in the playhouse.

As the use of the whistles suggested, however, this appeal to authority was also mediated by the comic world of the Italian stage on which it occurred. The Mezzetin/Parterre character might have spoofed the conventions of absolutist decision-making; it might also have satirized the absolute authority that audiences themselves frequently used in this period. Comparison of the two theatrical companies to suitors for a woman reminded observers that neither troupe was exempt from the mockery of the *commedia dell'arte* comic tradition, a reminder further emphasized by the fact that the focus of their attention was Colombine, another highly ambivalent product of the Italian stock of characters. Spectators and readers ordered the polyvalent meanings encoded in this staged Parterre personification in differing hierarchies. The many possible interpretations of this figure attested to the imprecise critical authority of the parterre, one which matched the uncertain nature of royal authority disseminating from court. Given the vacuum of royal authority within the playhouse at the end of Louis XIV's reign, the Comédie-Italienne chose to combat its rival not at

[19] Ibid., 509.

court, but at the box office. The commercial rivalry between the Comédie-Italienne and the Comédie-Française at the end of the seventeenth century led the former theater to seek the approbation of the parterre at the expense of its courtly patron. The increasingly large role the Italians and the fair actors accorded to the parterre in the production of meaning during performance in turn bolstered the pit's critical authority.

The Comédie-Française versus the Comédie-Italienne, 1680–97

Although the allegorical figure of the Parterre used in *Les Chinois* did not convey a stable political message, its appearance in 1692 made sense within the commercial context of Parisian theater after 1680. The "founding" of the Comédie-Française—Louis XIV's violent restructuring of the capital's theatrical establishments—altered the commercial and artistic activities of the two daily theaters left in the capital. At court and in the two remaining public theaters of the capital, each troupe measured success in terms of its competitor; this rivalry continued until the expulsion of the Italian troupe from the capital in 1697 left the Comédie-Française as the sole privileged Parisian theater. One result of this seventeen-year competition was that the French troupe triumphed at court while the Italians became the favorite of many public theater patrons.

As Virginia Scott points out in her study of the Comédie-Italienne in the second half of the seventeenth century, court performances by the troupe declined precipitously in the seventeen years between the creation of the Comédie-Française and the expulsion of the Italians in 1697. In the first quarter of 1683, the French actors played at court nine times to the Italians' six performances; in the first three months of 1685, court documents record thirty French performances compared to six Italian ones. By 1693 the Italians no longer made the annual trip to Fontainebleau with the court, and by 1696 they only played three times all year at Versailles.[20] The decline in the Italians' popularity at court was partly caused by the King's insistence that they play in Italian; because the influence of the Medici queens and Mazarin was only a memory by the end of the century, few courtiers could follow the Italians' dialogue. More fatal, however, was the court's growing scorn for anything that found favor in the public theaters. One observer commented in the early 1690s that "the

---

[20] Virginia Scott, *The Commedia dell'arte in Paris, 1644–1697* (Charlottesville, VA, 1990), 243–49, 317–18.

courtiers, especially the women, affect to be contemptuous of whatever the *bourgeois* has esteemed. [This behavior] has the air of quality and marks a superior intelligence."[21]

At the same time, there are indications that the Comédie-Française was losing favor with the Paris public, particularly from 1690 onward. Annual paid admissions, which had consistently reached 130,000 to 150,000 spectators in the 1680s, rose above 123,000 only once in the first half of the 1690s.[22] First-run, full-length plays (three to five acts) also declined in popularity during this period. Lough suggests that a first run of ten to fifteen performances in the late seventeenth century indicated a modest success, a string of fifteen to twenty-two performances a considerable success, and anything above twenty-two performances "striking" or "exceptional."[23] Based on these categories, we again see evidence of a decline in the Comédie-Française's popularity after 1689, when the troupe abandoned the Guénégaud theater for the newly constructed playhouse on the rue des Fossés-St-Germain-des-Prés. From 1680 to 1689, eight of fifty-six first-run plays exceeded twenty performances; only three of forty-four first-run plays in the 1690–97 period achieved this measure of success. The number of failures remained constant over the entire seventeen-year period. Before 1690, thirty of the fifty-six new plays, or 54 percent, failed to exceed ten performances, while from 1690 onward twenty-five of the forty-four plays, or 57 percent, also disappeared after ten or fewer performances. At the extreme, only one play before 1690 was withdrawn from the repertory after a single performance, while six plays in the 1690–97 period earned this dubious distinction. In summary, the Comédie-Française had fewer outright successes and more disasters after 1689, while over the entire 1680–97 period approximately 55 percent of their plays proved commercially unviable (ten performances or less).[24]

The Comédie-Française's attempts to suppress the use of parody and French-language scripts on the Italians' stage was another gauge of the heightened sense of competition between the two troupes. The Italian troupe had begun to integrate French-language scenes into their Italian improvisations as early as 1668, but this trend appeared more threatening after 1680 when there was only one French-language troupe jealous of its

---

[21] Jean Nicolas du Tralage, *Notes et documents sur l'histoire des théâtres de Paris au XVIIe siècle*, translated and quoted in Scott, *Commedia dell'arte*, 317.
[22] Lough, *Paris Theater Audiences*, 272. No attendance records exist for the Comédie-Italienne before 1716.
[23] Ibid., 52.
[24] Figures based on Lancaster, *Comédie-Française, 1680–1701*.

royal monopoly.[25] In 1683 the Comédie-Française addressed a petition to lieutenant general of police de la Reynie that demanded the suppression of spoken French on the Italians' stage. The most dangerous use of the French tongue, according to the French actors' appeal, occurred in the parodies of French plays staged by the Italians, particularly Jacques Pradon's parody of Racine's *Bérénice.* In spite of the "gentle warnings" that the Comédie-Française had issued after previous parodies of plays by Racine and by Pierre Corneille, the Italians continued "to try to destroy" the plays of the great classical playwrights through this war between the theaters. Rather disingenuously, the French actors argued that the King had established a single French-language troupe that was to have sole rights over plays written in French; they had sworn not to perform plays in Italian, and they simply asked that the Italians uphold their vow not to perform plays in French. In the view of the Comédie-Française, this was a business matter as well as an aesthetic one:

> The plays of Corneille, Racine and Molière are, so to speak, the patri-mony and the heritage of the supplicants. They have successively acquired this property through the payments they have made; therefore they have a great interest in opposing the parodies of the said Sr. Pradon.[26]

Thus, the battle between the Comédie-Française and the Comédie-Italienne involved issues of language, dramatic genre, and commercial appeal. The royally created Comédie-Française portrayed itself as a business venture that had made certain product investments to support itself. The troupe claimed that the Comédie-Italienne, with its rash parodies and disregard for commercial rules, threatened their livelihood. In this particular instance, the Crown sided with the Italians; a month later, Minister of State Pontchartrain told the lieutenant general of police that the Comédie-Italienne should be permitted to use spoken French onstage as long as it did not perform entirely in French.[27]

This 1683 conflict indicated the differing directions in which the two theaters were moving. The Comédie-Française, aware that it was unable to suppress the cutting parodies launched against it by the Comédie-Italienne, relied on its courtly pension and its monopoly over French-language plays.

---

[25] Scott, *Commedia dell'arte,* 192–220, 275–308, discusses the introduction and increased use of French at the Comédie-Italienne from 1668 through 1697.
[26] BN, ms 21625, September 1683.
[27] AN, O¹ 27, f.34, memo dated 19 October 1683.

The Italians, on the other hand, turned their plays into spectacles that integrated gestures, physical comedy, and the French language, thereby becoming a theater that achieved great popularity in the public playhouses while evoking scorn at court. By 1695, one journal noted, "It must be quite upsetting for the French troupe; even though abundance and popular taste are not always proof of the merit of plays nor of actors, they are in fact essential to theater companies, because it is these qualities which enlarge the receipts, and which make the whole enterprise run."[28]

In the same year, one writer had a Harlequin character comment that the Comédie-Italienne's success was owed entirely to its French-language repertory; were it to rely on the old *commedia dell'arte* routines, the public would soon grow weary of their spectacle.[29] Sources indicate that the Italians' transgression of linguistic restrictions and moral precepts continually undermined their position at court. A variety of explanations for their eventual expulsion from the kingdom in 1697 were put forth at the time. Some claimed that their failure to heed repeated warnings regarding obscene gestures and suspect language onstage sealed their fate. Others attributed their downfall to their insistence on producing a play, *The False Prude*, which lampooned the King's secretly married wife, Madame de Maintenon. Still others asserted that their suppression allowed a financially strapped King to save the eighteen thousand livres annual pension he doled out to a troupe that rarely performed at court.[30] Most likely, all of these reasons played some role in the expulsion of the actors. What seems certain is that the Crown could not erase their memory from the minds of Parisian theatergoers. On 6 December 1697, more than half a year after the closing of the Comédie-Italienne, the government included the following directions among its daily charges to the lieutenant general of police in Paris: "It is necessary . . . to efface the inscription which is on the theater of the Italian actors and destroy what intrudes there on the public way."[31]

Yet, while the Crown might have been able to erase the physical traces that the Italian troupe had left on the urban landscape, it could not so easily suppress the public memory of the entertainments that had diverted Parisian spectators. The government's determination to banish the popular troupe inspired at least three artists in subsequent years to memorialize the moment in ways that underlined the discontinuity between governmental

---

[28] *Journal de Hambourg*, 6 May 1695, quoted in Mélèse, *Le Théâtre et le public*, 51.
[29] Anonymous, *Le Livre sans nom*, 1695; quoted in Mélèse, *Le Théâtre et le public*, 51 n.2.
[30] Mélèse, *Le Théâtre et le public*, 49–56; Scott, *Commedia dell'arte*, 326–31.
[31] AN, O^{1}41, f. 182.

policy and theatergoer's pleasure. The best known of these images, an engraving based on Watteau's lost *Départ des comédiens italiens en 1697,* represents the actions of the Crown in the person of the wigged and robed magistrate in the right foreground of the image and in the young man on a ladder posting the King's orders at an entrance to the theater (figure 9).[32] The magistrate, whose back is to the viewer, appears to be striding toward the bill poster; four of the Italian characters, Mezzetin, Isabelle, Harlequin, and Polichinelle, also face the King's ordinance, the substitute for the King's body, with various stock expressions of dismay and supplication. At one level, therefore, the focus of the scene is the will of the King as expressed in his ordinance and enforced by his representative. Yet the cold efficiency of the anonymous magistrate who presides over the Italians' expulsion is undercut by the distraught young peddler of pies who stands behind him and lampooned in typical *commedia* fashion by the mock astonishment of Scaramouche, clad in black and positioned facing the viewer in the left foreground as a mirror image to the magistrate.

On further examination, one might argue, the scene is an idealized representation of the stock Italian characters in the midst of a performance.[33] The black-clad back of the magistrate is echoed to the left of the composition by the backs of two other men who have turned away from the players, and at the far end of the alley by two more men in dark cloaks striding away from the scene, one of whom sports a sword. Together, these five figures provide human reinforcement to the architectural boundaries imposed on the pictorial space by the building façades. The actors, each of whom strikes a theatrical pose, play out the scene within this human and architectural proscenium; the playing space they inhabit is set off from the rest of the composition by a shaft of sunlight that falls on them between the crowded Parisian buildings. From the windows above the street scene on the left, a bemused audience of two couples and a single woman survey the scene below them with the same detachment one might expect of loge occupants within the playhouse.

The scene on display, however, does not spring from any particular play performed by the Italians. Instead, each character responds to the news of the banishment within the improvisational framework familiar to afi-

---

[32] On the Watteau image, see Julie-Anne Plax, *Subversive Strategies: Watteau's Paintings and Cultural Politics in Early Eighteenth-Century France* (Cambridge, forthcoming), chap. 1. The other two images are *La Déroute burlesque des comédiens italiens chassés de Paris en 1697,* BN, *Cabinet des Estampes;* and *Le Renvoi des comédiens après la suppression de la Comédie-Italienne en 1697,* Musée du Havre.

[33] Crow, *Painters and Public Life,* 58, briefly analyzes the image.

Fig. 9. *The Departure of the Italian Actors in 1697*, after the painting by Watteau. (Courtesy of the Bibliothèque nationale de France.)

cionados of the Italians; Harlequin reacts to the news with a pointedly false, servile bow, Polichinelle's befuddlement is accentuated by his obesity, Columbine cunningly sobs into her handkerchief while plotting a way to turn the situation to her advantage, and so on. In other words, Watteau juxtaposes the "reality" of the King's ordinance with the "theatricality" of the *commedia dell'arte*. The authoritative text posted on the wall of the theater, which permits no alternative interpretation, confronts the improvisational techniques of the Italian actors, who relied on audience response to modify each lightly scripted performance. Within its fictive space, the image allowed the Italians to overcome the stigma of the royal dismissal; its mechanical reproduction in the form of an engraving suggests the presence of a theater public that required solace once deprived of the refreshing irreverence of the Italians.

The engraving of Watteau's lost painting thus provides another example of the popularity that the Italians had used to offset their steady loss of royal favor after 1680. In spite of their expulsion from the French capital, an expulsion that was reversed in 1716, a year after the death of Louis XIV, they continued to appeal to the increasing commercial and aesthetic authority of Parisian theatergoers in memory and in image; "posthumously," they persisted in flouting their disobedience of the King's orders. After 1697, the fair theater troupes appropriated many of the stock characters and comic situations of the Comédie-Italienne, in part thanks to a curious publication titled the *Théâtre Italien*.

The Publishing History of Gherardi's *Théâtre Italien*

In addition to the engraving of Watteau's painting, followers of the Italians could also turn to the textual traces of the Italian theater left behind after its expulsion. The troupe's Harlequin and nominal leader in the 1690s, a young actor named Evaristo Gherardi, had published the first edition of his *Théâtre Italien* in 1694; this work contained his edited versions of French-language sections of plays that the troupe had performed on the Parisian stages in the preceding two decades. Gherardi's editorial and authorial efforts ran into several telling difficulties, however, that provide insight into the disjunctions between the stage and the page in the commercial world inhabited by the public theaters at the end of the seventeenth century. The publishing history of this work demonstrates the ways in which the authority of the printed theatrical text had also lost ground since the outset of Louis XIV's reign; the difficulties encountered by Gherardi parallel those faced by actors such as Beaubourg in his quarrel with the spectator Mey.

Since the first half of the century in both England and France, playwrights had attended to the print versions of their scripts with increasing care; these editorial concerns formed part of a larger strategy to increase the respectability and social standing of the author. In England, Ben Jonson at the beginning of the century and William Congreve at its end carefully collaborated with printers in the production of standardized volumes of their theatrical work.[34] In France, the 1663 publication of Pierre Corneille's folio edition of his collected works established new typographical standards for dramatic publications.[35] In both countries, the aim of this editorial activity was to capture and reinterpret the theatrical moment within the pages of the printed book. These fixed-print versions necessarily clashed with the fluid interpretations generated nightly during performance. Typographical authority sought to eclipse the inconsistencies and irregularities encountered during the course of a play's run in the public theaters; authors used the finality of the printed page to reclaim their texts from uncontrollable actors and audiences. Playwrights and publishers thus explicitly based their authority and commercial enterprises on the reading public to which they addressed their books.

Given the hybrid nature of the Italians' spectacles, however, the players did not welcome publication with the same enthusiasm that their French counterparts did. In 1694, print and performance clashed in the first printing of *Théâtre Italien*, a single-volume work that contained many of the French-language plays performed at the Hôtel de Bourgogne by the Comédie-Italienne.[36] The Italian troupes in Paris had always relied more on *canevas*, or fixed plots and characterizations, than on published texts. The plots were often posted on the stage door, where the actors could review them before they entered the scene. Within the flimsy narrative structure of these set pieces, the actors combined various *lazzi*, or physical gags, to entertain the audience. The spectacle's suspense depended on the audience's need to see whether the next gag could possibly top the one just

---

[34] Timothy C. Murray, *Theatrical Legitimation: Allegories of Genius in Seventeenth-Century France and England* (Oxford, 1987), 39–93; Donald W. McKenzie, "Typography and Meaning: The Case of William Congreve," in *Buch und Buchhandel in Europa im achtzehnten Jahrhundert* (Hamburg, 1977), 81–125; and Julie Stone Peters, *Congreve, the Drama and the Printed Word* (Stanford, 1990). For a Europe-wide perspective on these issues, see Peters, *Dramatic Impressions: Print and the Stage, Text and Performance in Europe, 1480–1880* (forthcoming).
[35] Wallace Kirsop, "Nouveautés: théâtre et roman," in *Histoire de l'édition française*, eds. Henri-Jean Martin and Roger Chartier (Paris, 1984), 2:218–24.
[36] Evaristo Gherardi, ed., *Théâtre Italien ou Recueil de toutes les scènes françoises qui ont été jouées sur le Théâtre-Italien de l'Hôtel de Bourgogne* (Paris, 1694).

performed.[37] In the context of the heated commercial rivalry that arose after 1680, however, the Italian theater in Paris began to substitute complex narrative French scripts for the simpler Italian *canevas*, as was the case with *Les Chinois*. As the ratio of French to Italian onstage grew over the next seventeen years, commercial demands increased for a printed version of the Italian plays.

The troupe's young Harlequin, Evaristo Gherardi, attempted to satisfy these market pressures in the 1690s. In October 1689 he had replaced the company's long-time Harlequin and leading actor, Dominique Biancolelli, who had died the previous year. Gherardi had followed his father into the acting profession, but he had also received a classical education in a Parisian *collège*.[38] His training sensitized him to the importance of the printed text as a way of obtaining social status for the author and credibility for the troupe among the reading populace, which often wrote derisively of the Italians. He no doubt believed the Italians needed to combat opinions such as those expressed by Saint-Evremond in 1677:

> That which we see in France presented under the label of "The Italians" is not truly drama, at least not according to the rules of this Art, since it has no true plot, since the subject is not coherent, since one sees no character development, and since the composition reveals no genius. It is little more than a type of deformed concert undertaken by a number of actors, each of whom proceeds according to what is best for his character.[39]

To counter objections such as these, which suggested that the Italian stage had nothing to contribute to the corpus of dramatic literature as it had been defined in the seventeenth century and monopolized by the Comédie-Française, Gherardi obtained permission in May 1694 to publish a collection of French scenes played by the troupe since 1680. In his introduction to the volume, he noted that "all Paris" had admired the plays when first performed, and whenever played thereafter. The pleasure provided by the works was owed to the "fine and delicate satire" they displayed, as well as the "flawless" knowledge of the century's morals; in other words, the plays collected and published by Gherardi supposedly

---

[37] See Virginia Scott, "The *Jeu* and the *Rôle*: Analysis of the Appeals of the Italian Comedy in France in the Time of Arlequin-Dominique," in *Western Popular Theatre*, eds. David Mayer and Kenneth Richards (London, 1977), 1–27.

[38] See Campardon, *Les Comédiens du roi de la troupe italienne*, 1:240–41, for Gherardi's description of his educational background.

[39] Quoted in Marcello Spaziani, *Il Théâtre Italien di Gherardi* (Rome, 1966), 21.

displayed many of the same characteristics often attributed to Molière, the author whose work constituted the core of the Comédie-Française repertory. Gherardi also claimed that there had been a demand for these monologues in print for a long time and that he had agreed to shoulder the burdensome task only when none of his colleagues had stepped forward to prepare the corpus for publication.[40]

However, the young Harlequin's colleagues did not initially agree with Gherardi's justifications for publishing their precious *canevas*.[41] Sometime between May and September 1694, they presented a petition to the King in his council requesting that Gherardi's privilege be suspended and that the sale of the book be forbidden. According to the governmental decision rendered in mid-September, Gherardi had "adroitly swiped" the manuscripts from the individual charged with their safekeeping. The resulting volume, if placed on sale, would prove injurious to the interests of the public and the actors and would contravene the intentions of His Majesty. The actors argued that the "plays renew their charm, and thereby become new again, when they are not performed for several years, since the ideas in them are forgotten with the passage of time." If publication were to take place, however, the plays would become "public and common," to such an extent that the actors feared their theater would have to close owing to lack of interest. Furthermore, Gherardi had violated the property agreement among the players. These plays, acquired for cash over the course of thirty years from their authors, constituted the immovable property *(immeubles)* of the troupe; they belonged to all members of the Comédie equally, which was why one of them had been charged with their safekeeping.

This dispute, known to us through the legal documents it generated, is further evidence of the delicate interplay between the printed dramatic text and improvised performance at the end of the seventeenth century. Gherardi sought to publicize his troupe's activities in Parisian literary circles, as well as to burnish his own literary image; his colleagues, fearful for their livelihood, mistrusted the printed word. They conceived of their scenes and plots as their property, just as their competitors at the Comédie-Française had done in their 1683 plea to the King, and they imagined that the distribution of Gherardi's volume would flood the marketplace, leaving their performances redundant.

Between 1694 and 1700, the Gherardi text inspired printers in France and abroad to publish at least four unauthorized collections of French-

---

[40] Gherardi, *Théâtre Italien*, avertissement.
[41] Campardon, *Les Comédiens du roi de la troupe italienne*, 2:109–12; Scott, *Commedia dell'arte*, 276–79.

language Comédie-Italienne plays. In 1700, after the failure of his campaign to lift the King's 1697 ban on the Comédie-Italienne, Gherardi published a new and "definitive" six-volume edition of his *Théâtre Italien*. Seven more editions of *Théâtre Italien* appeared between 1700 and 1741; all faithfully reproduced Gherardi's 1700 text.[42]

The origins of Gherardi's desire to edit *Théâtre Italien* lay partially in his desire for literary fame. By publishing this work, he hoped to claim a place alongside Molière and his contemporary Dancourt, both of whom had achieved fame as stage actors and as dramatic authors of works in the Comédie-Française repertory. The two Latin encomiums to himself that Gherardi placed after the preface to his 1700 edition testified to his literary ambitions. But the preface that preceded them betrayed curious signs of the tension between print and performance that existed at the Comédie-Italienne. Although Gherardi devoted much of the preface to his version of the legal battles he had fought over his book since 1694, the first three pages contained a discussion of the relation between text and theater at the Italian spectacle. Indeed, the title of the preface, "Advertisement Which Must Be Read" *(Avertissement qu'il faut lire)*, foreshadowed the distinctions the author was going to make.[43] Even more mysteriously, Gherardi claimed in the preface's first sentence that "[o]ne should not expect to find whole plays in this collection, since it is not known how to print Italian plays."[44] The reason, he explained, was that Italian actors relied on improvisation rather than mindless memorization and that "the greatest beauty of the plays is inseparable from the action."[45] He then praised the Italian actors at the expense of their French counterparts, who simply recited memorized lines onstage: "Whoever says 'good Italian actor' refers to a man of substance, who plays more from imagination than from memory; who improvises, while acting, everything that he says; who knows how to work with whomever he finds onstage; that is to say that he marries his words and his actions so well with those of his colleague, that he is immediately attuned to the cues of his colleague and enters into the spirit of the scene in such a way as to make everyone believe that their actions had been previously coordinated."[46] The passage continued in this vein for another page and a half until Gherardi abruptly

---

[42] For a complete bibliography of all authorized and unauthorized editions from 1694 to 1741, see Spaziani, *Il Théâtre Italien*, 43–44.

[43] The words *qu'il faut lire* were added for the first time in 1700.

[44] Gherardi, *Théâtre Italien*, vol. 1, unpaginated preface.

[45] Ibid.

[46] Ibid.

shifted to publication issues by proclaiming, "But I stray tremendously from my subject."[47] This transition itself was reminiscent of the loose narrative structure of many Italian plays.

These laudatory remarks at the beginning of six volumes of printed play scripts, whose fixity on the page hindered improvisation, were puzzling, to say the least. Did Gherardi wish to negate his entire project at its outset? Later in the preface, he recanted by noting that many of the plays in the collection did not fall into the category of "plays that one does not know how to print" because they contained a preponderance of French over Italian.[48] In part, we can explain these contradictions by noting that Gherardi's praise of improvisation was yet another reflection of the furious commercial struggle between the Comédie-Italienne and the Comédie-Française. But the impossibility of Gherardi's task also stemmed from his wish to achieve literary immortality via a collection of texts that inherently defied the fixity of the printed page. As Gherardi so emphatically explained, the merit of the *Théâtre Italien* rested in its malleability; there was no way to translate improvisational genius to the well-regulated pages of an Old Regime typographical product. The fair theater troupes who built their spectacles in part on the riches they found in Gherardi's book challenged the authority of the printed word in ways that their audiences found even more compelling.

Fairs and Cultivation of Spectator Intervention, 1697–1719

The actors and entrepreneurs of the fair theaters fell heir to the Italians' legacy of raillery and satire after the latter's expulsion in 1697; their theatrical innovations further empowered the commercially potent parterre. Scholars typically side with the fair actors and entrepreneurs, who characterized themselves as clever but embattled underdogs fighting for their survival against the institutional power of the Comédie-Française and the Opera.[49] This David and Goliath historiography has rightly emphasized the *forains'* legal struggles for commercial existence in the face of Old Regime cultural and economic privileges. But with few exceptions it has also overlooked the radical challenge to the printed dramatic text posed

[47] Ibid.
[48] Ibid.
[49] Jules Bonnassiès, *Les Spectacles forains et la Comédie-Française d'après des documents inédits* (Paris, 1875); Campardon, *Spectacles de la foire*, 1:xv–xxv and 2:250–85; and Isherwood, *Farce and Fantasy*, 81–97.

by the fairs' theatrical innovations.[50] Legal restrictions on performance at these fair theaters caused their actors and playwrights to create spectacles that not only appealed to noncourtly audiences, but actively sought their participation in the production of meaning. The fair theaters took the old Comédie-Italienne's appeal to the parterre a step further; in so doing, they encouraged the pit to develop a repertory of cries and gestures that informed parterre response to spectacle throughout the eighteenth century. What was it like to watch these plays that created overtly political narrative strategies while they demolished all conventional standards of dramatic narrative? We will never entirely recapture this remarkable experience, of course, but contemporary police reports provide a surprisingly detailed glimpse of the audience that gathered to watch the plays performed in these "little theaters."[51] The documents show that constructive audience participation in the plays was an integral part of the theatrical moment at the fairs.

Since the late Middle Ages, Paris had hosted two annual trade fairs; one in the late winter and early spring on the grounds of the St-Germain abbey in the Latin Quarter, the other in the late summer and early fall under the jurisdiction of the St-Laurent abbey on the right bank. The late medieval Kings of France had suspended normal guild regulations and other privileges within the fairgrounds to allow Parisian merchants to compete with other fairs in the provinces and outside the kingdom. Theatrical entrepreneurs had successfully argued for centuries that the theatrical privileges enjoyed by the Confrérie de la Passion and later by the Comédie-Française and the Opera were also in abeyance within the fairgrounds. Many of the "theaters" built to house these fair performances in the late seventeenth century were makeshift affairs intended to accommodate the acrobats and tightrope walkers who provided the main entertainment before the expulsion of the Italians in 1697. Some of these spaces did not elevate the playing surface above the audience; one *procès-*

[50] The exceptions include Oscar G. Brockett, "The Fair Theaters of Paris in the Eighteenth-Century: The Undermining of the Classical Ideal," in *Classical Drama and Its Influence: Essays Presented to H. D. F. Kitto* (New York, 1965): 251–70; and David Trott, "French Theater from 1700 to 1750: The 'Other' Repertory," in *Eighteenth-Century French Theater: Aspects and Contexts*, eds. M. G. Badir and D. J. Langdon (Alberta, 1986): 32–40.

[51] These records from the AN are reprinted in Campardon, *Les Spectacles de la foire*. Marcello Spaziani, "I 'Foirains' plagiari degli 'Italiens'; overro quando la Polizia si rende utile alla storia del teatro," in *Gli Italiani alla 'Foire': Quattro Studi con Due Appendici* (Rome, 1982), 31–84, studies these reports for their recreation of plays whose scripts no longer exist. See also http://foires.net, a site maintained by Barry Russell, with many important transcribed resources.

verbal based on a 1707 performance notes that a curtain was all that separated the performance space from the area where the spectators stood.[52] A few performance spaces at the fairs became increasingly elaborate throughout the period, however, replicating the loges, pit, stage seating, perspectival stage sets, and elaborate ornamental decorations found in the privileged theaters; indeed, the *forains'* efforts to reproduce the physical experience of playgoing at the Comédie-Française was part of the charge leveled against them by their privileged competitors.[53]

The police reports echo contemporary testimony that indicates that these theaters were extremely crowded, often at the expense of the Opera and the Comédie-Française. One commissioner recorded the following impressions of the audience at the "Bel-Air" theater, once the home of the Académie royal de musique in the early 1670s, during the 1710 St-Germain fair:

> On either side of the stage one saw a double row of loges, and a parterre and an amphitheater, all of them entirely filled with spectators. On the stage itself, five rows of benches and chairs on both sides, also filled with people of both sexes, and such a large number of men standing around them that the stage was almost entirely covered, so that the actors had very little space to perform. From time to time during the performance, one heard the cry, "Make room on the stage."[54]

After the fair performance that evening, the Comédie-Française actors dragged the commissioner back to their theater, where he duly recorded that the receipts from a performance of Molière's *L'Avare* had only covered three-fifths of the evening's operating expenses. Historians of the fair theaters assume that the large crowds at these spectacles were drawn from the socially diverse mix of people who attended the fairs themselves.[55] The police reports offer little testimony to the social diversity of the audiences, but they do on occasion record the presence of courtiers and other members of the nobility one might not expect to find in such popular milieux. During the St-Laurent fair of 1712, for example, the police agents noted the presence of "many seigneurs and ladies of the Court, among them Mme la Duchesse de la Meilleraye and M. le Chevalier de Mesmes."[56] After the

---

[52] Campardon, *Spectacles de la foire*, 1:129.

[53] Ibid., see the description, 2:117.

[54] Ibid., 2:301; Lancaster, *Comédie-Française, 1701–1774*, 628, records ninety-five paying spectators at the Comédie-Française that evening.

[55] Isherwood, *Farce and Fantasy*, 29–34; Crow, *Painters and Public Life*, 51–55.

[56] Campardon, *Spectacles de la foire*, 2:346.

death of Louis XIV in 1715, the regent appears to have frequented the fair stages.[57] The presence of the court nobility, tired of rigid court etiquette by the end of the Sun King's reign, is not surprising; their attendance reinforced the popularity of the fair performances.

Although fair acrobats began to use spoken dialogue in their productions at least as early as 1678, they did not run afoul of royal monopolies until 1681, the year after the establishment of the Comédie-Française. That year marked the first of many efforts on the part of the *comédiens du roi* to shut down their fair competitors, who supposedly violated the privileged troupe's royal monopoly on spoken French drama. The conflicts escalated in 1697, when the fair theaters staked their claim to the Italian repertory and stock characters found in Gherardi's published collection that had been abandoned by the expelled *commedia dell'arte* troupe. For the next decade, the Comédie-Française pursued its exclusive privileges before the court at Versailles and in the Paris law courts, while the various fair entrepreneurs resisted the Comédie's claims, in part through appeals to patrons opposed to the Crown's official troupe. Characteristically, the Comédie-Française found support among the members of the King's council that had originally sanctioned its creation, while the *forains* appealed to the magistrates of the Parlement of Paris or Parisian ecclesiastical figures.[58] The fair theaters managed to continue their French-language performances until 22 February 1707, when the Parlement abandoned them in an *arrêt* that forbade the performance at the fairs of any "play, colloquy, or dialogue" in French. The Comédie-Française thought it had finally rid itself of its pesky competitors, but they did not take into account the fact that the court order had made no mention of "monologues." Although verbal exchanges amongst fair actors were forbidden by the Parlement, those between fair performers and their audiences were about to begin.

The day after the Parlement's ruling, the fair actors appealed the judgment before the "tribunal" of the audience gathered in their theater. The Comédie-Française, afraid that the *forains* would not abide by the court's ruling, requested that a commissioner record the performance that evening.[59] His report noted that after the tightrope walkers had opened the show, a Harlequin announced to the audience that a Parlementary *arrêt* forbade them to perform the play they had advertised

[57] Bonnassiès, *Les Spectacles forains*, 41.
[58] Campardon, *Spectacles de la foire*, 2:251.
[59] Ibid., 1:130–31.

for that evening; instead, they would play a variety of night scenes, a type of *lazzi* dependent on nonverbal, physical comedy.[60] The actors then performed a series of sketches, apparently unconnected, in which they cleverly avoided dialogue while conveying meaning to the audience. In one instance, an actor playing the Scaramouche character made a series of contortions and grimaces that Harlequin interpreted for the audience; in another, Scaramouche interrupted Harlequin's speech with "signs" that Harlequin then explained to the audience. Thus, the fair actors both alerted their spectators to the trials to which the Comédie-Française subjected them and also offered the option of a new type of fair diversion. The fair players gambled on the continuing support of the paying spectators in the face of official repression; spectators in turn received the promise of a new type of entertainment with legal and political overtones. The commissioner recorded the implications of this new genre when he noted the Comédie-Française's charge that the fair players' persistence in the face of the Parlementary *arrêt* was a "formal rebellion against the judicial authority."

At the St-Germain fair later that year, the *forains'* "rebellion" acquired greater subtlety. A commissioner's account of a September performance noted that the evening consisted of a pastiche of scenes lifted from Gherardi's *Théâtre Italien*.[61] The official, in the service of the Comédie-Française, argued that the scenes formed a unified comedy that mostly resembled the spectacles one might see at the Comédie-Française. He noted only one small difference: when an actor or actress had finished speaking, he or she withdrew into the wings while another player responded, returning to the stage to deliver the next line. By the following spring, at the St-Germain fair of 1708, the fair performers had developed other techniques to circumvent the prohibition of spoken dialogue on their stages. At times, one actor would simply remain offstage while reciting lines with the player remaining onstage; at other times, a player would whisper a response to the other, who would then speak it out loud.[62] In the following year, performers would recite nonsense verse in the grand style of the Comédie-Française, sing prose dialogues, or speak in abbreviations *(mots coupés)*. Through the use of these various techniques, developed on the fair stages between 1707 and 1710, the *forains* claimed to respect the royal privilege granted the Comédie-Française; the latter, faced with the

[60] See Mel Gordon, *Lazzi: The Comic Routines of the Commedia dell'arte* (New York, 1983), 47.
[61] Campardon, *Spectacles de la foire*, 2:117–18.
[62] Ibid., 2:176–77.

rising popularity of the fair theaters, continued to pursue legal remedies against their competitors.[63]

Although the fair players argued that they did not technically violate the French troupe's privileges, it was clear to both groups and the audience as well that they intended to succeed by mocking the Comédie-Française's overly legalistic claims. One performance observed by a commissioner in March 1708 recounted the comic tribulations of the Doctor, a stock character, who decided to improve his financial situation by organizing his servants into a theater company.[64] The servants rehearsed various tragedies and comedies from the Comédie-Française repertory in a parodical fashion, all the while using the techniques previously listed to avoid the appearance of dialogue. Furthermore, they poked fun at the Comédie's efforts to shut them down; at one point in the performance, Harlequin yelled out, "File a complaint, file a complaint!" in response to which an actor carrying a number of tomes read from a book titled *The Art of Speaking by Oneself, Invented by the French Actors.* He concluded the reading by exclaiming that when the French actors did not know what else to do, they reprised Dancourt's *Le Diable boiteux,* an overworked one-act play from the previous fall. Even the commissioner remarked that the play effectively mocked the Comédie-Française; significantly, he also reported that many spectators around him said the same thing.

These audience members were thus attracted to the fair performances by more than the usual sexual and scatological joking of the performers.[65] The tension in each day's performance arose from the *forains'* efforts to stage a spectacle without violating the ambiguous sense of "dialogue" insisted on by the Comédie-Française. At that latter spectacle, performances consisted of players reciting dialogues written by authors and often frozen on the printed page. At the fair theaters, however, performers were prohibited by the King's will, upheld in the law courts of the Old Regime, from staging these dialogues. Spectators' enjoyment derived from the ways in which the fair performers devised means to circumvent these restrictions. But if the fair theaters' actions constituted a "revolt" against the notions of monopoly and privilege cobbled together by the

[63] Ibid., 1:260–61, 2:121–22, 300–301. The fair players also requested *procès-verbaux* to prove that they were abiding by the letter of the law; see ibid., 1:85–87, 89–90, which reproduces two extremely detailed accounts of performances emphasizing the absence of dialogue.
[64] Ibid., 2:176–77.
[65] This humor undoubtedly also appealed to a theater audience seeking novel alternatives to the only authorized theater in town. Many of the *procès-verbaux* condemned the "obscenities" found on the fair stages; see ibid., 2:300.

government and the Comédie-Française, the spectators were also an integral part of this revolt.

The fair players acknowledged this role in their last major innovation, that of the *écriteaux*, or scrolls. The fair entrepreneur Allard first used them in 1710, apparently to circumvent the loss of the musical privilege that he had purchased from the Opera; it is also possible that fair audiences were tiring of the mute scenes and other performance techniques developed by the *forains*.[66] The following year, a police report from the St-Laurent fair dated 7 August 1711 detailed the uses of the scrolls during the performance of a play called *Arlequin à la guinguette*:

> [T]he players perform mute scenes concerning different subjects, with scrolls which are held by little boys suspended by ropes and moved up and down by machines. These scrolls contain songs which are sung by many parterre spectators as soon as the orchestra plays the accompanying air. The songs, which are written on both sides of each scroll, most often respond to each other and do not explain the mute scenes.[67]

The fair players had hit on the idea of having the spectators narrate the performance through song; instead of bearing silent witness to the spectacle staged before them, as the rules of French stagecraft had directed since the time of Richelieu, audience members now participated in the performance. A week later, a second commissioner attended a performance of the same play by the same troupe.[68] In his report, he noted that the players made themselves understood by means of "many large scrolls which contained, in large and very legible characters, their names and the vaudevilles." Again, the spectators sang the songs on the scrolls to the accompaniment of a small orchestra. The director of the fair production (the demoiselle Baron), had arranged to have *Arlequin à la guinguette* printed and distributed. The French actors, when they presented their complaint to the commissioner, showed the latter a copy of the printed text, whose physical appearance he described in great detail and initialed in the presence of the Comédie-Française representatives. The appearance of the fair play in print is telling; at the same time the *forains* asked their audiences to sing printed material displayed onstage during the performance, they also offered their spectators the opportunity to continue

---

[66] Isherwood, *Farce and Fantasy*, 87, points out that the Comédie-Française had pressured the Opera into canceling an agreement with Allard that allowed the latter to stage lyric drama. See also Bonnassiès, *Les Spectacles forains*, 36.
[67] Campardon, *Spectacles de la foire*, 1:90–91.
[68] Ibid., 91–93.

the reading experience outside the theater. By so doing, they created a new, print dimension to the experience of the fair theater.

Six months later, at the 1712 St-Germain fair, another fair troupe featuring Octave, one of the Italian actors expelled in 1697, performed a play "in three acts and in vaudevilles" titled *Arlequin Baron allemand, ou le triomphe de la folie*. This work had also been printed to coincide with its staging at the fair. The commissioner who reported on its 6 February 1712 performance was shown the printed book before the curtain; his report noted that the play he saw performed "followed the book brought to us which we initialed."[69] The play not only tracked the book, however; it relied on the scrolls to supply the dialogue and advance the plot: "The players used the scrolls, which supplied the words and by which means the dialogue was followed and the scenes linked throughout the play, with the singularity that *the parterre becomes an actor*, and that, taking its tone from the orchestra, itself provides the song and the words to the actors onstage [my emphasis]." Provided with the words and able to sing the common tunes that formed the vaudeville repertory, audience members became actors themselves, entering into the production of meaning within the theater.

From 1712 until the temporary suppression of the fair theaters in 1719, scrolls and singing audiences were a staple of fair theater productions. Socially diverse audience members came prepared to participate in the satire, mockery, and sexual allusions that characterized the fair stage. In 1718, another commissioner noted in a report:

> [T]he first act . . . was played as much by the actors as by the spectators, thanks to the placards which came down from above and on which were written the vaudevilles that composed the play: the actors gestured and by different pantomimes expressed what was on the placards, and the spectators sang and in several places, to link the couplets, the actors said some words, and when the placards came down, four violins, a bass, and an oboe played the vaudeville tune indicated on the placards and the public sang the vaudeville.[70]

The report indicated that the second and third acts consisted of similar spectator interventions. From the commissioner's perspective, actors

---

[69] Ibid., 2:188–89.
[70] Ibid., 2:363. For another contemporary who described the parterre as an actor, see Ardelle Striker, "A Curious Form of Protest Theater: The *pièce à écriteaux*," *Theatre Survey* 14 (1973): 67–68.

and spectators played equal roles in the staging of the play. The legal restrictions on the fair players prompted them to incorporate the audience into their spectacle in ways that followed logically on the Comédie-Italienne's appeals to the parterre at the end of the seventeenth century. In these spectacles, the parterre, in search of an identity since the beginning of the seventeenth century, finally came of age. For the remainder of the eighteenth century, the parterre considered itself an equal participant in the production of meaning on the Paris stage. Each night produced a new performance with different meaning; the experience of eighteenth-century theatergoing opposed the closure that the printed text claimed to impose on the experience of theatergoing. In the playhouse, audiences insisted on the right to shape the meanings of plays created by the King's Players; the theater was arguably one of the first forums in France where the subjects of the Bourbon Crown insisted on their place in French political culture.

In 1723, the newly anointed Louis XV invited one of the fair theater troupes to perform at Versailles; later that year, he attended the opening of the fair theaters while remaining absent from the Comédie-Française the same week. The King now followed his Parisian subjects in matters of theatrical patronage. These marks of royal favor caused the privileged theaters to cease their legal activities against the fairs; in turn, the fairs abandoned the placards. But parterre spectators did not forget the lessons they had learned while collaborating with the fair actors to circumvent Old Regime privilege.

The Parterre Rewrites Voltaire, 1724

Although the Comédie-Française turned primarily to legal sanctions in its struggles with the Italians and the fair theaters, it also tried to attend to the desires of Parisian theatergoers whom the other spectacles had lured away. The royal troupe continued to present new works during this period, some of which, by Crébillon, La Motte, Dancourt, and Lesage, attracted large audiences and remained staples of the repertory well into the century. But the French actors also panicked when confronted with deserted playhouses during the fairs; they occasionally used the same techniques as their competitors with less successful results. In August 1710, as the fair theaters unveiled the *écriteaux,* the Comédie-Française premiered Dancourt's three-act comedy, *La Comédie des comédiens, ou L'Amour Charlatan,* with the leads played by the troupe's best comic players dressed as Harlequin and Scaramouche. This novelty drew crowds away from the St-

Laurent fair for approximately two weeks, but disappeared from the repertory by the end of October.[71]

Later in the decade, in early September 1718 during that year's St-Laurent fair, the troupe advertised that it would play Racine's *Iphigénie* featuring "an extraordinary event never before seen, and perhaps never to be seen again."[72] When they finally performed the play on the ninth, their two leading male comic actors assumed the roles of Agamemnon and Achilles in the fourth act. It was a logical ploy; parodies of Racine and other classical tragedies had packed the house at the old Comédie-Italienne and the fairs. But when the Comédie-Française attempted to parody its own repertory and casting procedures, Parisian spectators balked. The audience's initial amusement quickly degenerated into displeasure and derisive calls, and the actors were unable to play the tragedy's final act. The experiment was not repeated.

Thus, by the 1720s, in spite of the royal privileges that the Comédie-Française continued to enjoy, the troupe had to contend with an interventionist audience nourished on decades of irreverency in the playhouses of its competitors. The consequences of this audience empowerment were evident by the early 1720s, as the Abbé Pellegrin noted in a 1724 play preface. That same year, the most controversial playwright of the period, Voltaire, saw *Mariamne*, his third tragedy, fall spectacularly in a single evening.[73] That night, 6 March 1724, Parisian theatergoers had eagerly awaited the

---

[71] See AD, 1:59–60 for details. Attendance figures in Lancaster, *Comédie-Française, 1701–1774*, 630.

[72] Chevalier de Mouhy, *Tablettes dramatiques* (Paris, 1752), 2 parts in 1 vol., 2:71; AD, 1:457.

[73] The playwright had taken his plot from the writings of Flavius Josephus, the Jewish historian of antiquity. Herod was a warrior-king of common birth whose son of the same name encountered the historical Jesus. The father had relied on his extraordinary military skills to defeat the Hasmonean Kings of Judea and seize the crown of the Jews. He married the female Hasmonean heir, the young and beautiful Mariamne (her name was derived from Latin translations of Josephus's original Greek), to solidify his hold on power. Mariamne, however, unhappy to find herself wedded to the murderer of her grandfather, father, and brother, fulfilled her conjugal duties but otherwise disdained the attentions of Herod. The latter's attraction to his wife grew stronger with each rebuff; when he returned from the court of Octavian in Rome in 29 B.C.E., Josephus relates that he found Mariamne unwilling to admit him to her presence. His suspicions fueled by his scheming sister, he ordered Mariamne to be brought before him. Each accused the other of breaching their marital trust; Herod sentenced his allegedly unfaithful wife to death. No sooner was he brought news of his queen's death, however, than he regretted his rashness; ultimately he sank into a deep depression that led him to wander the countryside unhinged. Only the passing of time and external threats to his kingdom allowed him to regain control of himself and the affairs of his realm. I discuss the 1724–25 response to Voltaire's play in greater detail in *"La Reine boit!* Print, Performance, and Theater Publics in France, 1724–1725," *ECS* 29 (Summer 1996): 391–411.

premiere of a new offering by the notorious author of the epic poem *La Ligue*; according to the *Mercure de France*, demand for tickets was so great that the loges were rented far in advance and the actors were able to charge double the normal admission price.[74] The huge audience, 1,257 people in all, listened attentively during the first three acts and a part of the fourth as the actors recited the Voltairean verse in the declamatory style adopted during the seventeenth century.[75] By the fifth act, however, the actors were having difficulty making themselves heard over the tumultuous reactions of the spectators. Finally, at the play's climactic moment, as the doomed heroine Mariamne raised a cup of poison to her lips, a spectator yelled out, "La Reine boit!" (The Queen is drinking!) This cry paraphrased the traditional shout, "Le Roi boit!" (The King is drinking!) associated with Epiphany celebrations. Despite the disruption, the players finished the tragedy, but Voltaire withdrew his work from the repertory.[76]

Both the *Mercure de France* writer and Voltaire, in an account the following year, agreed that the theater audience that saw the only performance of *Mariamne* in March 1724 had grown impatient with the tragedy long before the disruptive cry, "La Reine boit!"[77] These accounts, which situated the growing audience unrest in the third act when Herod first appeared onstage, suggested that some spectators were displeased with Voltaire's attempts to refashion a well-known story. The unsympathetic figure of Herod, who had murdered his way to the throne with little regard either for the wishes of his Queen or the needs of his people, posed nearly insurmountable challenges to an early eighteenth-century French playwright.[78] To make the story of Herod's murderous love for Mariamne more palatable to an audience sensitized to questions of the *bienséances*, Voltaire chose to delay Herod's entrance onstage until the middle of the third act.[79] In his place, the playwright created a Roman general named Varus, a character not

---

[74] MF, March 1724, 529–30.

[75] Attendance from Lancaster, *Comédie-Française, 1701–1774*, 679.

[76] This account of spectator response to the play's premiere is taken primarily from the MF, March 1724, 530, the only contemporary record of events that evening.

[77] MF, March 1724, 530; Voltaire, *Hérode et Mariamne* (Paris: Pissot & Flahault, 1725), unpaginated preface.

[78] In a review of Nadal's *Mariamne* in March 1725, the *Mercure* commented that "many people attribute the failure [of both Nadal's and Voltaire's *Mariamne* plays] to the subject; it is a waste of time to tell them that the old Mariamne of Tristan l'Hermite succeeded on the stage, since they will tell you that the two modern versions would also have succeeded in Tristan's time, and that Tristan's play would be rejected by today's audiences." (MF, March 1725, 549.)

[79] Herod appears onstage in the first act of both Alexandre Hardy's 1610 *Mariamne* and Tristan l'Hermite's 1636 *Mariamne*; he first enters in the second act of the Abbé Nadal's 1725 *Mariamne*.

present in either the Josephan narrative or in earlier French versions of the story. Varus, in charge of the Roman province while Herod is away in Rome, rules in a more just and civilized manner than Herod. In addition, Varus falls in love with Mariamne, who rebuffs his declaration of passion in the second act. Thus, when Herod enters the scene in the third act, Varus is already established as the play's most deserving male protagonist by virtue of his greater civility and his noble, yet unrequited, love. Consistent with this characterization, Voltaire has Varus chastise Herod in their act 3 confrontation. This dramaturgical strategy, however, failed to please the many members of the audience, who refused to accept the humiliation of the story's usual protagonist at the hands of a character fabricated by the writer.[80]

Given this response to Voltaire's authorial innovations, it is clear that the play's fate that night was already decided by the time the satirical cry of "La Reine boit!" rang out in the fifth act. Nevertheless, the collective theatrical memory subsequently collapsed the audience's response throughout the play to this single witty interjection. That moment, echoed repeatedly in print, parodies, and satirical references to the work, became one of the best-known theatrical anecdotes of the eighteenth century.[81] Why did this cry, which did not fully capture the audience's critical objections to the tragedy, acquire such importance in subsequent accounts of that disastrous evening? The carnivalesque potency of this three-word interjection, which recalled the raillery of the pre-1697 Comédie-Italienne and the fair troupes, offers an initial explanation.

Mariamne premiered two months to the day after Epiphany or in the midst of the great winter cycle of revelry that included the twelve days of Christmas and the period of carnival. This latter period ended forty days before Easter, or five days before the premiere of Voltaire's play in 1724. In a practice that continues today, the French in the eighteenth century celebrated Epiphany, otherwise known as the Feast of Kings, or as Twelfth Night in some Christian countries, on 6 January, twelve days after Christmas. Catholic doctrine specified that the three Magi had found the infant Christ in the manger in Bethlehem on this date, twelve days after his birth, hence the Feast of Kings.[82] A well-known rite associated with the Feast of

---

[80] In the preface to *Hérode et Mariamne*, Voltaire, who attended the 6 March 1724 performance, remarked, "[F]rom the moment Herod appeared onstage, I knew it would be impossible for the play to succeed." (Voltaire, *Hérode et Mariamne*, unpaginated preface.)

[81] Half a century later, the story was still so well known that it was unnecessary to provide the details to readers; see Abbé de la Porte and S. R. N. Chamfort, *Dictionnaire dramatique* (Paris, 1776), 2:172.

[82] See Arnold van Gennep, *Manuel de folklore français contemporain* (Paris, 1938–88), tome 1, 8:3551–86, for a discussion of French customs surrounding the *fête des rois*.

Kings in the eighteenth century, one practiced by commoners as well as Kings and Queens since the 1500s, involved the sectioning and distribution of a *galette*, or cake, which had a bean hidden in it.[83] The member of the family who received the portion of the cake containing the bean became the "king." This individual then chose a "queen" and established a "court" that was to rule during the period of carnival. The newly crowned King's first duty was to initiate the consumption of libations; as he emptied his glass, those around him cried, "Le Roi boit!" Van Gennep noted that in Paris the days' festivities often ended in *charivari*, with kings, queens, and their attendants pounding on copper drums and basins.[84]

Beyond the popular origins of the cry "La Reine boit!" however, there were many meanings that members of the diverse audience might have assigned to this carnivalesque intervention on the night of 6 March 1724. At one level, spectators that night certainly reacted with the Rabelaisian belly laugh called for by such a reference. The irreverent juxtaposition of the climactic moment in a French classical tragedy with a popular cry that signified the onset of gluttony and physical excess drew the inversionary response spectators had learned at the old Comédie-Italienne and in the fair theaters. The spectators' eruption meant that many of them relished the thought of substituting the crowning of the King of Fools and the beginning of riotous celebration for the death of Mariamne and the end of this particular classical tragedy. In addition, the cry had an element of black humor; when the "king" drank on the Feast of Kings, all those at the table had to follow him. But if the characters onstage quaffed the same beverage as Mariamne, they would imbibe poison and then expire, perhaps an outcome desired by theatrical connoisseurs displeased with both play and players.

The pandemonium that followed the cry of "La Reine boit!" however, indicated disapproval for more literary reasons as well; the response to this cry undoubtedly signaled some spectators' displeasure with Voltaire's violation of theatrical *bienséance*. The literary codes of the French classical stage, familiar to exacting spectators such as Mathieu Mey, prohibited a playwright from depicting the death of a protagonist onstage; typically, dramatic authors would have another character narrate the tragic demise in rhymed verse for the audience. In the original version of *Mariamne*, however, Voltaire chose to stage the Hasmonean Queen's death, violating a rule observed not only by Tristan l'Hermite in his seventeenth-century

---

[83] See the historical survey of French *fête des rois* practices in Alfred Franklin, ed., *La Vie privée d'autrefois*, ser. 1, vol. 8, *Variétés gastronomiques* (Paris: Plon & Nourrit, 1891), 164–73.
[84] See Ravel, "*La Reine boit!*" 408 n. 20.

version of the tragedy, but also by Corneille and Racine in the most canon-
ical works of the French tragic repertory. An audience wag let loose with
"La Reine boit!" at precisely the moment when the actress playing Mariamne brought the cup to her lips; audience members, already displeased
with Voltaire's earlier revisions to the Josephan narrative, seized on this
witticism to complete their rejection of *Mariamne*.

Alongside the carnivalesque inversion and the formalist critique implicit
in this cry, an element of masculine aggression also existed. The parterre,
which most likely was the source of the fifth act intervention, was an
exclusively male space within the playhouse; many male youths in attendance made little effort to mask their desires.[85] The male bodies packed
into the parterre on 6 March 1724 had jostled and shoved each other for
three hours by the time the actress playing Mariamne brought the cup of
poison to her lips. They were able to gaze at the women seated above them
in the loges, as well as at the actresses performing before them onstage.
The latter, in particular, represented a striking contradiction: while they
might play chaste tragic heroines, they enjoyed unsavory sexual reputa-
tions offstage. By the fifth act, the all-male parterre had watched the character of Mariamne, played by a sexually suspect actress, jilt both her
virtuous suitor and her husband. For these men the cry, "La Reine boit!"
served to puncture the actress's illusion of sexual fidelity by suggesting that
she was, after all, as accessible to the men of the parterre as their female
drinking partners in a Parisian tavern or brothel. This *mauvaise plaisan-
terie* gave voice to male anxieties always present in the eighteenth-century
parterre yet usually suppressed by the conventions of playhouse behavior.
Once released from their normal obligations by Voltaire's and the players'
transgressions of the agreements between audience and actors, parterre
spectators engaged in a display of masculine unruliness for the remainder
of the evening. In so doing, they reinforced what the Abbé Pellegrin and
many other observers already knew: public theater spectators, especially
the men who stood in the pit, had become irrevocable participants in the
making of meaning in the playhouse. Parterre spectators, perhaps never a
tranquil group, paid silent homage no longer.

[85] On the origins of the cry that evening in the parterre, see Ravel, *"La Reine boit!"* 409 n. 25.

4

Policing the Parisian Parterre, 1697–1751

I have the honor to report to you today, Sir, that . . . between the two plays at the Comédie-Italienne, two disorderly officers insulted everyone before them in the parterre, even to the extent of threatening to "throw them all the fuck out the window." I requested, with as much politeness as I could muster, that they leave the theater; the insults, oaths, and violent propositions which followed were incredible. They caused many parterre spectators to take refuge in the café.

—Report to the Lieutenant General of Police, 5 December 1743.

One afternoon in the 1660s, according to a colorful anecdote from the Sieur de Grimarest's 1705 *Life of M. de Molière*, a group of soldiers and attendants from the royal household stormed the Palais Royal theater fully armed.[1] These men were outraged that the actors had convinced the King to eliminate their free entrance to the parterre of the theater. When the porter surrendered his weapon to them after briefly resisting their onslaught, they brutally slaughtered him, "piercing him a hundred times with their swords." They then rushed into the theater, determined to take their revenge on Molière and his colleagues. But Grimarest recounts that Louis Béjart, a member of the troupe, dashed onstage at this moment in his costume, that of a seventy-five-year-old man, and asked the pugilists to spare the life of an "aged man" with few years left. This humorous improvisation "calmed" the youths, according to Grimarest, and in the interlude Molière successfully reminded the turbulent soldiers that their insistence on free admission violated the King's orders.

After smiling at Béjart's quick-witted improvisation, one is struck by the absence of any armed police intervention when reading this account. Where was the muscle necessary to back up the King's orders on which Molière insisted? Why did troupe members have to rely on their wit and character to save their lives, much less secure their incomes? How could

[1] Jean-Léonor Le Gallois, Sieur de Grimarest, *La Vie de M. de Molière* (Paris, 1705), 82–89.

actors and spectators come together in the public theaters with the threat of such random violence hanging over them? By the time Grimarest's work appeared in print in 1705, however, the absolute monarchy had begun to fashion an answer to these questions. In the first decade of the eighteenth century, the police of Paris were taking steps to prevent the types of violence that had plagued the theaters at the height of the French stage's classical period in the 1660s and 1670s. The playhouses at the turn of the eighteenth century were more violent and unpredictable than ours are today; but after 1700, for the first time, guards armed with weapons and authorized to arrest troublemakers patrolled the parterres of the Paris theaters.

The government's efforts to police the public theaters, which were carried out with mixed success in the first half of the eighteenth century, must be understood within the context of the history of "policing" in Paris in the seventeenth and early eighteenth centuries. The verb *policer*, in a pre-revolutionary context, included but was not limited to the suppression of violent and malevolent acts against individuals or corporate entities. State officials charged with policing responsibilities regulated various forms of commerce, worked to eliminate unsanitary practices that threatened the well-being of city dwellers, and organized aid to the poor; in short, their functions included what we might call administrative and judicial tasks as well as disciplinary ones.[2] It is a commonplace of seventeenth-century French historiography that Colbert's initiatives, which resulted in the 1667 establishment of one central policing officer, the lieutenant general of police, successfully transformed the previously backward or nonexistent practices of administration and security in the city of Paris.[3] But work by the historian Paolo Piasenza convincingly argues that the Parlement of Paris, largely independent of the Crown, had organized an urban policing force of significant size and competence in the first half of the seventeenth century.[4] Agents of the Parlements met in consultative "assemblies" with Parisian nonaristocratic professionals, merchants, and master artisans to

[2] The most thorough description and justification of the absolute monarchy's police is Nicolas de la Mare, *Traité de la police*, 4 vols. (Paris, 1705–38).

[3] See, for example, Marcel Marion, *Dictionnaire des institutions de la France aux XVIIe et XVIIIe siècles* (Paris, 1923), 441–42.

[4] Paolo Piasenza, *Polizia e citta: Strategie d'ordine, conflitti e rivolte a Parigi tra Sei e Settecento* (Bologna, 1990); summarized in Piasenza, "Juges, Lieutenants de Police, et Bourgeois," 1189–1215; see also Roland Mousnier, *The Institutions of France under the Absolute Monarchy, 1598–1789. Vol. 1: State and Society*, trans. Brian Pearce (Chicago, 1979), 574–79.

form policing policies; furthermore, these assemblies were careful to build into their procedures formal means of protection and appeal for Parisians drawn into this policing "system."

According to Piasenza, the reform of 1667 that created a lieutenant general of police responsible solely to the King and his ministers of state was part of the Crown's effort in the first decade of Louis XIV's personal rule to undermine the urban-based, "paternal" authority of the Parlement of Paris and the urban bourgeoisie who had challenged the Crown during the Fronde. Nevertheless, the first lieutenant general of police, Nicolas de la Reynie, devoted his attention primarily to political and religious matters as they pertained to the nobility and to Protestants resident in the capital; he did little to challenge the administrative and disciplinary procedures of the police established under the Parlements. In 1697, however, De la Reynie's successor, Marc René de Voyer de Paulmy, Marquis d'Argenson, used the powers granted to him by the King to establish an invasive system of clandestine police who were armed with "orders" from the King, orders that did not have to pass through normal legal channels. Piasenza suggests that d'Argenson wished to serve the merchants and master artisans of Paris by creating an urban space in which these *honnêtes hommes* would not be disrupted by the supposed "dregs" of society. On a city-wide scale, d'Argenson's forces pursued prostitutes, vagabonds, "sodomites," and other members of the lower orders with a vigor not previously seen in Paris. In the public theaters, he attempted for the first time to control the behavior of some spectators inside the playhouse, precisely at the moment when theatergoers had begun to intervene forcefully during the performance of plays in the theater. With the death of Louis XIV in 1716, the Parlement of Paris repealed some of d'Argenson's initiatives; d'Argenson himself left the lieutenancy general of police to become keeper of the seals in 1718. In the theater, however, his legacy lingered on until 1751, when the Crown formally altered the personnel and policing of the public theaters.

In the aftermath of Michel Foucault's analysis of eighteenth-century disciplinary initiatives, other historians have renewed their interest in this topic, without necessarily agreeing with Foucault that changes in the policing system resulted in more sinister "micro-techniques" of control. Daniel Gordon has argued that the absolute monarchy's theoretical justification for its "policing" force symbolized the French state's commitment to its own progress and well-being in the seventeenth and eighteenth centuries, while David Garrioch has suggested that the Paris police of the eighteenth century were directed from above by enlightened reformers and served the needs of many different constituencies within the capital, sometimes against the inclinations of the police themselves.[5] The case of the public theaters in the first half of the eighteenth century permits one to expand on these arguments. The policing of playhouses, which the government placed under the rubric of *discipline des moeurs*, or the regulation of manners and behavior, was intended to eliminate potentially fatal scenes such as the one described by Grimarest. In so doing, the state claimed that it allowed spectators to witness French playwrights and actors perfecting the dramatic arts under the auspices of royal patronage. Inside the playhouse, however, the consequences of daily policing practices proved more ambivalent. The activities of the police had eliminated the most violent spectator behavior by the early eighteenth century, but the abuses of policing agents, who capriciously arrested spectators under the vague terms of the King's Ordinances concerning the Theaters, provoked audience criticism of their tactics. By the 1740s, this criticism of the police had reached such a pitch that the King and his highest ministers began to contemplate reforming the system. These reforms, enacted in 1751, provided further evidence of the strength of the audience's collective critical voice in public affairs; the spectators, who had learned to intervene collectively in the theatrical moment from 1680 to 1730, now forged a common voice critical of the state's policing policies in the following two decades.

A Disorder at the Comédie-Française in 1691

On 6 November 1691, approximately a quarter of a century after the episode recounted by Grimarest, four soldiers, almost certainly drunk, forced their way into the parterre of the Comédie-Française without paying.[6] These military men were probably on leave from the battlefields of the War of the League of Augsburg, a conflict that pitted France alone against most of the other European powers. Jean Fortier, a royal official stationed at the door to the parterre to prevent such an abuse, challenged the men. In response, one of the soldiers, reportedly a captain by the name

---

[5] Gordon, *Citizens without Sovereignty*, 9–24; David Garrioch, "The Police of Paris as Social Reformers," *Eighteenth-Century Life* n.s. 16 (February 1992): 43–59; Garrioch, "The People of Paris and Their Police in the Eighteenth Century: Reflections on the Introduction of a 'Modern' Police Force," *European History Quarterly* 24 (1994): 511–35.

[6] Campardon, *Les Comédiens du roi de la troupe française*, 290–97; Bonnassiès, *La Comédie-Française*, 331; and Lancaster, *A History of French Drama in the Seventeenth Century* (Baltimore, 1940), pt. 4, 1:48–49.

of Sallo, drew his sword against the weaponless official and wounded him on his right side. A number of Sallo's colleagues rushed with swords drawn to their comrade's aid in the theater's foyer. Sallo and his tipsy companions then reentered the parterre, where they caused such a ruckus that the actors could not, or would not, begin the performance. Charles Varlet de La Grange, the troupe's senior member and *orateur,* appeared onstage to ask the audience if it wished the performance to begin. When the spectators responded affirmatively, the actor and actress featured in the first scene appeared onstage to start the play.

Before the scene got underway, however, Sallo managed to take some of the lighted candles from the foot of the stage and heave them at the players. This action prompted the actors to withdraw from the stage. In due course, La Grange reappeared to beg pardon of the public and ask if the actors might begin the performance again. Having received the requested permission, LaGrange retreated into the wings and the performance started. Not far into the first act, however, Sallo interrupted the performance anew. According to the theater's concierge, he yelled, "Get off the stage, you sons of bitches, or I'll break your skulls with a shot from my pistol!"[7] This time, the actors left the stage definitively, and La Grange appeared for the third time to announce that the troupe had canceled the performance and that the spectators could obtain a refund at the ticket booth.

Sallo and company then climbed on stage, extinguished all the candles at the foot of the playing area, destroyed the stage decorations, and ripped several boards out of the playing surface in an attempt to destroy the overhead chandeliers that held the remainder of the candles. Sallo threatened to set the whole building on fire, kill actors and actresses, and pin any other theater employees to the stage wall after running them through with his sword. In spite of the warnings of one of his comrades, Sallo continued his rampage as the other spectators cleared the theater. In the wake of this violence, the theater remained closed for the next two days while the troupe sought additional protection from the King and the lieutenant general of police. The day the theater reopened, a bill poster for the privileged spectacles reported harassment from an unidentified man dressed in a manner similar to Sallo when he tried to affix the day's playbill for the Comédie-Française to a building on the rue St.-André-des-Arts near the theater. Sallo was finally arrested six days after his rampage at the Comédie-Française, and in January 1694 a police sentence ordered him to pay fifteen hundred livres in damages to the troupe.

---

[7] Campardon, *Les Comédiens du roi de la troupe française,* 294.

Sallo's physical and verbal violence, directed against the exempt charged with maintaining order and the privileged troupe of actors performing onstage, seemingly indicates that the establishment of the Comédie-Française and twenty years of policing activity in the capital had done little to ensure tranquility in the public theaters. Sallo threatened not only the actors and spectators present in the theater that day, but also the tenuous claims of civil order necessary for the maintenance of the absolutist state under the Bourbons. In this sense, his disruptions posed a threat similar to that of the youths whom Grimarest claimed had violently invaded the Palais Royal twenty-five years earlier. Had the royal government's capacity to respond to such defiance changed over two decades? If we return to Sallo's rampage, we can see that even while he wreaked havoc within the theater, his challenge was not unanswered. Fortier, the royal official at the door, was an exempt, or the head of a Parisian policing unit who was exempt from paying taxes; his presence at the entrance to the theater, a new development since the days of Molière, indicates that the Crown had decided to commit its own personnel to the policing of the playhouse. In an account of the events that transpired at the door to the parterre, the ticket taker reported that Fortier told Sallo, "Sir, you cannot enter the theater without paying. I am here by order of the King to prevent any disturbance."[8] This statement, no matter how self-serving, suggests the government's heightened commitment to the maintenance of order at the spectacles. Fortier believed that a mere reminder of royal authority would serve to reign in overly aggressive behavior.

The theater's concierge related an equally telling moment when he recounted the confrontation between Sallo and three of the troupe's male actors as the former destroyed scenery and the stage itself. The actors pointed out that Sallo's actions were an offense to the King's orders, but Sallo, drunk with wine and flushed with adrenalin, responded that "he [didn't] give a fuck about the King's orders."[9] According to the concierge's account, this statement was too much for one of Sallo's colleagues, identified as his brother. The latter apparently told Sallo, "That's not right, we must respect His Majesty's orders."[10] It was not surprising that the actors fell back on the threat of reprisals by their royal patron to try to calm the enraged soldier. But it was telling that the soldier's colleague, probably also drunk and carried away by the momentary disruption, realized that Sallo's actions risked the threat of severe reprisals by the state.

[8] Ibid., 292.
[9] Ibid., 295.
[10] Ibid., 295.

In this incident, then, it would appear that two decades of royal responses to disorder in the theater had made some inroads. The statements by the exempt and Sallo's colleague suggest that the disturbance caused by Sallo and his friends was, by 1691, an exception to the generally civil behavior of late-seventeenth-century theater spectators who attended the Comédie-Française. Sallo's capture and subsequent financial penalty also demonstrated the resources wielded by the state in its efforts to curb unauthorized violence in the theaters. The parterre, and other sectors of the playhouse as well, had become somewhat safer for the Parisian *bourgeois* and others who attended the theater by the end of the century. After 1697, under the administration of the second Parisian lieutenant general of police, d'Argenson, the state posted policing agents inside the playhouse itself in an effort to head off disturbances that disrupted performances. In so doing, it increased the profile of the monarchy in the public theaters, thereby raising the stakes for the crown's policing forces.

D'Argenson's Reforms and Excesses, 1697–1718

In January 1697, d'Argenson assumed the responsibilities of the Paris lieutenant general of police; four months later, the King ordered him to close the Comédie-Italienne. The police commissioner, Nicolas de la Mare, in a section of his *Traité de la Police* written in 1701 or 1702, claimed that the Italians' expulsion increased audience sizes at the Comédie-Française and the Opera, thereby necessitating "stronger measures to maintain the tranquility necessary for public entertainments."[11] De la Mare did not specify these measures; rather, he reprinted a dozen ordinances that the King or the police had issued in the previous thirty years concerning the policing and administration of the public theaters. These royal proclamations, referred to by officials, actors, and disruptive soldiers during Sallo's rampage in 1691, publicized the King's will on the matter of theater disruptions in the main public places of the capital; they were also posted outside each of the privileged theaters. The most current of them, dating from 19 January 1701, slightly modified the King's prohibitions against the disruption of performances. A previous ordinance, issued in November 1691 just after Sallo's rampage at the Comédie-Française, had prohibited "all those who enter the theaters from commiting any disorder, or from inter-

[11] De la Mare, *Traité*, 1:404–5. Although the first volume of de la Mare's treatise was published in 1705, the approbation is dated 1702, and the last ordinance on theater policing that he reprints is dated 30 August 1701.

rupting the performers in any way." The 1701 ordinance expanded on these prohibitions: "The King forbids . . . all those who enter the theater to interrupt the performers in any fashion, or to commit any disorder, either during the performance or the intermissions, or before or after the play, at the risk of disobedience."[12] The lieutenant general of police, d'Argenson, was ordered to "attend to the execution" of the 1701 ordinance. But both de la Mare and the ordinances themselves remained silent on the methods d'Argenson was to use to enforce the King's will.

Soon after d'Argenson took up his duties in 1697, he began to reorient the forces at his command.[13] Thieves, mendicants, and prostitutes faced much harsher forms of repression; night patrols arrested vagabonds more often; and even lackeys had to carry certificates from their masters when out in public. Posters reproducing police ordinances appeared throughout the city with a greater frequency that underlined the new campaign against those who troubled the repose of neighborhoods or who menaced the safety of Parisian homes. Individuals who violated these ordinances were arrested according to the authority of the "King's orders"; use of this expedient in arrests, a measure that circumvented normal judicial procedures involving the Châtelet or the Parlement of Paris, rose dramatically in the decade after d'Argenson took office. These actions and others fell under the category of *discipline des moeurs*, the rubric under which de la Mare also placed the policing of spectacles.[14]

D'Argenson drew personnel from existing police units to staff his forces devoted to the correction of morals. He selected exempts from groups such as the watch and the office of the lieutenant *criminel* of the Short Robe, a judicial and administrative bureau that was superseded by the establishment of the lieutenant general of police in 1667 but which continued to exist. He obtained separate funds from the minister of state to pay his exempts their salaries, thereby making them dependent on him and breaking their previous institutional loyalties. He then reassigned these individuals to the policing functions that particularly concerned him, also allowing each exempt to hire additional men to enforce policies or act as spies. It was to this new corps of policing agents that d'Argenson turned when he designed a system to police the interior of the playhouses.

---

[12] BN, 21625, 11 November 1691; BN, 21625, 19 January 1701.

[13] The following paragraph summarizes Piasenza, "Juges, Lieutenants de Police, et Bourgeois," 1197–1205.

[14] For the phrase *discipline des moeurs*, see de la Mare, *Traité*, tome 1, page 6 of the unpaginated preface.

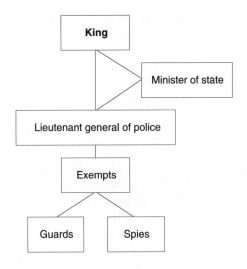

Chart 1. The hierarchy of theater discipline from Louis XIV to 1751.

The language in the King's ordinance of 1701 that directed d'Argenson to suppress theater disturbances was reinforced in 1706 by a royal edict granting the lieutenant general of police exclusive jurisdiction over the public theaters.[15] Even before 1706, however, d'Argenson had begun to create a system to police the interior of Parisian public theaters (chart 1). This system included a hierarchical structure wherein power flowed from the King downward to the exempt in the theater, and a strategy of deterrence that began with the omnipresent royal ordinances concerning the theaters and then relied on the tactic of singling out for arrest certain spectators accused of starting any disorder. Through this bureaucracy, d'Argenson, operating in the name of the King, invested his agents in the theater, the exempts, with the judicial authority to arrest and imprison "disorderly" spectators. This authority passed from the King through the Count of Pontchartrain, the minister of state charged with overseeing Parisian affairs, to the lieutenant general of police.[16] Letters from Pontchartrain to d'Argenson in November 1707, for example, emphasized the King's vivid interest in the "tranquility of the playhouses," and instructed d'Argenson to send Pontchartrain from time to time "very exact accounts

---

[15] Nicolas Toussaint le Moyne, dit des Essarts, *Les Trois théâtres de Paris* ... (Paris, 1777), 147.
[16] On the powers of the lieutenants general of police, see Alan Williams, *The Police of Paris, 1718–1789* (Baton Rouge, 1979), 48.

of everything that happens at the theaters."[17] Armed with these guidelines, d'Argenson then instructed the exempts, who made decisions regarding arrest and imprisonment and commanded the guards and spies who carried out these orders. Information also flowed in the opposite direction: the exempts addressed their reports on theater disturbances to the lieutenant general of police, who in turn communicated this intelligence either to the minister of state or directly to the King.

This hierarchical system was largely in place by the end of Louis XIV's reign in 1715, as the following excerpt from a 1713 letter from Pontchartrain to d'Argenson attests. Although Pontchartrain was here more concerned with disorderliness among the spectators seated on the stage than among those standing in the parterre, the assumptions detailed in this section characterize royal directives to the lieutenant general of police:

> [A]ttached you will find the new ordinance; His Majesty recommended that I add some articles and at the same time tell you that all these precautions will be useless if you do not closely adhere to their execution and if you do not try to make examples of those who dare to contravene them. This will be easy for you to do if you expressly order Rivière [an exempt] to station himself on the stage of the theater, to observe those who make noise or who remain outside the barriers and the balustrade, to determine their names and standing and to declare them to you, so that upon the advice that you will give me I can report to His Majesty, who will determine the appropriate action.[18]

This letter, occasioned by the issuance of a new ordinance in 1713, detailed the hierarchy of power involved in the policing of spectacle.[19] In this instance, the King himself, via his agents the minister of state and the lieutenant general of police, positioned the exempt (Rivière) in the theater. The King also specifically stated that his ordinance lacked teeth without the example of several arrests; Rivière was ordered to imprison spectators to fill what amounted to a quota. The King himself would then decide the appropriate punishment for the unfortunate audience members singled out by the Crown's deterrent policies.

There appear to have been one or two brigades of seven to fourteen archers of the Short Robe assigned to the two privileged Comédies during the first half of the eighteenth century. At times, men drawn from the munic-

---

[17] BN, ms ff 9326, f. 77, Pontchartrain letters of 9 and 16 November 1707.

[18] BN, ms ff 9326, f. 84.

[19] AN, O¹57, f. 200–201, for the ordinance in question, also dated 28 November 1713.

ipal watch may have joined them in the theaters.[20] These individuals had responsibility for enforcing the King's ordinances both inside the theater and out, where they had to prevent unruliness on the part of carriage drivers as well as scalping and the sale of counterfeit tickets. They were assisted in this task by *mouches*, or spies, who were secretly stationed in the theater audiences as early as 1689.[21] In compensation for their services, the men of the Short Robe were well rewarded by the royal treasury, and perhaps by the actors as well; one historian indicates that the post of policing the theaters was sought after by other soldiers, but given to the lieutenant criminel's men because they were more sensitive to the "civility" of the theaters.[22]

The policing structure established at the Opera in this period did not place as much power in the hands of the lieutenant general of police as that created at the Comédie-Française. In June 1700, Pontchartrain indicated to d'Argenson the need to maintain order at both spectacles: "The King being informed that the Opera is often disturbed by whistles, hand-clapping and other similar practices, His Majesty has ordered me to tell you to take the same pains to maintain order at this spectacle as you take at the Comédie-Française; it is no less necessary to maintain the order at one of these spectacles than it is at the other."[23] Nevertheless, around this time the Crown decided to station a regiment of forty musketeers and their commanding officers from the Paris royal garrison at the Opera house on performance evenings. Twenty-four of these men were positioned inside the playhouse, four of them in the parterre itself.[24] Several factors accounted for the state's weightier display of force at the Opera. First, this spectacle staged performances only three nights a week, hence it was cheaper to police but more crowded on performance evenings. Second, the Opera, as the Royal Academy of Music, enjoyed a more prestigious cultural status than the Comédie-Française, and was therefore entitled

---

[20] LaGrave, *Le Théâtre et le public*, 57; Chevalier de Mouhy, *Tablettes dramatiques* (Paris, 1752), 2:73. See BN, ms Joly de Fleury 376, "Mémoire pour les lieutenants, guidon, exempt, & archers de la compagnie du Sieur lieutenant-criminel de Robe courte . . ." for details on the responsibilities of the Short Robe and the watch; and the description of the watch in Jean Chagniot, "Le Guet et la garde de Paris à la fin de l'Ancien Régime," *RHMC* 20 (January–March 1973): 58–71.

[21] Lancaster, *Comédie-Française, 1680–1701*, 15; AN, O¹44, f. 112, 17 March 1700; Cottin, ed., *Rapports de police de Réné d'Argenson*, 191–92, 19 October 1706.

[22] Chagniot, *Paris et l'armée*, 133; BA, ms 10010, f. 170–71, 11 February 1740.

[23] AN, O¹44, f. 268, 21 June 1700.

[24] The precise date at which the *gardes françaises* began to police the Opera is difficult to establish; AN, O¹618, f. 73, suggests that the guards may have been at the Opera since 1704; this impression is reinforced by AN, O¹620, f. 466, which lists dozens of military interventions at the Opera in the 1700–15 period.

to greater protection. And third, the performances took place within the confines of a royal residence, the Palais Royal, which required greater proprieties from spectators entering its confines than the commercial site on which the Comédie-Française had built its theater in 1689.

This notion of the Opera house as the King's property was voiced in a police report from the 1720s. Describing a brawl that had occurred in the Opera house, the guard remarked, "This is an affair between young men of the same condition which has nothing to do with the public welfare except with respect to the place where it occurred. *It is a lack of respect for the Opera house which belongs to the King.*"[25] The nobler tones of the Opera house thus placed it beyond the exclusive jurisdiction of the lieutenant general of police, who was expected to assist in the maintenance of order at this spectacle, yet was required to share his authority with the commanding officer of the Paris garrison. The problems with this arrangement would become manifest in the second half of the century, particularly once the royal soldiers also took over policing duties at the Comédie-Française and the Comédie-Italienne as a result of the 1751 reforms.

By 1708, Parlement and court opposition to d'Argenson's clandestine police operatives led to a restructuring of the police; a royal edict in that year created a corps of forty-eight *inspecteurs de police*, later reduced to twenty.[26] These inspectors still served under the lieutenant general of police, but the latter could no longer choose them nor pay them out of a slush fund set aside by the minister of state. Furthermore, the royal edict carefully defined the inspectors' responsibilities and the legal authorization under which they acted. When Louis XIV died in 1715, the Parlement took its revenge on d'Argenson by trying many of his exempts on charges of extortion and abuse of royal authority; the most corrupt individuals were stripped of their offices, imprisoned, and in one case sentenced to the galleys. D'Argenson himself, in spite of his tacit conviction during the trial, ascended to the more powerful office of keeper of the seals in 1718. Before the trial, many of d'Argenson's clandestine police force became inspectors; those who escaped Parlementary revenge during the early years of the regency went back to their positions in the watch or the Short Robe. By midcentury, these two forces seemed to be at odds. These men often continued their "criminal" policing activities, albeit under changed conditions. The 1716–19 trial of their comrades had demonstrated that their secret activities might be made public at any point.

[25] BA, ms 10856, f. 222, my emphasis. For examples of similar claims, see AN, O¹620, no. 466; and Johnson, *Listening in Paris*, 9.

[26] Piasenza, "Juges, Lieutenants de Police, et Bourgeois," 1203–5.

Quantitative Aspects of Theater Policing after D'Argenson

The tension between the efficiency of secret policing procedures and the need for public intervention to expose potential abuses haunted the men who policed the Comédie-Française and the Comédie-Italienne from the mid-1710s to 1751. Exempts and archers from the Short Robe continued to provide a police presence at the theaters during this period; their primary source of authority became the King's Ordinances concerning the Theaters, which Versailles continued to issue on a regular basis for the remainder of the century. The last major change in the text of this ordinance occurred in 1728, when the provisions regarding disorder in the theater written in 1701 were modified for the last time. The revised section of the ordinance reads as follows: "The King's ordinance . . . also forbids all those who attend these theaters, and especially those who place themselves in the parterre, to commit any disorder there, either when entering or leaving, to cry out or make noise before the play begins or during the intermissions, to whistle, hoot, have a hat on one's head or to interrupt the actors during the performance in any way or under any pretext at all, under pain of disobedience."[27] Whereas the 1701 ordinance failed to specify that a particular area of the theater was subject to its restrictions, in 1728 the phrase "those who place themselves in the parterre," identified the area of primary concern for royal officials. Similarly, the 1728 ordinance offered more explicit guidelines for the identification of unacceptable behavior. The 1701 phrase "aucun désordre" was unpacked to include cries, noises, whistles, and shouts before the play began and during intermissions, and spectators were specifically enjoined not to wear hats. Likewise, royal officials in the spectacles received greater discretionary power in 1728 by the addition of the clause "in any manner and under any pretext," which allowed them to intervene in the parterre when they saw fit.[28]

Armed with these instructions, but chastened by the fate of their colleagues who had been convicted by the Parlement and faced by a group of spectators well aware of their past abuses, the exempts and their brigades continued to police the parterres of the public theaters after the death of Louis XIV and the end of d'Argenson's service as lieutenant general of police. The first archival traces that directly record their activities appear in 1717 while the trial in the Parlement was still in progress; they continue

---

[27] BN, ms 21625, "Ordonnance de Sa Majesté concernant les spectacles du 7 décembre 1728."

[28] In 1780, the clause regulating the behavior of parterre spectators used exactly the same language; AN, AD^{VIII}10, 2 April 1780.

through 1765.[29] Analysis of these incidents reveals three noteworthy patterns: first, that parterre arrests were more likely to occur at the Comédie-Française, the Comédie-Italienne, or the Opera than at the nonprivileged spectacles in this period; second, that those arrested in the parterres tended to be young men in relatively marginal positions, such as apprentices, legal clerks, students, or soldiers; third, that two peak periods of arrests occurred in the mid-1730s and around the year 1750.

In the forty-eight-year span represented by these dossiers (1717–65), seventy-three instances of police intervention in the parterres of both privileged and nonprivileged Parisian spectacles exist; forty-four, or more than half, of these arrests occurred in the parterre of the Comédie-Française. The next most active site of police activity was the parterre of the Comédie-Italienne, where nineteen separate incidents occurred from 1720 to 1761. Only three incidents at the Opera, where a different policing regime prevailed, remain in the archives, and the nonprivileged spectacles account for seven instances of police interference. Thus, d'Argenson's policing apparatus, which had existed in part to satisfy the old King's desire to survey the public theaters, continued to serve the needs of the absolutist state well beyond d'Argenson's tenure in office. In spite of the reputation that the boulevards and the fairs subsequently acquired for criminality, police officials operating within this bureaucracy were more concerned with the privileged spectacles during the 1717–65 period.[30]

Thanks to the diligence of the Paris police, who almost always noted the name, occupation or title, domicile, and age of those they arrested, it is possible to identify some patterns emerging from the biographical backgrounds of spectators arrested by the police. In the seventy-three incidents of arrest whose records survive, the police detained a total of ninety-four spectators. Because women were excluded from the parterre,

---

[29] A total of almost two hundred police dossiers that detail penal actions taken against spectators, their servants, theatrical employees, counterfeiters, scalpers, and others accused of violating the King's ordinances survive in the Bastille archives at the Bibliothèque d'Arsenal and the "Y" series at the Archives Nationales. Roughly half of the reports memorialize instances of police action taken against actors, spectacle workers, or individuals outside the theaters, such as scalpers, rebellious coachmen, or unwitting *colporteurs*; I discuss some of these incidents in chapter 1. The remaining dossiers all record disputes within the theater hall, but approximately thirty of these involved disturbances occurring in parts of the theater other than the parterre. Therefore, a little more than a third of these two hundred episodes occurred in the parterres.

[30] On the "criminality" of the boulevard actors later in the century, see Michèle Root-Bernstein, "The Moral Criminality of the Popular Actor in Eighteenth-Century Paris," *Eighteenth-Century Life* n.s.10 (January 1986): 48–70.

the sample contains only men; the vast majority were young men or adolescents in subservient social positions. Only twenty of the men arrested in the capital's parterres in this period were lawyers, bureaucrats, master artisans, or merchants—that is to say, men of some power and standing. The other spectators plucked from the parterre as examples to disorderly crowds and dragged off to prison were shopworkers, students, clerks, soldiers, or visitors from the provinces. Because of its proximity to the Sorbonne, the parterre of the Comédie-Française attracted more students than the other spectacles; otherwise, the parterres of both Comédies seem to have been laced with an equal number of these younger, less powerful men. In keeping with the general goals of d'Argenson's policing strategy, the theater police rarely arrested noble or wealthy men who chose to stand in the parterre.

Finally, a year-by-year breakdown of recorded police intervention in the parterre suggests that police activity was at its height during two periods. In the first, which lasted from 1733 to 1738, the police intervened nineteen times, fourteen of which occurred in the parterre of the Comédie-Française. The second period, a five-year span lasting from 1747 to 1751, saw the police arrest parterre spectators twenty-six times. More than a third of all interventions for which documentation exists took place approximately midcentury, and the two periods together account for more than 60 percent of the surviving instances of police activity in the parterres of the capital. The relative scarcity of these recorded parterre arrests, on average less than two incidents per year, and the incompleteness of existing records cautions against staking too great a claim on the quantitative evidence alone. But the irregular pattern with which they are distributed across almost half a century corresponds to evidence of heightened conflict in these periods found in sources such as spy reports and memoirs.

The quantitative and prosopographic evidence contained in these records thus provides important information about policing practices in the Parisian parterres, particularly that of the Comédie-Française. But these same dossiers also preserve rich narrative accounts of the confrontations between spectators and guards in the public theaters; the authorial voices of exempts, detained spectators, and witnesses to these events offer a qualitative commentary on the nightly interactions in the playhouses. The dossiers from the 1730s and 1740s in particular tell the story of audience members, increasingly united in their opposition to the exempts' policing practices, who found a variety of means to articulate their criticisms of the theater police. Eventually, their combined critical weight contributed to the government's decision to change its tactics in the theaters in 1751.

Officer Bazin at the Comédie-Française in the 1730s

In the not quite faceless world of eighteenth-century French bureaucracy, the psychologies of individual officials and spectators did matter, particularly within the familiar confines of the privileged theaters. Not only did audiences who came regularly to the theater establish a rapport with the performers they watched again and again; they also came to know members of the supporting cast of characters at their favorite spectacles. The booksellers, the food vendors, the ticket sellers, and the ticket takers were all well known in the playhouses, and the exempts, the soldiers, and even the *mouches* were no less recognizable to theater regulars. For example, an exempt named Etienne Pannetier, assigned to the Comédie-Française in the 1720s, earned the enmity of both performers and audience. In one instance, Pannetier arrested Moligny, a former actor, for an incident in a third balcony loge. In a letter to the lieutenant general of police stating the case for his release, Moligny asks that the evidence provided by Pannetier be disregarded, because the latter "is my enemy."[31] More telling still, in November 1728, several *mouches* stationed in the Comédie-Française parterre reported the following audience sentiments: "Although there were many people in the parterre, nothing happened. Everyone said, however, that they did not want M. Pannetier to show up, and they decided that if he appeared they would demand that the actors throw him out of the theater."[32] It is hard to know whether Pannetier had earned this reputation on his own or whether he suffered from the general dislike of the exempts dating back to d'Argenson's days as lieutenant general of police.

A change in personnel, therefore, could upset the fragile equilibrium constantly renegotiated between spectators and royal officials. The upturn in arrests at the Comédie-Française in the mid-1730s (thirteen arrests from 1733 to 1737) can be explained in part by the arrival of a new exempt at the theater in 1733. In a letter written to curry the favor of newly appointed Lieutenant General of Police Feydeau de Marville in February 1740, the exempt Bazin, by his own account a forty-year veteran of theater policing, described the circumstances of his move from the Comédie-Italienne to the Comédie-Française seven years earlier:

> [P]ersuaded that I could better control the tumultuous parterre than [the previous exempt], the Count of Maurepas [then minister of state] and M.

---

[31] BA, ms 10954, f. 77–78.
[32] BA, ms 10295, f. 87.

Hérault [then lieutenant general of police] honored me by saying that I had to place many officers in the parterre to observe those who disturbed the spectacle and to arrest them, and in those cases where I could not arrest them in the spectacle or at the exit that the spies should follow them and discover their names and residences so that they could be arrested the next day, which was punctually executed.[33]

Although the letter was certainly self-serving in its account of the reasons for Bazin's reassignment, it also reveals the disciplinary assumptions common in the spectacles and Bazin's particularly aggressive application of official policy. Writing from the vantage point of seven "successful" years of service at the Comédie-Française, Bazin stressed the active role he was encouraged to take to suppress disorder on the parterre. The task confided to him by Maurepas and Hérault was to survey troublemakers in the parterre and arrest them at all costs. Neither here nor elsewhere in his surviving correspondence did he question the policy of arrest or the role he was assigned in this system. Instead, Bazin concentrated on increasing the efficiency of his men's ability to identify and arrest unruly spectators.

As his letter to Marville suggests, one of the most important tools at Bazin's disposal was the deployment of *mouches* in the parterre. Of the thirteen arrests that we know he carried out in the Comédie-Française parterre during the mid-1730s, reports on seven of them contained explicit references to the role played by the spies in identifying and arresting spectators charged with disturbing the spectacle; it was possible that the other cases of arrest could also have resulted from the activity of Bazin's spies.[34] Bazin relied on the spies because they provided him with access to the frequently impenetrable mass of bodies crowded into the parterre; they also provided a means to keep tabs on the activities of those in the parterre when he and his uniformed soldiers had to attend to other responsibilities. Their presence, however, did not add to Bazin's popularity with the spectators.

Another facet of Bazin's aggressive attempts to enforce the King's orders were his continued pleas to Hérault and Marville, the lieutenant generals of police under whom he served, to stiffen the penalties of those arrested to reinforce deterrence. In his first year on the job in 1733, Bazin con-

---

[33] BA, ms 10010, f. 170–71, 11 February 1740. By the time of his promotion to the Comédie-Française in 1733, Bazin already had at least two decades of policing experience in the spectacles; see Campardon, *Spectacles de la foire*, 1:262–63 and 2:346–47.

[34] BA, ms 11301, f. 275–76; BA, ms 11292, f. 70; BA, ms 11317, f. 182; BA, ms 11322, f. 144; BA, ms 11326, f. 467; BA, ms 11365, f. 170.

cluded a report to Hérault on disorders occasioned by an apprentice and a clerk who were dancing in the parterre with the following observations:

> Both of them deserve an exemplary punishment, which is why, given the circumstances, their detention could not be too long. Perhaps, Sir, you will even judge it appropriate to take a more rigorous stand by locking them up for a while at the Hospital [Bicêtre]. It is your usual prudence, Sir, which will determine this matter, but I will take the liberty of pointing out to you that severity is necessary at the beginning of winter in order to contain the parterre during the most difficult season of the year.[35]

Similar enjoinders can be found in Bazin's reports for the rest of the decade.[36] It is interesting to note the origins of the call for discipline; in 1713, it was Louis XIV who had called for a "quota" of spectators arrested. By the 1730s, the cry came from the ranks of the exempts; as we shall see, they were buttressed by the supposed acclamation of parterre members who opposed the troublemakers.

In part, these cries were a response to the continued confrontations between exempts and the parterre audience, clashes in which each side attempted to tip the balance of authority in its favor. On 3 January 1734 at the Comédie-Française, Bazin encountered a difficult situation before the commencement of the spectacle.[37] That night, the crowd in the parterre would not cease its cries and chants before the performance, in spite of the efforts Bazin claims he put forth in his report to Hérault: "I had appeared many times in the parterre, crying out, 'A little silence, Sirs.'" In the construction of the event found in Bazin's account to the lieutenant general of police, the failure of these pleas justified his entry into the parterre: "Not having made any impression on them, it gave me occasion to enter the parterre almost to the orchestra, where I was not noticed." Bazin then proceeded to describe his intervention in the following terms: "[M]any young people were saying, 'we can scream, he won't get as far as us'; and at the same time one of them took to crying, 'Take off your hat'; and this was repeated many times, which gave me reason to arrest him in plain view of the whole parterre, of which part cried out, 'Well done!'"

This report thus justified Bazin's actions in selecting a single individual for punishment when the entire parterre was screaming; the spectator was subject to arrest because Bazin heard this one individual consciously "vio-

---

[35] BA, ms 11218, f. 388–89.

[36] Most notably, BA, ms 11262, f. 163; and BA, ms 11292, f. 70.

[37] BA, ms 11249, f. 407–10. All quotes in this paragraph and the next are taken from the same dossier.

late" the King's ordinance. Furthermore, this "well-deserved" detention occurs in such a manner that the rest of the men in the parterre serve as approving spectators to Bazin's exercise of royal authority; he concludes his report by saying, "this example constrained the parterre in such a way that the three plays were performed in perfect tranquility." Bazin's justification for his actions, the approbation of a portion of the parterre spectators, implicitly granted them the right to critique his policing actions. Bazin's narrative tactic was interesting, for in some sense it violated the absolutist conceit that the state could act without the approval or advice of the people. Instead, Bazin here claimed that his actions were justified in part because some members of the parterre desired them.

As the decade wore on, the exempts' appeal to this line of reasoning appeared more frequently in their reports to the lieutenant general of police. On 16 March 1738, the exempt at the Comédie-Italienne justified his intervention into the parterre in much the same terms, saying that a good number of the almost seven hundred people in the parterre that evening requested his presence to stifle disruptive cries.[38] He arrested the son of a tailor who had cried out "ouvrez les loges" many times, "even when [the exempt] was standing next to him." After trotting his victim off to prison, the exempt reported that he was obliged to remain in the parterre for the remainder of the performance, "to everyone's satisfaction."

But the appeal to spectator approbation carried its own dangers for the police; by this logic, the parterre's displeasure could undermine the exempts' authority. In a written plea addressed to the lieutenant general of police seeking his son's release, the father of the man arrested in the incident just described claimed that his son found himself in the middle of a large group of people shouting and carrying on, without necessarily doing so himself. He contested the actions of the exempt, saying that he acted "without investigating the situation." As the 1730s turned to the 1740s, criticism of the police became a more frequent refrain among spectators whose actions were recorded by the police. In a sense, the police's reliance on spectator approval empowered these critiques.

Criticism, Disorder, and Reform, 1740–51

From 1713 to the early 1740s, France was rarely at war on the European continent or elsewhere in the world. Although courtly intrigues and the

---

[38] BA, ms 11394, f. 15–18. All quotes in this paragraph and the next are taken from the same dossier.

religious and constitutional struggles prompted by the papal bull Unigenitus placed pressures on the absolute monarchy and alienated some of the King's subjects, the government avoided the strains occasioned by the seventeenth-century wars of Louis XIII and Louis XIV. With the passing of the Prussian and Austrian rulers in 1740, however, and the rise of overseas tensions with the United Kingdom, France, as well as most of the other European states, found itself drawn into the international conflicts generally known as the War of Austrian Succession. The French government needed tax revenues and male recruits to pursue its foreign policies; the King's subjects approached the war with a combination of patriotic fervor and mistrust of the King and his ministers, prompted in part by the increasingly public knowledge of the King's sexual infidelities.[39]

In the capital's playhouses, these external anxieties served to heighten the crisis of authority experienced by the theater police. On the one hand, the exempts relied more and more on crowd approbation as justification for their activities, perhaps because fewer and fewer spectators were inclined to approve of enforcing the King's ordinances. On the other hand, police patterns of arrest began to seem more arbitrary and abusive to skeptical spectators and royal officials alike. In a letter to Lieutenant General of Police Marville in 1744, Minister of State Maurepas wrote: "For a long time I have been aware of the lack of good sense on the part of the officers of the guard of this spectacle, who, far from preventing disorder, frequently cause problems which are difficult to remedy."[40] Maurepas's displeasure pointed to the inadequacies of the theater police by the 1740s; the failures of the King's government on the battlefields of the 1740s made these ministers doubly sensitive to shortcomings in the monarchy's domestic policy. And if these problems in the theater were obvious to the minister of state and the lieutenant general of police, how must they have appeared to parterre spectators who had suspected the authority exercised by the exempts since d'Argenson's time?

Maurepas based his comments in part on the increasingly troublesome information contained in reports written by the exempts. On 10 June 1741, during the second act of a play called *Mélanide* at the Comédie-Française, Bazin decided that cries of "place aux dames" from the parterre to the loges had reached a level that justified his intervention.[41] He wrote in his

[39] On the mistrust of the King and his court, and its amplification as a result of the war, see Merrick, *Desacralization of the French Monarchy*, 49–77; Farge, *Subversive Words*, 153–61; and Thomas E. Kaiser, "Madame de Pompadour and the Theaters of Power," *FHS* 19 (Fall 1996): 1025–44.

[40] Boislisle, *Lettres de M de Marville*, 1:181.

[41] BA, ms 11489, f. 2–11. All cites in this paragraph and the next are from the same dossier.

report that as he entered the parterre he "observed there one spectator in particular, and [he] approached him," but he did not indicate why he noticed this particular audience member. Bazin verbally reproached this man by saying, "[Y]ou [have] to be more circumspect and not disturb the spectacle; if not I [will] be obliged to carry out the King's orders and make an example of someone." Bazin obviously considered this statement to be adequate warning of potential police action; he had invoked the King's orders, his justification for action, and he had reminded the wayward spectator of the well-known policing strategy that singled out individuals to serve as examples to the rest of an unruly parterre. Bazin then remained in the parterre for a while, according to his report, until other duties recalled him to the stage. No sooner did he leave the pit than the same disruptions broke out again, at which point he returned to the parterre and arrested the same man he had warned before. Bazin's report claimed that this man had once again provoked disruptive cries in the parterre by renewing the cry of "place aux dames."

The victim, a law student from the provinces named Briquet du Marcy, emphasized the seeming arbitrariness of the procedure in his plea for release addressed to the lieutenant general of police. He claimed that it was those around him who cried, not he; when Bazin entered the parterre the first time, he singled him out because, as Briquet du Marcy said, "[M]y head stood out among those around me." In any event, when Bazin began to warn him, those around Briquet testified to Bazin that Briquet had not been one of those crying out. Much to his astonishment and disbelief, he had been seized by the guard and hauled off to prison in spite of his protests of innocence and his demands to see the lieutenant general of police. His *placet* to Marville concluded with this summation: "I dare to assure you that I am the victim of an example they wanted to give to the public that I had not in any way offended." Was it true that Bazin arrested Briquet because the latter was the tallest man standing in his section of the parterre?[42]

The exempts had done little to correct this impression of random arrest by 1749. On 5 October of that year, a carriage-maker's apprentice named Jean Maignan was arrested at the Comédie-Française for allegedly crying louder and longer than other parterre spectators "ouvrez les loges."[43] In the *procès-verbal* drawn up by Commissioner LeComte to memorialize his

---

[42] The rest of the administrative correspondence suggested by inference that Briquet was unfairly singled out of an unruly crowd. BA, ms 11489, f. 6, 9, 11, emphasized that the sword Briquet illegally sported was the major justification for the five days he spent in prison, not his activities in the Comédie-Française parterre.

[43] BA, ms 11683, f. 23–34. All cites in this paragraph from the same dossier.

interrogation of Maignan, the latter confessed that he had joined others in the parterre in this cry, but that "it [was] the first time he attended the theater, that he [had] only been in Paris for six weeks, that he did not at all know that this was prohibited, that he had heard others yell the same thing and that he did not think it was a crime." His master, however, who needed him back in the shop, made an even more telling point in defense of his apprentice. Noting that Maignan was a black man from the "American isles," he observed in his petition to the lieutenant general of police that because Maignan was "visible because of his color[;] the supplicant presumes that this was the only reason which caused the officer to seize him." Although the cases of Briquet and Maignan might have been exceptional in that both had obvious physical characteristics that set them apart from the rest of the parterre spectators, it was possible that other spectators, and officers who received these reports, felt more than a twinge of discomfort at the exemplary justice practiced by the exempts.[44]

The inaccuracies and injustices of the exempt system became well known in many circles. In September 1741, Bazin had arrested a law clerk and his friend for instigating "tumult" in the parterre. Fortunately for the law clerk, the lawyer who employed him, a man named Barthelemy, had witnessed the entire incident that evening from the second balcony. In his letter to the lieutenant general of police requesting his clerk's release, Barthelemy noted that the theater was particularly stuffy on the late summer night in question. When the parterre cried out "ouvrez les loges" to remedy the situation, Bazin and company had responded by arbitrarily arresting two members of the crowd. His account of the exempts' actions was scathing:

> Meanwhile the actors presented themselves for the beginning of the second act, and the same cries as before began again. This shocked the delicate ears of the exempts. Instead of going to open the loges, as it seemed to me natural to do, they wanted to play one of their tricks on us. One of them, at the head of three or four valorous champions who kept looking behind to see if others might not come to lend a hand, seized two of the scruffiest-looking young men, made a huge scene, and almost caused a riot . . . it would be quite pointless to tell you that they did not fail to lead the two youngsters off to prison.[45]

Barthelemy's need to secure the release of his imprisoned clerk certainly colored his account, but the sarcasm with which he recounted the arrest

---

[44] The guards may also have arrested individuals whom they thought could be conscripted into the military; see BA, ms 11760, f. 209–17.

[45] BA, ms 11481, f. 273–74.

also betrayed the low opinion that many held of the exempts. It was becoming increasingly difficult to respect the Crown's policing activity in the spectacles.

Incidents in late 1743 and early 1744 illustrate the erosion of exempt authority in the pit, and the corresponding rise in audience "sovereignty" by the mid-1740s. On Sunday, 17 November 1743, at the Comédie-Française the actors played Crébillon's *Electre* and Molière's *Le Médecin malgré lui*; this double bill attracted a full house of 1,008 paying spectators.[46] The police report for the evening, signed jointly by four police agents, began with an account of a disruption during the interval between the two plays.[47] According to the officers, a number of individuals formed a large circle and began to dance in the midst of the crowded parterre. The police responded to this disruption by entering the parterre with the guard, where they arrested two of the revelers. One of the detainees was a furniture restorer (*marchand fourbisseur en chambre*), the other a young man living in a lawyer's household and most probably a student or a clerk.

The account of this disciplinary procedure emphasized two points. First, the police depicted themselves as being very cautious: "among the great number of people dancing, we arrested only two at first." Second, the account stressed the approving role played by the parterre looking on. When the men began their dance, which caused a "very great uproar" (*un très grand tapage*), it resulted in the "displeasure" of "all the parterre." This hyperbolic description excluded those members of the parterre who chose to participate in the dance. Then, when the police did make two arrests, they did so to "the satisfaction of all those assembled" (*à la satisfaction de toute l'assemblée*). This construction of the event cast the police in a reasonable and restrained light and suggested that the united voice of the parterre applauded a performance in which the police enacted the ceremonies of social control. Excluded from the report was the performance of the dancers. These men, disciplined and rebuked by the police, had staged a spectacle of their own in the parterre, one which emphasized their bodily presence and carnivalesque festivity.

The police officers' account then reported that as two officers led the two carousers off to prison, a third, unidentified man, dressed in red, began to cry out, presumably in protest. The police quickly arrested him as well; the remark noted earlier in the report by the authors indicated that they were predisposed to arrest many more spectators to reestablish order in the pit.

---

[46] Lancaster, *Comédie-Française, 1701–1774*, 742.
[47] BA, ms 11534, f. 231–37. All quotes in this paragraph and the next two are taken from the same dossier.

At this point, however, the man in red intervened in the officers' performance of social discipline. "In acknowledgement of his folly," the officers
wrote, "he threw himself to his knees to ask for pardon." This gesture may
have had religious overtones, but it also reads surprisingly like a scene from
the *drame bourgeois* genre advocated by Diderot later in the century, or a
Greuze painting depicting *bourgeois* sentimentality.[48] The unknown spectator's gesture of supplication found a receptive audience in a surprising place:
among the players gathered onstage to observe the arrest. The officers
noted that the sight of the kneeling spectator "excited the compassion of
Mlle Dumesnille and the other actors and actresses, who all begged Bazin
and Chevery [the police officers] to release him." At this moment, then, the
stage and the parterre enacted a total inversion of the presumed spectator-
spectacle relation; the "official" actors onstage assumed the role of spectators, observing the performance played out in the pit, while the two officers
and the repentant spectator became the players of the scene. Furthermore,
the theater professionals onstage found the playgoer's performance quite
convincing, as they chose to intervene with the officers on his behalf.

How did the two officers improvise their roles in light of this intervention? They chose to release the pleading spectator from custody, which
explains why his name and occupation were not recorded in the report.
Their account, however, did contain an explanation for their clemency:
given the example of the previous two arrests they had made "vis-à-vis the
public," they thought themselves justified in releasing the third spectator.[49]
Thus, the "public" had become an important arbiter of policing actions in
the parterre. Final authority rested not with the lieutenant general of
police, the intended reader of the report, or with other individuals in the
royal administration, but with the theatergoers in attendance at the playhouse. The latter could be swayed by those who performed more convincingly than the police.

Half a year later, on 27 May 1744, a new actor debuted in the Crébillon
tragedy *Rhadamiste et Zénobie*. As the performance wore on, the parterre
became more disorderly, until Bazin and his colleague Cheverry felt
obliged to take action. Bazin characterized the young law student they

---

[48] On the art of Greuze and the dramatic theories of Diderot, Mercier, Beaumarchais, and
others, see Anita Brookner, *Greuze: The Rise and Fall of an Eighteenth-Century Phenomenon* (Greenwich, 1972); Norman Bryson, *Word and Image: French Painting of the Ancien
Régime* (Cambridge, 1981), 122–53; Michael Fried, *Absorption and Theatricality: Painting
and Beholder in the Age of Diderot* (Berkeley, 1980), 55–70; and Crow, *Painters and Public
Life*, 134–74.
[49] BA, ms 11534, f. 231.

arrested, named le Sueur, as an author who wrote poetry and even plays; he claimed that le Sueur was yelling at the top of his lungs in the parterre, crying that two of the troupe's best known thespians were "god-damned actors."[50] After the completion of the Crébillon tragedy, spectators in the parterre arose in protest, some of them perhaps remembering the incidents that had occurred the previous November; they informed the officers that they would prevent the rest of the performance if le Sueur was not released. Bazin reported that the actors and actresses also called for the young student's release, as they had six months earlier. But Bazin and company held the line this time, claiming somewhat lamely that they could not release an individual once arrested without an order from the lieutenant general of police. The account vaguely reported that the audience lingered on in the parterre, in the loges, and on the stage until eleven o'clock without the actors resuming the play.

Apparently, however, the tumult spilled over into the streets and cafés surrounding the theater. Bazin recorded that Cheverry was attacked by a man carrying a sword on the Pont-Neuf and was saved from further insult only by the guards who were accompanying him at the time. The harried exempt concluded his report with a call for two squadrons of soldiers from the Paris garrison at the Comédie-Française for the following evening, because the *tapageurs* in the parterre reportedly planned to return the next evening with two hundred other spectators to resume the struggle.[51] Another dossier recorded the discontent of a part of the audience who had retired to the nearby Café Baptiste after the theater was cleared.[52] One of them, the composer Philidor, was arrested several days later for having "blamed the exempt who arrested le Sueur, like many others." Although Philidor claimed he did not enter the parterre until ten o'clock that evening, having noticed the lights still on in the theater on his way home from a late-night music lesson, the order for his release notes that he was arrested "for having been one of those who most contributed to the tumult at the Comédie-Française."

The abuses and inconsistencies in the practices of parterre policing were building to levels intolerable to playhouse patrons or royal officials. At the same time, however, these practices called into being a spontaneous critical response from spectators who wished to redefine their prerogatives in the playhouse. Audiences grew increasingly imperious; Morand's tragedy

[50] BA, ms 11554, f. 232–33.
[51] Apparently, this threatened disturbance never came to pass; see BA, ms 11554, f. 236.
[52] BA, ms 11556, f. 189–96. The remaining quotes in this paragraph are taken from this dossier.

Mégare in 1748 and Saint-Foix's work *La Colonie* in 1749 were chased off the stage after one performance by tumultuous parterre spectators, and in 1750 the pit demanded on several occasions that the actors perform Legouvé's *Attilie,* a tragedy that had been performed in private but not submitted to the Comédie-Française; once the play was printed and publicly available, the request was dropped.[53] Furthermore, as noted above, the years from 1747 to 1751 constituted a high point for police arrests in the parterre. Around 1747, the old exempts, Bazin and his counterpart at the Comédie-Italienne, were replaced by newer men who had less hesitation about using the power of arrest to make their point. It was also significant that most of the disturbances in which parterre members were arrested in this period took place on Sundays or holidays, days when the social composition of the parterre differed from weekdays.[54] Because of the Sunday audiences' increased reputation for violence, the exempts were more prepared than usual to resort to arrest.

The events that transpired at the Comédie-Italienne on the evening of 12 January 1749, a night when the exempt detained six parterre spectators, the highest single-night arrest total found in the police archives, testified to the chaotic experience of theatergoing in these years.[55] Two points from the account left by Duveau, the exempt, of the evening's events merit special attention. First, the harried officer recorded an interesting exchange between himself and the two men he arrested during his second excursion into the parterre. When Duveau asked these two spectators, one the son of a printer at the royal press and the other an *écuyer,* why they created such a disturbance, they had no "excuse" to offer. Instead, they told the exempt that he should have arrested the other hundred spectators who had also shouted. Duveau responded that: "[he] did not have a hundred hands, and that [he] had grabbed those who were closest to him, seizing them as soon as they cried out." The spectators' retort to Duveau amounted to a declaration that they were no more guilty than the hundreds who indulged in forbidden cries on any evening at the Comédie-Italienne. As for Duveau's response, it constituted a tacit admission that state resources prohibited an equitable enforcement of the King's ordinances.

The second noteworthy aspect of Duveau's report was his appeal to the public to justify his response to the chaotic events at the Comédie-Italienne that evening. At the end of his report, he added an explanatory

[53] Mouhy, *Tablettes dramatiques,* 1:28, 56, 154; AD, 1:126, 215–16, 536.
[54] Lagrave, *Le Théâtre et le public,* 244–52; and chapter 1.
[55] BA, ms 11681, f. 282–88. Quotes in this paragraph and the next are taken from the same dossier.

comment to the description of his activities that evening: "If these impris-
onments make me the enemy of those whom I have arrested or of those to
whom they belong, I will find solace in the approbation of many *seigneurs*
who were at the theater, who saw me in the foyer and told me that if a similar action were tolerated, it would not be possible for decent people to
attend the theater, and the majority of the parterre told me the same
thing." Duveau's comment broke the theater public into two groups. The
first was the traditional group of elites for which spectacle typically was
staged at court. The second was the majority of people standing in the
parterre, who reportedly expressed the same noble opinions to Duveau. In
each case, in the mind of Duveau, the goal of policing spectacle was to
make the privileged theater a reliable rendezvous for the "decent" (*honnête*) spectator to appreciate the spectacle on stage.

At least in Duveau's mind, therefore, if not in the understanding of the
theatergoers themselves, two types of parterre spectators existed. One was
unruly and disrupted the performance; the other was deeply disturbed by
these disorderly interventions on the part of the audience. The goal of policing the spectacles had become that of disciplining the former for the benefit
of the latter, who were sometimes referred to as the "public." No longer did
police agents worry about insults to the King or the King's responses to
reports of his agents' activities. Now they simply puzzled over how to ensure
the comfort of the decent spectator. But while the goals of spectacle policing
had clearly changed since the beginning of the century, the system created
fifty years earlier had not adapted to these new conditions.

In an effort to address these concerns, the monarchy decided to do away
with the old system of exempts and their brigades during the Easter recess
of 1751. When the new season opened on 26 April 1751, spectators at the
Comédie-Française and the Comédie-Italienne found themselves face to
face with a company of soldiers from the royal garrison, just as they had
for half a century at the Opera.[56] The exempts and their men gave way to
thirty musketeers supervised by seven officers; four of these armed soldiers
were stationed permanently in the parterre. Some observers welcomed the
change; the Chevalier de Mouhy, himself a *nouvelliste* for the police,
wrote in 1752 that the change in policing regimes began "a happy epoch
where order and tranquility would reign in these spectacles."[57] But the
sentries posted in the theaters had little sense that they were performing a
public service. Their presence, armed and in uniform, necessarily changed

---

[56] AN, AD^VIII 10 (30), "Ordonnance du Roy concernant les Spectacles des Comédies Françoise
et Italienne du 25 avril 1751."
[57] Mouhy, *Tablettes dramatiques*, 2:79.

the theatrical ambiance. When they first appeared in April 1751, the playwright Charles Collé noted their advent with a sigh of despair:

> Today, by ordinance of the King, a military guard was established at the Comédie-Française and the Comédie-Italienne; it replaced the archers who had formerly guarded these spectacles. There are actually soldiers now, just as at the Opera; this provides a great deal of calm, but it also cloaks the playhouse in a certain sadness, which makes me fear at times that I am in a foreign country. I no longer find that French gaiety; the parterre at present has a German air about it. These soldiers restrain a nation as lively as ours a little too much, and a little too pedantically. . . . It all breathes an air of despotism down to the littlest details; one is almost no longer permitted to feel that one is a man.[58]

[58] Collé, *Journal et mémoires sur les hommes de lettres*, 1:310–11. Collé, a man of letters whose greatest theatrical successes came on the private stages of the Parisian elite and in provincial playhouses, kept this diary of theatrical and literary events from 1748 to 1772. In this journal, he often recorded his grievances against the actors and administrators of the Comédie-Française, who repeatedly refused to stage his plays, which had proved successful in other venues.

5

Policing the Parterre in Paris and the Provinces, 1751–89

Those insolent riflemen, stationed to the right and to the left in order to temper my outbursts of enthusiasm, sensibility, and joy, make our theaters into places quieter and more proper than our churches. They offend me extraordinarily.

—Denis Diderot, 1758

After 1751, when the royal government placed soldiers in the privileged Parisian theaters, confrontations between police and spectators in the parterre became more violent. The Comédie-Française actor Henri LeKain, in a 1754 letter in which he discussed a recent premiere, alluded to the severity of the soldiers: "The most hazardous audience response [at the opening] consisted of two whistles sounded in the midst of the parterre, in spite of all the gun blows dispensed so inhumanely by the police in the parterre. Is it such a great crime to boo bad plays and bad actors?"[1] Four years later, Diderot also complained about the police in a letter to the novelist Mme Riccoboni. After the Maupeou crisis of 1771–74, however, spectators often responded in kind to military aggression in the theaters. These violent clashes between spectators and armed agents of the Crown were quantitatively and qualitatively more serious than the confrontations between drunken spectators and policing agents that had occasionally marred performances since the days of Louis XIV. The antics of Sallo in 1691, for example, seemed tame in comparison to the battles that left spectators dead and wounded in provincial theaters from Beauvais to Marseilles after 1774. The heavy-handed policing activities of the state in turn caused parterre spectators to cast their grievances in the political language of the day; audiences came to believe they were resisting the Crown's tyrannical administration of the theaters.

[1] Henri Louis LeKain to the Comte d'Argental, 26 July 1754, in Voltaire, *Correspondence and Related Documents*, ed. Theodore Besterman (Oxford, 1968–77), 15:210.

161

Collective parterre resistance to governmental interventions in the pit brings to mind historians' analyses of "crowd behavior" outside the walls of French Old Regime theaters. The pathbreaking work of Georges Rudé and E. P. Thompson in the 1960s and 1970s taught historians of the eighteenth century to move beyond unthinking, reflexive epithets when discussing the actions of the crowd.[2] In the intervening decades, historians of the crowd in eighteenth-century France have taken the discussions begun by Rudé and Thompson in directions relevant for a discussion of late-eighteenth-century parterre confrontations.[3] The parterre clashes discussed in this chapter coincided chronologically with the period of the Flour War and the turbulence generated by the government's second effort to liberalize the grain trade under Turgot; good reason exists to believe, as we shall see, that they played a part in the political education of the "faces" in the prerevolutionary crowd. Parterre riots differed from other forms of collective action at this time, though, to the extent that parterre spectators did not obviously represent local or community interests before police actions taken against them. The groups of men gathered together in the parterre each night did not convene to protest price gouging by local bakers or nefarious actions by neighborhood spies and police agents, although many of them may have shared these grievances. Rather, they congregated for aesthetic and commercial reasons. They sought distraction, sexual titillation, or the stimulus of intellectual and literary exchange; they had, in most cases, paid to enter the theater. In addition, they expected the commercial element of the public theater to grant them certain rights over the spectacles they patronized. Official administration, or policing, of these theaters took into account neither intellectual freedoms nor commercial rights. Instead, local and national bureaucrats sought to control theater audiences the same way they dealt with food rioters: through the use of force.

Policing the Parisian Parterre, 1751–89

The number of soldiers deployed at the three privileged spectacles was substantial in 1751 and grew larger in the decades that followed. Accord-

---

[2] Georges Rudé, *The Crowd in History, 1730–1848* (New York, 1964), esp. 195–213; E. P. Thompson "The Moral Economy of the English Crowd in the Eighteenth Century," in *Customs in Common: Studies in Traditional Popular Culture* (New York, 1993), 185–258.

[3] See especially Steven L. Kaplan, *Bread, Politics, and Political Economy in the Reign of Louis XV* (The Hague, 1976), 2 vols.; Cynthia Bouton, *The Flour War: Gender, Class, and Community in Late Ancien Régime French Society* (University Park, PA: 1993); William Reddy, "The Textile Trade and the Language of the Crowd at Rouen, 1752–1781," *Past and Present* 74 (February 1997): 62–89; and Colin Lucas, "The Crowd and Politics between *Ancien Régime* and Revolution in France," *JMH* 60 (September 1988): 421–57.

ing to the annual almanac *Les Spectacles de Paris*, the government posted a squadron of thirty soldiers under the direction of a sergeant-major, two majors, and a corporal at the two Comédies in 1751. These numbers remained the same until the early 1780s, when each troupe moved into a new theater. In 1782, the government assigned eight officers and thirty-nine soldiers to the Comédie-Française; in the next seven years, the number of soldiers never dipped below forty-six. At the Comédie-Italienne from 1783 to the Revolution, the numbers remained constant at eight officers and fifty-two soldiers. The Opera, which only performed three nights a week, saw its military force increase from forty to sixty soldiers in 1765; on nights when this theater was converted into a ballroom, the state increased the military presence by forty more soldiers.[4]

Of course, some of these men were stationed outside the theater to supervise the routing of carriages around the buildings. But the military presence within the theater was also considerable. In 1751 at the two Comédies, the government posted fourteen of the thirty soldiers inside each theater. We can compare this distribution of soldiers with that at the Opera twenty years later; a document prepared for the opening of the newly reconstructed Palais Royal Opera in 1770 called for ninety riflemen within and outside the building.[5] The military augmented its presence because of the opening; normally it dispatched only two-thirds this number of troops to the Opera house. Of the ninety soldiers, twenty-four soldiers, or ten more than at the Comédie-Française or the Comédie-Italienne in 1751, were distributed throughout the building. Strikingly, the parterre drew the greatest number of riflemen; in both instances, four soldiers were stationed in the pit, the largest number of armed guards in any area of the theater, although at the Opera in 1770 four soldiers were also placed on stage and in the *paradis*.

As with the exempts and their men, the government and each of the three privileged troupes shared the cost of maintaining the military at the spectacles. At the Comédie-Française, for example, guard expenditures became a line item in the annual budget from 1755 until the Revolution; the French actors spent between 2 and 3 percent of their yearly budget, or approximately ten thousand livres per year, on pay for the soldiers.[6] Beginning in 1760, the Comédie-Française would occasionally hire extra guards for specific performances, usually for controversial premiers. For the opening of Dorat's *Régulus* on 31 July 1773, a play with a patriotic theme bound to

---

[4] In addition to Abbé Jean-Barthélemy de la Porte, ed., *Les Spectacles de Paris* (Paris, 1759), see Chagniot, *Paris et l'armée*, 181, for figures in 1788.

[5] SHAT, Y^a 272, chemise "gardes françaises," dossier "théâtre." On the 1770–81 Palais Royal theater, see Jean Gourret, *Histoire des salles de l'Opéra de Paris* (Paris, 1985), 61–79.

[6] Alasseur, *La Comédie-Française*, 180–92.

create controversy during the Maupeou ministry, the Comédie employed the staggering figure of 320 extra guards.[7] The opening attracted 1,100 paying spectators; if one counts the normal complement of soldiers, the Comédie established a ratio that evening of one guard for every three spectators in attendance, perhaps the quantitative high point for theater policing during the Old Regime. This situation was exceptional, however, during the reign of Louis XV; the next highest single-night total of supplemental guards procured was 202. The actors deemed that only fourteen other evenings from 1760 to 1774 merited extra manpower, and in all but four other cases they brought in fewer than a hundred extra bodies.[8] Early in the reign of Louis XVI, the 1776 premiere of Beaumarchais' *Barber of Seville* warranted an additional 184 soldiers during each of its forty-six public performances.[9] From 1751 until the Revolution, therefore, the number of guards at the privileged spectacles underwent periodic increases; this escalation may have furthered resentment among theatergoers already troubled by the military presence in and around the playhouse.

The annual theater almanac *Les Spectacles de Paris*, edited by the Abbé de La Porte, tried to mollify the fears of its readers in 1759 when it reported that the soldiers drawn for duty at the playhouses were "the best-mannered, the bravest, and the most handsome" in the entire garrison; these men were instructed "to behave as though they were guarding the King at court."[10] Neither the spectators nor the performers were entirely convinced, however. In 1762 the Comédie-Française's leading actress, Mlle Clairon, complained to governmental administrators that the guards failed to carry out their duties adequately, while placing too large a strain on the troupe's annual budget.[11] La Clairon requested that retired soldiers now living at the Invalides replace the guards, but her proposal was never approved.

At times it did indeed appear as if the guards did nothing to alter the slapstick atmosphere of pre-1751 spectacle policing. In 1759, the same year as La Porte's printed praise for the guards, an actor at the Comédie-Italienne received a gunshot in the upper thigh when a soldier, participating in a performance of the play *Camille magicienne*, fired a supposedly empty gun backstage. The evening's performance stopped and the actor, Antoine-Etienne Balletti, was taken to a nearby doctor. Balletti ultimately

---

[7] On *Régulus* and its contemporary reception, see Lancaster, *French Tragedy in the Time of Louis XV and Voltaire* (Baltimore, 1950), 2:522–25.

[8] Lancaster, *Comédie-Française, 1701–1774*, 800–838; information on *Régulus* at 837–38.

[9] Alasseur, *La Comédie-Française*, 31.

[10] La Porte, ed. *Les Spectacles de Paris* (1759), 19.

[11] Ernest Boysse, ed. *Journal de Papillon de la Ferté* (Paris, 1887), 74.

survived, but the incident aroused such curiosity that the bullet that had caused the injury was retrieved and taken to Versailles for display before a court that still remembered the attempt on the King's life by Damiens two years earlier.[12] Several entries in La Porte's *Anecdotes dramatiques* also ridiculed the literal-mindedness of the soldiers assigned to parterre duty. In one instance, a parterre partisan of Lulli during the midcentury *Querelle des Bouffons*, when requested by a guard to tone down his comments, supposedly replied, "Monsieur est donc Bouffoniste? (So, you're a Bouffoniste?)" The guard, apparently confused and certainly the butt of the story, returned to his post without making an arrest.[13] In another anecdote, the audience burst into laughter when a guard posted on the stage of a provincial theater became so involved in the story that he repeatedly tried to draw the attention of the tragedy's protagonist to advise him of his fictional wife's treachery.[14]

The guards' treatment of spectators and others in the general vicinity of theater, however, was often less comical. Only months after the installation of the soldiers in 1751, the lieutenant general of police received accusations that the military was arresting parterre spectators primarily to recruit them for military service. One father claimed an officer in disguise visited his son in prison to offer him his freedom if he agreed to join the Paris regiment; the youth was told he would be permitted to serve in the squadron that policed the interior of the playhouses, as he was so fond of the theater.[15] Not surprisingly, allegations of excessive guard violence also were made; in 1773, Lieutenant General of Police Sartine complained in a letter to the commander of the guards that the soldiers, in an effort to control the riotous lines at the Comédie-Française ticket window, were hitting waiting spectators on the head with their rifles.[16] On the eve of the Revolution, a military administrator's daily report from the Opera mentioned in passing that "all had gone well, aside from one spectator who complained to me that a soldier had conked him on the head."[17] The soldiers may also have been too overt in the use of their firearms when attempting to detain unruly spectators; again in 1773, Sartine called on the commander to respond to an accusation that a spectator had been forced from the parterre at gunpoint.[18]

[12] Campardon, *Les Comédiens du roi de la troupe italienne*, 23–28; AD, 2:168.
[13] AD, 1:259.
[14] Ibid., 3:501–2; see also ibid., 2:189.
[15] BA, 11760, f. 215–16.
[16] SHAT, Yª 272, chemise "gardes françaises," dossier "théâtre," memo dated 1 February 1773.
[17] SHAT, Yª 274, chemise "Délits par des particuliers contre les gardes françaises," "Copie du rapport du 24 mars 1787."
[18] SHAT, Yª 273, 16 June 1773.

Writing in the 1780s, Louis-Sébastien Mercier recounted the conditions of theatergoing under martial rule:

> Inside the soldiers squeeze you into each row like sardines, make you sit down, challenge the more portly spectators, wrangle with them, insist that each row contain a certain number of rear ends without taking into account their proportions. They silence those who scream that they're suffocating. One must listen to our good Molière under the mustache of a grenadier. Laugh or cry too much, and that grenadier, who never, ever laughs or cries, will decide if you have been too demonstrative.[19]

Once detained, one's fate was determined by "barely civil and poorly-coiffed" majors in the pay of the actors. In fairness, Mercier's account does not mention the continued confrontations with unruly coachmen outside the theater, confrontations that the soldiers had inherited from the exempts. Throughout the 1770s and the '80s, military commanders continually complained of the alacrity with which carriage drivers applied their whips to the soldiers on duty at the spectacles. Even officers were not immune to such insults; an unruly spectator at the Comédie-Italienne in 1785 seized the collar of a corporal on duty and ripped off his epaulette.[20]

The military's own description of its travails, however, did not inspire confidence in its personnel and procedures. A testy 1773 letter to Sartine detailed military procedure, including the authorized use of firearms against spectators, in the following fashion:

> We order the soldiers to control those found in the square that they guard by saying 'Move along.' When this doesn't work, as it never does with a crowd, it is absolutely necessary that they use their rifles in order to implement their given orders. When someone gets upset by this, it compromises the guards' authority by exciting a rumor which must be stopped immediately.[21]

Thus, the guards' authority ultimately rested on the threat of violence; in spite of the government's intention to reform theater policing in 1751,

---

[19] Mercier, *Tableau de Paris*, 6:121–22; quoted in John Lough, "A Paris Theatre in the Eighteenth-Century," *University of Toronto Quarterly* 27 (April 1958): 296–97.

[20] SHAT, Yᵃ 274, chemise "délits par des particuliers, 4 mai 1785." For other whipping incidents outside the spectacles, see documents dated 30 April 1774, 2 August 1775, and 30 August 1775 in the same chemise; and SHAT, Yᵃ 273, entries for 17 December 1779, 13 August 1781, 26 April 1782, 30 December 1785, 31 December 1787, and 14 February 1789.

[21] SHAT, Yᵃ 273, entry for 16 June 1773.

the presence and the practices of the soldiers served to heighten tensions at the spectacles.

When the state installed the soldiers in the theater in 1751, it also took another step to correct potential policing abuses. Sometime around mid-century, the lieutenant general of police and the Paris commander of the guards agreed to a procedure, first put in place on a partial basis as early as 1749, whereby spectators arrested by the soldiers for disturbances during performance were led before the neighborhood commissioners for judgment. Early in the century, these officers had drawn up the *procès-verbaux* describing fair theater performances. They were widely regarded to be more impartial than the exempts or the military officers because they were not subject to audience heckling in the theater and thus offered the promise of a more objective review of each audience disturbance. The commissioners were charged with a dizzying array of responsibilities; in a given day, a commissioner might inventory the property of a deceased resident, conduct a criminal investigation, inspect foodstuffs being sold in the neighborhood, and accompany the watch on its nightly rounds.[22] In addition to the myriad legal and administrative responsibilities these men performed, they contributed to the separate sense of community in each quarter. In the first place, the commissioner was required to wear a special judicial robe in his residence and in public; this robe immediately marked him as an agent of the Crown. Second, the government required the commissioner to reside in the quarter to which he was assigned. This residence rule meant that the commissioner's house was a well-known feature of the local urban topography; neighborhood inhabitants turned first to the commissioner during commercial or domestic disputes, to report criminal activity, or to complain of inadequate city services or obnoxious neighborhood activity.

During the flurry of arrests from 1749 to 1751, the documentary record indicates that two commissioners were involved in five disciplinary procedures.[23] For the period from 1751 until 1760, there are no surviving records of arrests at the privileged spectacles with interventions by the commissioners. The new system seemed to be working; perhaps there were fewer disturbances, or perhaps the commissioners decided to send fewer spectators to prison. But it was also the case that the commissioners and

---

[22] On the commissioners, see Williams, *Police of Paris*, 119–24; Steven L. Kaplan, "Notes sur les commissaires de police de Paris au XVIIIe siècle," *RHMC*, 28 (October–December 1981): 669–86; and Garrioch, and *Neighbourhood and Community*, 7–8, 144–46.
[23] For Lecomte: BA, ms 11700, f. 230–39; and BA, ms 11708, f. 8–15, 233–51. For Grimperel: BA, ms 11706, f. 280–90; and BA, ms 11728, f. 120–27.

the military clashed as a result of the administrative reforms. In 1763, Sartine, then lieutenant general of police, reached an agreement with Cornillon, the commander of the guards.[24] Under the terms of this accord, the military agreed that it would release arrested spectators into the custody of the city guards, who would then lead the detainees to the commissioner's residence. The guards who accompanied the suspect would also present the commissioner with a "bulletin" completed by the sergeant in charge of the soldiers at the spectacle. This account was to contain the name and quality of the spectator in question and a description of the incident that had led to the arrest. The commissioner would then make a complete report of the incident and decide what penal action, if any, was to be taken against the spectator. This system had one seeming advantage over that previously in place: no longer would the guards, who might have tussled with the person under arrest, be permitted to pass judgment on the culpability of the spectator.

This delicate balance of power between the military and the commissioners frequently broke down. For their part, the military complained that riflemen stationed at the spectacles, particularly those positioned outside the theater to direct the flow of carriages before and after the spectacles, were subject to verbal and physical abuse from carriage drivers and other people in the streets, as we have seen. In these instances, the military appealed to the lieutenant general of police for stiff penalties against those guilty of insulting the soldiers. They also attacked the practice of leading offenders before the commissioners because of the supposed leniency of the latter group. A 1780 military memo, probably addressed to the lieutenant general of police, set forth the problem:

> Instead of leading the guilty parties directly to prison, in conformity with existing ordinances on this subject, the Watch (to which the Guard confides them) leads them to the Commissioners. These latter officials claim the right to inform themselves of the circumstances surrounding arrest and to render a verdict. They cast themselves as sovereign judges in the execution of the King's orders and they release the guilty parties on their own authority; they play favorites under the pretext that the guilty ones have a residence, or that they belong to well-known people.[25]

---

[24] AN, Y13396, papers of Grimperel for 1768, document marked "Lettres de M. le Lieut. Général de Police."

[25] SHAT, Yᵃ 274, chemise "discipline," document entitled "Délits des particuliers contre les gardes des spectacles et les patrouilles dans Paris," 2. See a similar complaint at SHAT, Yᵃ 273, 3 February 1773.

In the 1780s, the military continually argued for harsh punishments for those who assaulted the guards; stays of two or three months in prison or calls for the stockades were not uncommon.[26]

For their part, the commissioners were quite wary of the unrestrained authority exercised by the military in the spectacles. More troublesome to the commissioners, however, were threats posed by the military's willful violation of the procedure agreed to by the lieutenant general of police and the commander of the guards. An incident that occurred at the Comédie-Française on 15 December 1765 underlined this danger for Commissioner Chenu.[27] That evening, the guard arrested an officer named Saint-Romain, who was standing in the parterre, for crying out against the play onstage and then quarreling with the armed sentry who asked him to tone down his criticism. According to several sources, the soldiers then detained him illegally in their guardroom at the theater for more than an hour. Finally, instead of turning their prisoner over to the Paris watch to be led before a commissioner, they forced a police inspector ignorant of the accord governing arrest and imprisonment of theater spectators to take Saint-Romain off to jail without first being brought before the commissioner.

The next day, Chenu addressed an angry letter to Sartine in which he detailed the improper handling of the case and demanded that renewed orders be issued to the guards to prevent further abuses.[28] In his letter, he pointed out both procedural and ethical abuses committed by the military in their handling of Saint-Romain. Not only had the sergeant denied Saint-Romain the opportunity to appear before a commissioner, he had threatened Villegaudin, the inspector who led Saint-Romain off to prison. Furthermore, an escort of soldiers had inappropriately accompanied Saint-Romain and Villegaudin in the coach that led the latter off to prison; Chenu claimed that the task of this escort was to ensure that Saint-Romain was not brought first before Chenu. And this one instance was not an isolated affair; the commissioner heard daily complaints about the conduct of the military assigned to the Comédie-Française. In sum, Chenu wrote, "the soldiers are in general very insolent, and it is shocking that the sergeants base their decisions to arrest decent people solely on the reports of these same soldiers." The abuse, according to the enraged commissioner, was greater than a merely procedural one. The military's method of proceeding, an arrangement whereby they refused to listen to other wit-

---

[26] SHAT, Yª 273, 13 August 1781; 26 April 1782; 30 December 1785; 31 December 1787; 14 February 1789.
[27] BA, ms 12258, f. 276–83.
[28] Ibid., f. 280–81.

nesses who saw the incident, established the sentries and their sergeants as both judge and plaintiff *(juge et partie)*. This method exposed innocent theatergoers to the "caprice" of a soldier or a sergeant:

> In effect, the public would be exposed to major improprieties and injustice if the liberty of each citizen depended on a soldier or a sergeant who, under the pretext, be it true or false, that he had been insulted, could send decent people to prison. On the contrary, these people frequently have grounds to complain about [the guard] based on the insolence and the brutality which they display all too often.[29]

In the heat of the moment, and perhaps in self-interested defense of his own venal prerogatives, Chenu articulated an essential problem inherent in the Old Regime's attempts to police spectators in the Paris public theaters. From the beginnings of Louis XIV's interest in disciplining the public theater audience, paying spectators had no recourse against over-zealous policing agents, whether they were exempts or soldiers. The procedures designed to involve the commissioners in the 1750s and '60s appeared in theory to provide some safeguards for wrongly accused spectators, but in practice these procedures too often broke down, leaving theater patrons exposed to the disciplinary impulses of the royal army. The system instituted in the beginning of the century by d'Argenson had, by the reign of Louis XVI, evolved to the point at which soldiers directly confronted spectators on a nightly basis in the theaters. The results of this confrontation did not offer comfort to reformers who hoped it might be possible to modify absolutist practices of government according to enlightened principles.

Provincial Theater Riots during the Reign of Louis XVI

Tensions generated by policing abuses continued to build in the Parisian theaters after the Maupeou years. But by the end of the Old Regime, the problem was not confined to Paris; similar difficulties arose in many of the kingdom's provincial playhouses after the ascension of Louis XVI to the throne. These confrontations occurred in a network of provincial theaters that had undergone a rejuvenation in the eighteenth century. Perhaps the surest guide to the provinces' theatrical renewal after 1750 was the rate at which permanent playhouses, often built of stone to withstand the fires that constantly plagued Europe's early modern urban centers, were

[29] Ibid., f. 280–81.

built after 1750. From 1750 to 1773, the last quarter-century of Louis XV's reign, twenty-three major new provincial theaters were constructed.[30] In this regard, the provinces surpassed Paris, where new structures for the privileged troupes did not appear until the early 1780s. Innovative architects constructed new-style theaters in towns such as Lyon, Marseille, and Besançon well before they applied their new techniques and designs to the established theaters of the capital. These new playhouses served as civic monuments and as the cornerstones of urban renewal projects throughout the provinces.[31] In the final fifteen years of the Old Regime under Louis XVI, however, only four more new theaters were built outside Paris, although a number of others were refurbished. By the late 1770s and '80s, the municipalities and regional authorities had found ways to resist demands to build costly and "elitist" playhouses. Newspapers, printed pamphlets, and administrative correspondence after 1774 were filled with arguments against building expensive civic monuments that served primarily, they argued, to increase the income of morally corrupt players who frequently failed to honor their contractual obligations.

One detects here the influence of Rousseau, whose views on the evils of theater may have been more persuasive in the French provinces than in his native Geneva.[32] When Rousseau published his *Letter to d'Alembert on the Theater*, of course, no public theater existed within the city. His essay was prompted by d'Alembert's suggestion that the town fathers construct a public theater; d'Alembert's remarks, in turn, were prompted by Voltaire, then residing just outside the Republic, who wished to see his dramatic works staged in a Genevan playhouse. The impetus to build a theater in Rousseau's Geneva came in the wake of his book from the aristocratic classes who sought control of the city's political and cultural life. The playhouse itself became a potent sign of the Republic's turbulent class politics in the latter half of the eighteenth century, as aristocratic, bourgeois, and disenfranchised commoner factions sought symbols with which to wage their political battles. Unlike the Republic of Geneva, however, disputes over public playhouses within the French kingdom did not yet overtly engage questions of individual political liberties. Instead, debates

---

[30] Fuchs, *La Vie théâtrale*, 105–7.

[31] Daniel Rabreau, *Le Théâtre et l'embellisement des villes de France au XVIIIe siècle* (Paris, 1978).

[32] R. R. Palmer, *The Age of the Democratic Revolutions* (Princeton, 1959), 1:111–39; Franco Venturi, *The End of the Old Regime in Europe, 1768–1776*, trans. R. Burr Litchfield (Princeton, 1989), 340–50; Haydn Mason, *French Writers and Their Society, 1715–1800* (London, 1982), 128–45; Jeffrey S. Ravel, "Rousseau and the Construction of French Provincial Playhouses," *Pensée Libre* 6 (1997): 183–90.

surrounding these theaters focused on the relation between the centralizing state and local authorities, or the role of government in providing "public services" and assuring "public security" in these buildings. In other words, the theaters served as vehicles for exploring, and contesting, the state's obligations to its subjects.

Not surprisingly, policing problems similar to those experienced in Paris also arose in the provincial theatrical centers, where military officers or Crown administrators battled for jurisdiction with local officials.[33] The latter, often jealous of their local rights and privileges, refused to cede to agents of the central government, whether military or civilian. In many cases, however, particularly in garrison towns, the problems posed by theater policing proved beyond the capacity of local or royal officials. As in Paris, provincial administrators issued and reissued ordinances and regulations governing spectator behavior throughout the century, often to no avail. Instructions distributed in Cambrai in 1783, for instance, directed the military commander of the guard to march his troups through town from the barracks to the theater at four in the afternoon each day.[34] The commander was then ordered to place each grenadier inside the theater and to instruct his men to maintain tranquility in the theater by arresting those who whistled, demanded plays not previously announced, or brought their dogs to the playhouse. In addition, the regulations specifically directed sentries stationed in the parterre to discipline spectators who wore hats or hissed the play; details were also provided for sentries posted at the entrance and on the stage.

These directions were not substantially different from those contained in the King's ordinances issued for the privileged Parisian theaters in the eighteenth century, but a police ordinance issued by town officials in Bordeaux in 1759 offered significantly greater discretionary powers to the local theater police.[35] In this document, the town officials repeated the usual proscriptions against hissing and hats, but they also forbade spectators to assume "indecent postures" or to walk across the stage during the performance. Assistants to surgeons and wig makers were prohibited from wearing powdered wigs, and the police were instructed to remove dogs from the theater and shoot them in a designated area nearby. Theater personnel who through their tardiness caused the performance to begin after five were fined heavily. In spite of these draconian measures, audiences continued to behave in a

[33] Fuchs, *La Vie théâtrale*, 167–82.

[34] Ibid., 208–10.

[35] Lagrave, et al., *La Vie théâtrale à Bordeaux des origines à nos jours. Tome 1, Des origines à 1799* (Paris, 1985), 203.

"disorderly" manner in Bordeaux; after 1775, the Bordeaux ordinances wearily repeated the standardized language of the Parisian edicts.

Although space prevents a thorough examination of all provincial parterre riots in the 1774–89 period, we can look at two particularly spectacular incidents that typify these clashes.[36]

Angers, 30 March 1775

The sixteenth- and seventeenth-century history of Angers, located just off the Loire on the Mayenne River midway between Nantes and Tours, had been turbulent; but with the expulsion of the city's last Protestant elements in 1685, the Angevins acquiesced to monarchical tutelage.[37] The city's population remained at twenty-five to thirty thousand during the late seventeenth and eighteenth centuries, failing to rise as many of its provincial counterparts did after 1750. Angers struck visitors and outside observers in the second half of the eighteenth century as a stagnant provincial town; the receiver general of finances for the Generality of Tours noted in 1783 that the current generation of Angevins, "deprived of energy, vegetate, just as the previous generation vegetated and the one to come will vegetate."[38] The development of Angers' theater exemplified French provincial patterns in the eighteenth century.[39] Ambulatory troupes stopped for limited engagements in the town in the first half of the century, where they played in an old, uncomfortable building that contemporary accounts referred to as the *parc des jeux* or *théâtre des jeux*. This structure, located on the same

[36] In addition to the two incidents that follow, see Fournel, *Curiosités théâtrales*, 94–95, for Marseille in 1772 and 1775; Jean Quéniart, *Culture et société urbaines dans la France de l'Ouest au XVIIIe siècle* (Paris, 1978), 510–11, for Nantes in 1779; Fuchs, *La Vie théâtrale*, 172, for Grenoble in 1783; MS, 31:229, 246–48, 251–52, 259–60, 263–65, 32:39–42; and MF, 8 and 15 April 1786, for Beauvais in 1786; Lagrave, et al., *La Vie théâtrale à Bordeaux*, 258, 260, for two conflicts in Bordeaux in 1787; and Quéniart, *Culture et société*, 511, for Rouen in 1788.

[37] François LeBrun, et al., *Histoire d'Angers* (Toulouse, 1975), 39–130. See also François LeBrun, "Une Source de l'histoire sociale: la presse provinciale à la fin de l'Ancien Régime. Les *Affiches d'Angers*, 1773–1789," *Le Mouvement Social* 40 (July–September 1962): 56–73; and John McManners, *French Ecclesiastical Society under the Ancien Régime: A Study of Angers in the Eighteenth Century* (Manchester, 1960).

[38] Quoted in Lebrun, et al., *Histoire d'Angers*, 101. See also the remarks of various English visitors to the town in McManners, *French Ecclesiastical Society*, 1–2.

[39] E. Queruau-Lamérie, *Notice sur le théâtre d'Angers (1755–1825)* (Angers, 1889); Jacques Maillard, "Le Théâtre à Angers au XVIIIe siècle," *Revue de la société d'histoire du théâtre* 43 (1991): 107–18. For a general discussion of eighteenth-century theatrical growth in western France, see Quéniart, *Culture et société*, 485–95.

square as the central marketplace, was almost certainly constructed for nontheatrical purposes. In 1762, two town merchants acquired a wooden tennis court on the same square. It was not surprising that they chose to situate their theater in the market district. In addition to the older precedent, this neighborhood was surrounded by the residences of many of the town's wealthiest families; it was also the site of local executions. The new theatrical proprietors remodeled the tennis court by adding two rows of loges at the end opposite the stage and two rows of balconies along either side of the hall; a standing parterre occupied most of the ground floor of the building, yielding to an amphitheater at the back of the hall. In spite of these alterations, the "new" theater remained crowded and dangerous, because there was only one exit for the entire building.

In 1768, the government accorded the right to organize the Angevine theatrical season to Mlle Montansier, an enterprising actress who had already acquired exclusive permission to mount theatrical productions in Versailles and Nantes. Montansier used her provincial theaters to polish performers and productions that then played in the public theater at Versailles, and after 1775, at court; her Angevin audiences thus benefited from a steady diet of aspiring performers and a repertory composed of seventeenth-century classics, well-known operas, and many plays of contemporary composition.[40] A parterre ticket to these performances cost twelve *sous*, with first and second loge tickets running forty and twenty-four *sous*, respectively. Although evidence is hard to locate, it appears that these prices permitted those well below the nobility and the merchant classes to attend the theater. Secondary and university students particularly enjoyed the Angevin stage, and law students profited from an ancient privilege that granted them six free tickets to each evening's performance.[41]

The violent parterre outburst of 30 March 1775 had its origins in the jurisdictional conflict between the commander of the Company of Invalides at the Chateau, the medieval fortress that dominated the southern ramparts of the city, and the mayor and the municipality.[42] In some ways, the dispute

[40] Quéniart, *Culture et société*, 503.

[41] LeBrun, *Histoire d'Angers*, 129. Depositions taken by the police after the fact indicate that on 30 March 1775, the evening in question, the following were among the spectators standing in the parterre: three town officials, two students, a doctor from the medical faculty, a glove merchant, and a *bourgeois*. ADML, 49 3.E.9.

[42] Queruau-Lemérie, *Notice*, 29–37, is the most complete and accurate narrative of the events of the evening; see also Celestin Port, *Inventaire analytique des archives anciennes de la mairie d'Angers* (Paris, 1861), 493–98, which reprints the town's official report of the event drawn up the day after the conflict. ADML, 49 3.E.9., contains, inter alia, a manuscript version of the town's report and twenty-two of the twenty-three police depositions of townspeople on which the report is based.

resembled that between the military and the commissioners in Paris. In early 1774, the commander of the Invalides and forty of his armed soldiers had unsuccessfully attempted by force to replace the town's watch at the theater. In May 1774, the new commander of the Invalides, a man named Renty, notified the mayor that he intended to renew the claim of the Invalides to police the public theater. The mayor protested this maneuver, but ultimately agreed to back down until Versailles decided the matter definitively. By the end of the year, however, when no response was forthcoming from the King and his court, the municipality disbanded its theater policing corps and ceded its authority to the Invalides. Subsequent events, however, were to prove the court negligent in its failure to act.

Toward the end of March, the manager of Montansier's troupe refused to stage a benefit performance for an actress particularly well liked by the Angevin public. On the afternoon of 30 March, in anticipation of trouble, or perhaps in search of an excuse to assert his authority, Captain Renty and his lieutenant, Cazeau, gathered forty men at the Chateau, more than three times the normal policing contingent at the theater, and ordered the men to load their rifles. The officers then marched through the streets of Angers at the head of their squadron. Along the way, according to police depositions, the soldiers had verbal altercations with citizens; in one instance, the soldiers menacingly pointed their guns at two townsmen as they walked past, claiming that they would "blow their brains out" (*voilà de quoi vous bruler la cervelle*).[43]

Renty, Cazeau, and their charges reached the marketplace square in front of the theater at approximately 4:30, at which point the troops formed two lines, performed several maneuvers, and made a show to the public of their loaded rifles, an act reminiscent of the Parisian drills recorded by Mercier. Several townspeople heard the officers instruct their troops to fire at the first signal, although some of the troops may also have protested this order. The officers then distributed the soldiers throughout the theater. Before the performance, some actors told several spectators not to buy tickets for the parterre, because there might be violence in the pit that evening. The scheduled performance of Charles-Simon Favart's *Acajou* began at 5:30; several observers noted that the parterre was only half full. The first act went off without disturbance. During the intermission, spectators in the parterre briefly cried to a man in livery in the second loges to remove his hat, which he did, stopping the jeers. The men in the pit then tapped their feet to the music played by the orchestra during the interlude, as they had before the play began, and some of them jumped up and down on a loose board in the floor that functioned like a teeter-totter. None of the witnesses later interviewed by the police thought that this behavior was provocative.

Just then, however, much to the surprise of the audience in the parterre and those watching from the first and second loges, the two officers and eight or ten of their men, rifles fitted out with bayonettes, charged into the pit. Renty and Cazeau, armed with pistols that they waved wildly about, swore foully at the parterre spectators: "Do you think, you miserable, fucking beggars and rednecks, that you can force your law on us?" (*Croyez-vous, gens-foutus, foutus gueux, foutus manans, nous imposer la loi?*) The official municipal report stated that they repeated these oaths, "and many more much worse, in a rage," beside themselves, "foaming at the mouth"; they stood in the center of the parterre swearing, while the spectators shrunk back to the corners of the room.[44] Meanwhile, ominously, the remainder of the soldiers appeared on the stage, in the amphitheater, and in the second loges, with their rifles trained on the pit. The officers told them to prepare to fire. Cazeau appeared especially crazed; he repeatedly pointed his pistols at the heads and chests of spectators and threatened to kill them on the spot. One fourteen year old in the pit, the son of Bancelin, the *secrétaire-greffier* of the town, "trembling" and fearing for his life, turned to a friend of his father and asked to be boosted out of the pit and into the loges. As the latter began to lift him up, Cazeau advanced to within a few feet of the boy and shot him in the chest with one of his pistols. The adolescent, aided by other spectators, somehow managed to escape the theater and find his way to a nearby doctor who dressed the wound. In the next few days he suffered from a fever as doctors bled him thirteen times, but he ultimately survived.[45]

Either just before or just after Cazeau shot the youth, a soldier stationed in the amphitheater named La Tulippe, cried out to Renty to move away from the parterre spectators, because he was going to begin firing. Fortunately for the spectators, his rifle jammed; instead, he attacked audience members who attempted to flee the pit with his bayonet. Some of the witnesses deposed by the police reported that other soldiers' rifles also failed to fire at this point, but one witness also said that he spoke with a soldier afterward who claimed that, wiser than his commanders, he knew not to shoot. Although no more shots were fired, the soldiers, at the behest of

[44] Port, *Inventaire analytique*, 495.
[45] ADML, 49 3.E.9., deposition of Charles Pierre Jean Baptiste Bancelin, 2 April 1775. A letter in the same dossier, written by his father at the end of the month, indicates that the boy was back on his feet. Maillard, "Le Théâtre à Angers," 117, incorrectly asserts that the youth was killed.

their commanders, blocked the exits to the theater; several spectators sought refuge backstage. Some semblance of order returned to the theater, and the actors began the second act of the play. A few minutes into the performance, however, Bancelin *père*, father of the wounded adolescent, entered the parterre and politely but firmly asked Renty whether the gun fired at his son had contained powder or a ball. One or more parterre spectators immediately shouted that Cazeau, not Renty, had fired the fateful shot. Renty ordered several of the parterre informants arrested, Bancelin *père* sought out Cazeau, and the actors decided to forego the rest of the performance. The soldiers continued their attempts to arrest parterre spectators, although they did not fire again, and the rest of the audience members fled the theater. Three Angevins were imprisoned by the soldiers, and several others escaped the grasp of Renty's troups.

In the wake of these events, the town elders called an emergency meeting to calm local outrage, and a local court (the Présidial) ordered the arrest of Renty and Cazeaux, who had gone into hiding. Several days later, the municipality dispatched a delegation to Versailles to request punitive action. For six weeks, this delegation encountered resistance from the national commander of the Invalides; but toward the end of April, the court ordered the troop of Invalides to cease policing the theater in Angers. At the beginning of May, the troop was dispatched to St. Malo; and their successors, a group of sixteen men and one officer, were forbidden to interfere in the theaters. The Crown appears not to have recognized the guilt of the two officers, however, who were neither captured nor punished for the events of 30 March.

At one level, this affair might be dismissed as the unfortunate escapade of an overzealous provincial military commander anxious to assert his authority amongst the local inhabitants. Renty's insistence on supplanting the local theater police with his troups, and his eagerness to provoke violent confrontation with parterre spectators on 30 March, attest to his lack of good judgment. But his comments and actions during the events indicate that he saw the spectators gathered in the parterre as representative of the town's disobedience of his authority. Ironically, his determination to "impose the law" on the parterre led not to a reestablishment of order in the theater, but to a situation more dangerous than that in the pit before his intervention. Whereas in Molière's day the disorderly soldiers had acted outside official sanction, the excessively violent troops now claimed the authorization of ministers at Versailles for their actions.

At another level, the premeditated disruption of the spectacle, and young Bancelin's chest wound, indicated the monarchy's negligent attention to provincial theater policing. The mayor's willingness to back down in the face of Renty's demands to police the theaters reflects the pacification of the town in the previous century; Anger's inhabitants had been stripped of the political and military resources to oppose willful commanders such as Renty. But the Crown was unwilling or unable to provide safeguards against abuses its own personnel might commit. In the wake of the tragedy in the theater, royal officials at Versailles took weeks to respond to the pleas of local Angevine officials, who sought redress against the Invalides troops and their commanders, as the affair became tied up in court intrigue. Meanwhile, back in Angers, the town watch resumed its policing responsibilities at the theater, to the satisfaction of local residents. As Bancelin *père* emphasized in a letter written at the end of April 1775 to one of the Angevin delegation at Versailles, the watch policed the spectacle "with all the decency and honor that one enjoys when one leaves men free, as they were meant to be."[46] In this aggrieved observer's mind, abuses in theater policing invoked more abstract questions of political liberty.

Bordeaux, 26–30 May 1783

If Angers represented stagnation in the French provinces at the end of the Old Regime, Bordeaux typified the opposite. This Atlantic port outstripped all its eighteenth-century competitors to become France's leading commercial maritime center on the eve of the Revolution.[47] Its economic dynamism also led to significant demographic increases. Although estimates of the city's population at the end of Louis XIV's reign vary from 45,000 to 55,000, most demographers agree that the number of the town's residents had approximately doubled to 110,000 by 1790.[48] The contrast with the Angevin theater was also striking. Bordeaux's theatrical institutions up to 1739 had resembled those of Angers in that they had consisted of a dozen or so ambulatory troupes who played on an irregular basis in the town's provisional wooden playhouse.[49] In 1739, however, the municipality constructed a theater of stone, and four years later the town council established

---

[46] ADML, 49 3.E.9., letter from Bancelin *père* dated 29 April 1775.

[47] François-Georges Pariset, et al., *Histoire de Bordeaux*, vol. 5, *Bordeaux au XVIIIe siècle* (Bordeaux, 1968), 191–323. See also P. Butel and J. P. Poussou, *La Vie quotidienne à Bordeaux au XVIIIe siècle* (Paris, 1980), 21; and William Doyle, *The Parlement of Bordeaux and the End of the Old Regime, 1771–1790* (New York, 1974).

[48] Pariset, et al., *Bordeaux au XVIIIe siècle*, 327.

[49] Lagrave, *La Vie théâtrale à Bordeaux*, 191; Henri Lagrave, "Les Structures du théâtre dans la province française: le cas exemplaire de Bordeaux," *SVEC* 192 (1980): 1425–31.

a sedentary troupe to perform in this theater. This troupe also obtained exclusive rights over the performance of spoken and lyric drama in the province from the regional governor and the Opera in Paris; from this time forward, tensions manifested themselves between the local Bordelais authorities, who claimed policing power over the theater, and the central powers, who asserted their right to license public performances.

These conflicts escalated in 1755, when the Maréchal de Richelieu, a military commander and one of the First Gentlemen of the King's Bed-chamber at Versailles, became governor of Guienne, the province in which Bordeaux was situated. In 1760, Richelieu encouraged the establishment of a second permanent troupe, founded as a joint venture among nine of Bordeaux's leading lights. Their ranks included the Maréchal, two town councilmen, two Parlementary judges, a high-ranking naval officer, and the Polish and Prussian consuls. Control of the theater had slipped away from the municipality to a conglomerate of directors assembled and con-trolled by Richelieu, a representative of royal power. The Grand-Théâtre of Bordeaux, designed by the architect Victor Louis at the behest of Riche-lieu and completed in 1780, characterized the conflict between the Maréchal and the city's leaders on a grand scale. The building itself, a monumental construction in the heart of the city, was "by far the most magnificent" theater in France, as Arthur Young noted in his diary during a visit to the city in 1787.[50] The engravings that Victor Louis published in 1782, in a book intended to justify the expense of the theater, attest to the theater's opulence (see figures 6 and 10). Some observers, however, wondered about the appropriateness of such a monument in a provincial city; their fears were echoed by the town council, which thought that Richelieu's activities in this sphere had reduced the town to a policing agent without control over its internal affairs.[51]

It was in this atmosphere that a major conflict between parterre specta-tors and policing authorities broke out in late May 1783.[52] The confronta-tion originated with the decision of the theater's directors not to welcome a minor opera singer named Durand, expelled from the Paris Opera in 1781, into their company.[53] Durand, on the verge of leaving town, had so impressed some Bordelais at a concert performance that they promised to

---

[50] Quoted in John Lough, *France on the Eve of the Revolution: British Travellers' Observa-tions, 1763–1788* (Chicago, 1987), 95.

[51] See the discussion of this point in Lagrave, *La Vie théâtrale à Bordeaux*, 177.

[52] MS, 32:321–24, 326–27; and AMB BB 179, "délibérations de la jurade du 31 mai 1783," contain accounts of the events; Lagrave, *La Vie théâtrale à Bordeaux*, 259–60, discusses the affair in passing.

[53] On Durand, see Spire Pitou, *The Paris Opera: An Encyclopedia of Operas, Ballets, Com-posers, and Performers* (Westport, CT, 1985), 2:16, 25, 288, 482.

Fig. 10. *Perspective View of the Interior of the Bordeaux Playhouse Facing the Audience,* from Victor Louis, *Salle de spectacle de Bordeaux* (Paris, 1782). (By permission of the Houghton Library, Harvard University.)

pursue the matter on his behalf with the theater's directors. Consequently, on the evening of Monday, 26 May 1783, when the troupe's orator presented himself at the end of the evening's performances to announce the next day's schedule, a number of youths in the parterre demanded that Durand be allowed to sing in the current production of Rameau's opera *Castor et Pollux*. Several town councilors present at the performance, however, forbade the troupe to respond to the public's demand. The curtain was lowered and the lights in the theater extinguished without further response. The enraged parterre spectators who made the demand on Durand's behalf, however, refused to leave the theater. Their actions prompted the soldiers on duty to arrest a young man named Etienne Alliez, described by town officials as one of the "principal troublemakers" (*principaux tapageurs*). The guards hustled Alliez into a carriage and drove him off to prison surrounded by soldiers who brandished their unsheathed swords through the streets of Bordeaux.

The next night at the theater, parterre spectators demanded the release of Alliez. They also recognized spies whom the town council had planted in the parterre and began to attack them. In response, armed soldiers of the town watch entered the parterre, swords drawn, and began to injure some of the mutinous parterre spectators. The youths in the pit, reportedly rallied by cries of support from the loges and the parquet, fought back and eventually chased the soldiers from the theater; the youths then became, in the words of the *Mémoires secrets*, "the absolute masters of the hall." The spectators then renewed their demand for the release of Alliez and also insisted on punishment for the town's soldiers and the director of the theater.

Eventually, both sides appealed to the Comte de Fumel, commander in chief of the royal forces stationed in Guienne, who was in attendance that night. In response, Fumel ordered the punishment of the soldiers who had invaded the parterre. But the spectators, mistrustful of the commander, continued their tumultuous behavior. In particular, they forced the town councilors to leave their loge. One young man, hoisted on the shoulders of his parterre comrades, called for all concerned spectators to meet in the Royal Garden near the theater the next day to take further action. The crowd also ordered the actors to give the night's receipts to the hospital, because the performance had not taken place. The *procureur sindic de la ville*, recounting these events to town officials the next day, labeled the parterre insubordinate and suggested that in their disobedience they had forgotten "the respect due to the places where the public assembled, to the police regulations, to the paternal voice of the magistrates [the Parlement], to the king's ordinances and the laws of the kingdom, whose object is the maintenance of public order."[54] In other words, the *procureur sindic,* in his demonization of the pit, amalgamated the authority of the law courts, the Crown, and an abstract public into a unitary entity whose legitimacy was threatened by the parterre discontents. The conflation of royal, municipal, public, and military authority was striking, if not confused.

The crowd that gathered the next day in the Royal Garden, however, thought its actions were justified by the incarceration of Alliez and the brutality of the soldiers in the theater. Both the *Mémoires secrets* and the police reported that "at least three thousand youths" gathered in the garden, where they celebrated the release of Alliez that morning.[55] The latter, however, had secured his release by agreeing to press the crowd to drop its grievances against the town officials and the military. According to a *procès-verbal* he dictated to the police later that day, he attempted to calm the crowd by "admitting" his guilt and expressing his gratitude to the town officials, who supposedly had granted his liberty after listening to his distraught mother's pleas. According to Alliez, though, the assembled individuals told him that his freedom was not their only objective; they also wanted further action taken against the soldiers who had battled them the night before, and they sought punishment for the theater director who had failed to respond to their requests on Monday, the first night of the crisis.[56] They then decided to boycott the theater for three months and to impede other residents from entering the playhouse until their other demands were met.

By five in the afternoon, the youths had barricaded all the streets leading to the theater and chased away most of the evening's theatergoers, as well as another squad of the town's guards. The *Mémoires secrets* suggested that the protesters discouraged local *femmes du monde* from attending the theater by threatening to whip them in public. In spite of these precautions, a few theater subscribers managed to slip through the barricades to watch the evening's performance. When the protesters realized that the performance had begun, they crashed into the theater and physically prevented the continuation of the performance. The following day, Thursday, the town council closed the theater. Fumel, the army commander, ordered two hundred dragoons who were stationed in a nearby town to march on the city, in spite of a prohibition against royal troops in the town that dated back to the medieval period. And the Parlement issued an order prohibiting "all sorts of tumultuous assemblies" and authorizing the "insulted" town council to determine the names of

[54] AMB, GG 1004b.
[55] MS, 22:323; AMB, FF 70, 28 May 1783.
[56] AMB, FF 70, 28 May 1783, procès-verbal d'Etienne Alliez.

those behind the recent events at the theater. The combined actions of the town council, the royal commander, and the Parlement appeared to have finally stifled protest; on Friday, the theater reopened, but almost no one attended the performance. A week later, according to one report, the troupe was still performing to a largely empty house.

One historian analyzing these events concludes that the whole affair was rapidly forgotten.[57] But it is difficult to imagine that a disruption that led first to violent confrontations between town guards and residents in the playhouse and the following day to the physical seizure of the area around the theater could be easily dismissed by those who participated in the events. The contemporary accounts of the affair seem to agree that the youthful partisans of Durand who were initially responsible for the tumult acted out of a mischievous desire to see their favorite onstage; no underlying political motivation emerged.[58] But the escalation of events from Monday through Wednesday suggests a pattern familiar from Angers and other theaters around the kingdom: local and royal officials, uneasy with the potentially disruptive forces at play any time an audience gathered in a playhouse, often fueled civil disruptions through their confused interventions. By the Wednesday gathering in the Royal Garden near the theater, the parterre spectators and other participants were prepared to battle not only for their aesthetic preferences in the theater, but also for their legal and political claims against the town council and the military.

In the aftermath of another confrontation between soldiers and townsmen in the public theater of Beauvais in 1786, a conflict that proved fatal, an anonymous local writer penned an inflammatory poem titled "Stances or Ode on the Massacre at Beauvais."[59] In his verses, he decried the soldiers' actions, implored vengeance from the King, and chastised his fellow townsmen for failing to expel the "perfidious barbarians" who had assaulted them. The final stanza of his poem attacked the virtue and the masculinity of those who failed to respond to playhouse violence in kind:

---

[57] Lagrave, *La Vie théâtrale à Bordeaux*, 260.

[58] Ironically, CS, 14:364–65, commented just days after the Bordeaux incidents that parterres in all the kingdom's major provincial cities were composed of "lively, impatient, and undisciplined individuals who were difficult to contain." The entry then described an incident in Toulouse in which a group of students in the parterre, partisans of a particular actress, caused a disturbance that the local police had to quell.

[59] One evening in late March 1786, a squadron of royal soldiers provoked an incident in the parterre of the city's public theater that ended with one young man dead and as many as twenty others grievously injured. As with the Angers affair, which it closely resembled, word of the incident found its way to Versailles, where the King ultimately took action against the troops. (Sources cited in note 36.)

Cowardly inhabitants of a town
Formerly filled with valor;
Go ahead, grovel, you imbecilic people,
You deserve your misfortune!
To the insolent soldiery
Offer up your wives unblushingly,
And caress the bloody hand
Which takes your life and your honor.[60]

These lines, influenced by the melodramatic style of the late eighteenth century, nevertheless bespoke the passions that bloody playhouse confrontations could evoke. In provincial towns where weapons were drawn in the final fifteen years of the Old Regime, the threat was understood in visceral terms. Armed tyranny in the theaters had escaped the control of the central state; policing forces now threatened spectator-citizens with loss of life, honor, and masculine pride. Spectators who failed to rise to the challenge, this local poet and patriot implied, deserved the fate that audiences in Angers, Bordeaux, Beauvais, and elsewhere met.

Paris, 26 December 1787

By 1787, events beyond the world of the theater were beginning to echo the violent, disturbing incidents taking place in the provincial theaters. By the late 1780s, the government's financial solvency had begun to erode at a rapid rate. The crown's plans for tax reform roused vigorous opposition, first in the newly convened Assembly of Notables, then in the Parlements.[61] In the midst of this governmental crisis, the most subversive Parisian theater riot before 1789 occurred in the parterre of the Comédie-Italienne. On the night of 26 December 1787, the Italian troupe attempted to introduce a new three-act comic opera entitled *Le Prisonnier anglais*, with words by Desfontaines and music by the popular Grétry.[62] By the third act, the whis-

---

[60] MS, 32:42, 13 May 1786.
[61] Jean Egret, *The French Prerevolution, 1787–1788*, trans. Wesley D. Camp (Chicago, 1977), 86–123; William Doyle, *The Oxford History of the French Revolution* (Oxford, 1989), 66–85.
[62] Detailed accounts of the evening include MS, 36:275–79; MF, 5 January 1788, 39–43; CL, 4:3–4; Siméon-Prosper Hardy, *Mes Loisirs, ou Journal d'Evenements, tels qu'ils parviennent à ma connaisance*, in BN, ms ff 6686, f. 328–29, 332; Rétif de la Bretonne, *Les Nuits de Paris* (Paris, 1987), 301–7; and an anonymous pamphlet written sometime after 26 December 1787 but before 15 January 1788, *Le Parterre justifié, ou précis historique et réflexions sur la représentation du 26 décembre 1787* (London, 1788).

tles and catcalls from the displeased pit had grown so loud that the actors abandoned the stage; as the author of the *Mémoires secrets* commented, "there was little to keep the play from dying a tranquil death."[63] Because it was only 7:30 when the actors gave up on Desfontaines' play, the audience demanded another. This request was fully within the spectators' rights; according to the company's statute, the troupe was required to have a second play ready in case the announced play failed. Nevertheless, the actors did not respond to these calls for at least twenty minutes. When one of the leading male actors, Thomassin, appeared, he told the crowd that the players had already sent the orchestra home. Although the audience was upset, it proposed that the actors play a comedy without music first performed two weeks before, *Les Etourdis ou la Mort supposée*. Thomassin went off to see if the necessary actors were still in the theater.

During his absence, according to one account, the orchestra reappeared and began to play symphonies. After another half hour without any sign from the troupe, however, the tumult began anew. When Thomassin finally reappeared, he only increased the audience's displeasure by announcing that owing to the absence of two actors the troupe could not comply with the public's request; instead, they proposed to play a third piece, Favart's 1756 comedy, *La Servante maîtresse*. Despite the public's vociferous objections to this plan, two players, Mlle Renaud and M Chenard, appeared onstage to begin the substitute performance. Some accounts speculated that the actors had hoped to pacify the angry crowd by sending out Renaud, an attractive young actress who was one of the parterre's favorites.[64] Although a portion of the pit did applaud her, particularly when she began to shed tears to gain sympathy, the majority of the audience was so vocal in opposition to the play that the actors could not begin the scene. Chenard exacerbated the standoff when he taunted the parterre by making cuckold gestures (*faire les cornes*) in its direction.

Although the situation was spinning out of control, it was still one with Parisian precedents up to this point; audiences not infrequently demanded an entirely new play by the 1780s, and the privileged troupes had been regularly callous in their disregard for the public's wishes since the time of the hyper-patriotic play *The Siege of Calais* in the mid-1760s.[65] What followed, however, went beyond any previous Parisian theater disturbance to bring to the surface the contradictory expectations of the theatrical Old

---

[63] MS, 36:276.

[64] MS, 36:277; *Parterre justifié*, 4.

[65] Nine days before at the Comédie-Française, for example, the audience had rejected a translation of Richard Brinsley Sheridan's *Rivals*. MF, 5 January 1788, 40.

Regime and the assembled theatergoers. As the audience continued to react to Chenard and the actors' general neglect, a squadron of fifty soldiers, equipped with bayonettes at the end of their rifles, entered the parterre. At least two spectators were arrested; the soldiers divided the rest of the parterre into two parts and forcefully drove the spectators out of the pit by blows from their rifles.[66] One commentator characterized this military action by writing that the soldiers pushed people out of the parterre "like butchers forcing the animals they wanted to slaughter out of the pen."[67] In less than five minutes, the soldiers had cleared the parterre; they had not, however, conquered the hall, for sympathetic spectators in the amphitheater, the balconies, and the *paradis* welcomed the dispossessed pit spectators. The soldiers, now in possession of the empty parterre, found themselves face to face with a theater full of angry spectators throwing food and furniture and yelling insults at them.[68]

It is unclear whether the actors, the soldiers' commander, or one of the government's administrators in attendance ordered the troops to occupy the pit. In any event, this risky action, which could have resulted in fatalities if the parterre spectators had chosen to resist the soldiers, demonstrated the great divide separating the assumptions of the actors and the government from those of the spectators. The players, backed by military force that they had purchased from the government, insisted on dictating the plays they would perform for the theatergoing public. The spectators, who had paid the price of admission, thought they had purchased the right to reject unacceptable theatrical products. As one outraged observer put it, "Isn't it unheard of, indeed unimaginable, that mercenaries, hired to support the players' insolence, made people who had paid for their places leave them by force?"[69]

When armed soldiers displaced the bodies of mutinous spectators from the parterre, the theatrical Old Regime had also reached a tangible crisis, as it had earlier in Angers and Bordeaux. As the soldiers faced the jeering audience, the authority of the King, which supported the actors by decree and by physical force, directly confronted a public that claimed an aesthetic, commercial, and above all political right to veto the performance onstage. In this case, those supported by the authority of the King blinked; the soldiers withdrew, leaving the embarrassed players to respond to the triumphant public now in possession of the playhouse. Mlle Gonthier, one

[66] MS, 36:277; Hardy, *Mes Loisirs*, in BN, f. 332; La Bretonne, *Les Nuits de Paris*, 306.
[67] *Parterre justifié*, 5.
[68] *Parterre justifié*, 5; MS, 36:277–78; Hardy, *Mes Loisirs*, in BN, f. 329.
[69] *Parterre justifié*, 7–8.

of the company's senior actresses, threw herself to her knees at the front of the stage with her hands clasped, indicating that she demanded pardon for herself and her colleagues. The audience, however, rejected this gesture of supplication; some of the public demanded an apology from Chenard, who had disappeared, while others apparently cried out that an apology would be accepted only from one of the male actors.[70] Slowly, the idea began to take shape among the audience that the actors could make amends by donating the proceeds from a single performance to the poor.[71] By then, Rosière, one of the troupe's leading actors, was attempting to mollify the spectators; faced with this request, he withdrew to discuss the matter with his colleagues.[72]

When he returned several moments later, Rosière stated the troupe's desire to submit to the wishes of the audience but hastened to add that the company could not agree to donate the evening's receipts to the poor because they had not been authorized by their "superiors" (i.e., the First Gentlemen of the King's Bedchamber, a group of courtiers given administrative responsibilities over the privileged troupes). The actors were effectively caught between two masters. They knew it would be difficult to explain any capitulation to the First Gentlemen and other royal ministers who insisted on strict crowd control in the playhouses. The author of the *Mémoires secrets* seemed to confirm this suspicion when he wrote several days later, "The First Gentlemen of the King's Bedchamber did not want the actors to receive their orders from the Public, since they regard this as contrary to their own supremacy."[73] But the spectators that night, emboldened after facing down the soldiers, were unrelenting with Rosière as he shuttled back and forth between stage and wings. According to one account, each time that he reappeared to inform the crowd that the actors had no authorization to meet their wishes, they responded that "the Public was their supreme master and that they had to submit to its decrees."[74]

In the short term, neither the King's authority nor the will of the public prevailed in this playhouse confrontation. Rosière finally abandoned the scene and the actors lowered the curtain. A group of mutinous spectators

---

[70] Hardy, *Mes Loisirs*, in BN, f. 328; MS, 36:278; *Parterre justifié*, 5–6.

[71] The MS reported that the audience wanted the receipts from that night's performance donated, but the author of *Parterre justifié* suggested that the spectators demanded another performance specifically for charity. Hardy suggested that some had wanted the actors to give three performances for charity.

[72] The MS claimed that one voice from the hall had cried out for Rosière to sink to his knees, (*à genoux*), in expiation.

[73] MS, 36:284.

[74] MS, 36:278.

who climbed onstage, however, forced the troupe to raise the curtain again when they threatened to tear it to shreds. But the actors did not return to the stage, and the audience's request for a charitable donation did not receive a definitive response. At approximately eleven in the evening, the crowd finally dispersed, reportedly threatening that the "war of the whistles would start up again the next night."[75] The bookseller Hardy concluded his account of the evening's affairs by noting that the same disturbances would probably occur the next night unless the administration took sufficient precautions.[76] Indeed, matters on 27 December were hardly less tumultuous, although both actors and audience finally negotiated an arrangement whereby the play could proceed.[77]

Despite this standoff, the decay of police authority within the playhouse dramatized the general breakdown of the Old Regime in the waning days of 1787; the will of the people confronted the crumbling façade of the King's authority. Henri Meister, the acutely observant if somewhat selective author of the *Correspondance littéraire*, captured the deeper implications of this moment in his account of the evening's events. Writing with the political uncertainties of late 1787 and early 1788 in mind, he reported that one of his neighbors at the Comédie-Italienne that night had made a metaphoric leap from parterre to political spectacle; this move was unsurprising in a country contemplating the reassembly of the three Estates after a long hiatus. Viewing the audience that had asserted its supremacy over the players and the royal administrators, Meister's neighbor had concluded that "[the parterre] is the nation which serves as prelude to the Estates-General."[78]

The pregnant political observation by Meister's neighbor found further elaboration in a pamphlet entitled *The Parterre Justified, or Historical Précis and Reflections on the Performance of 26 December 1787*, authored by an anonymous theatergoer and political observer who signed himself "E. M. L." This ten-page tract, which appeared no later than two and a half weeks after the incident, contained a partisan description of the events of 26 December and stinging criticism of the government's theatrical administration. The players had made the first mistake, the author asserted, by "ordering" the public to watch a play they had not requested. This had been an insult to the public, to "imagine that it would submit to the will of the actors."[79] But the military had compounded the wrong by forcibly interven-

---

[75] MS, 36:279.
[76] Hardy, *Mes Loisirs*, in BN, f. 329.
[77] For events the next evening, see Hardy, *Mes Loisirs*, in BN, f. 332; and MS, 36:284.
[78] CL, 14:4. Meister, writing for select courtly circles outside France, failed to mention the police intervention in the parterre that evening.
[79] *Parterre justifié*, 7.

ing in the conflict. E. M. L. claimed that the soldiers, responsible only to the King, lacked authority to arrest spectators or to clear the parterre. This "despotic and revolting" situation had obtained in the parterre for too long: "How is it that because a man whistles at a play he doesn't like in order to inform the actors of his displeasure, he is then arrested, seized by his collar, led to the guardroom, and often imprisoned?"[80]

Why should the pleasures of French theatergoers be accompanied by terror and bayonets, he continued, when actors and audiences in Italy and England interacted without military intervention? In London, flying oranges, onions, and apples kept both rebellious actors and disruptive spectators in line; surely these techniques were preferable to the vexations of the military. But E. M. L. also acknowledged that Parisian theatergoers, "living in a country where liberty was entirely unknown," might not be capable of an English-style system of self-regulation. It was necessary to maintain a policing force in French theaters so that liberty would not degenerate into license, but only under the condition that this force be submitted to a constitutionally established authority. Mindful of the rights the Parlements were currently claiming in their constitutional struggles with the monarchy, E. M. L. proposed the Paris Parlement for this task. In this "patriot" view, it was a violation of the Parlement's prerogatives to deprive a citizen of liberty without recourse to legal structures:

> It is up to Parlement to take charge of reforming these abuses, which effect the preservation of people's rights. It is Parlement which has an interest in preventing a portion of the policing authority, which is exercised every day, from escaping its own authority. And it is Parlement which must assure the tranquility of its citizens against the innumerable oppressions and injustices that result from a military force not subject to any tribunal.[81]

Thus, E. M. L. inscribed the tumult in the theater within the larger constitutional struggles between Crown and Parlement. The events of 26 December 1787 at the Comédie-Italienne, like those earlier in Angers, Bordeaux, and elsewhere in the kingdom, emphasized the difficulties faced by the monarchy in its efforts to police the theaters. Bourbon governments from the time of the Sun King to the eve of the Revolution never satisfactorily reconciled the desire to maintain order with the need to protect the

[80] Ibid., 8.
[81] Ibid., 10.

persons of the king's subjects. But while the monarchy failed to come to grips with the pit, writers, playwrights, and other observers proposed new discursive strategies for understanding the actions of the men in the pit; the most important of these constructions, like that of Meister's neighbor, equated the parterre with the nation.

6

The Parterre and French National Identity in the Eighteenth Century

It is this . . . parterre which acquits the debt of the nation; it is this parterre which welcomes heros and rewards them; it is this parterre which distinguished Prince Henry; it is this parterre, finally, which pays an authentic tribute to every sort of talent. The King of Sweden arrived at the Opera after it had started; the parterre made them lower the curtain and begin again. No other nation is as susceptible to these vivid demonstrations that honor one by one men who have become famous in all genres. Sensitivity and enthusiasm are communicated there in an instant; hommage is prompt, and never mean-spirited: no other people knows how to pay tribute in this manner, and certainly not with as much grace and vivacity. It knows how to create the finest and most delicate allusions; the most ingenious turns of spirit come all at once from these assembled men; it is the eruption of a volcano; the acclamations form but a single voice.

—Louis-Sébastien Mercier, *Tableau de Paris*, 1788

Not long after the events that occurred in the parterre of the Comédie-Italienne in late December 1787, Mercier published this passage in his widely circulated underground work. The parterre that he invoked was not characterized by its fierce resistance to the policing agents of the state, although, as we have seen earlier, Mercier was well aware of disciplinary abuses in the pit. The playwright and patriot of the 1770s chose instead to praise the ability of hundreds of men to send, unanimously and instantaneously, subtle messages to the performers and political figures who appeared before them. By the late 1780s, he suggested, the parterre as a collective entity had become more politically self-conscious than the spectators who had jeered the *Hérode et Mariamne* of Voltaire off the stage in 1724, and it had transcended the disorderly image that the police constantly invoked to justify their violent incursions into the pit. The parterre, according to Mercier, exercised the sovereign power it had acquired in the theater to express the sentiments of the French nation. His remarks indicate that outside the circle of

191

royal ministers, military officers, and municipal officials who understood the parterre as a place of sedition, it was possible to perceive assembled parterre spectators as representatives of the French people.

The theater, of course, had never occupied an apolitical position within the political culture of Bourbon absolutism. We have seen the uses to which both Richelieu and Louis XIV put the theater in their own time; after the death of the Sun King, theatrical apologists formulated a secular doctrine that emphasized the moral benefits that a properly administered theater might bring to civil society and, by implication, to the welfare of the state itself. Beginning in the 1740s, theater became a tool of foreign conquest for French generals such as Maurice de Saxe and the Comte de Lowenthal. After 1750, playhouses signified the potential hegemony of Parisian culture on the provincial urban landscape, and in the overseas colonies public theaters reinforced the imperial claims of French civilization.[1] By the end of the 1770s, as we shall see, the progressive perfection of the morals and aesthetics of the French stage had become a key component in the writings of those who sought to glorify the cultural identity of the French nation and the monarchy that ruled over it. In contrast, those who believed in the aftermath of the 1771–74 Maupeou crisis that the Crown had become a tyrannical institution that threatened the liberties of the French pointed to the allegedly abusive government tutelage of the public theaters in support of their arguments.

Neither side had much to say specifically about the occupants of the parterre before the 1770s; they understood the theater, as it related to French national identity, to consist of performances by morally virtuous performers and plays written by elegant, entertaining men of letters. Theatrical history and practice, as many writers understood them, did not include the actions of spectators in the theaters; these interventions were confined to the realm of the anecdotal, a popular genre even before 1750, to be sure, but one that lacked the *gravitas* of works devoted to performers and playwrights. After the reign of Louis XV, however, exclusion of audiences from French theater history began to change, first in the 1775 publication of the *Anecdotes dramatiques*, a sprawling three-volume compendium of theater anecdotes that often highlighted the actions of spectators in the theater, and then in the debates that began in 1777 regarding the value of installing benches in the parterres of the Parisian public theaters. In both these instances, writers and readers began to understand the

---

[1] Anne Boes, *La Lanterne magique de l'histoire: essai sur le théâtre historique en France de 1750 à 1789*, published as SVEC 23 (1982), 93–94; Fuchs, *La Vie théâtrale*, 105–7; Joan Dayan, *Haiti, History, and the Gods* (Berkeley, 1995), 182–86.

assembly of parterre spectators, diverse in its composition yet imperious in its judgment, as a metaphor for the nation whose political sovereignty was gaining momentum. Mercier's claims for the parterre should be understood within the context of these developments in the theaters and the kingdom at large.

Theater and French National Identity

In the seventeenth century, in spite of Richelieu's activities and Louis XIV's intervention in the public theater in 1680, most individuals who discussed the merits of the theater did not do so in terms of its usefulness to the state. Rather, from Corneille's earliest successes to the *querelle* between Bossuet and a priest named Caffaro in 1694, observers praised or condemned the stage based on its contribution to Christian morality. After the turn of the century, however, and particularly after the death of the old King in 1715 and the onset of the regency, the terms of the debate began to change.[2] Perhaps as a result of the victory of the "Moderns" in their quarrel with the "Ancients," perhaps owing to an increasingly progressive, secularized outlook on the part of educated French individuals after the exhausting wars at the end of the reign of Louis XIV, apologists and attackers alike began to evaluate the stage in terms of its value for civil society, independent of Christian moral imperatives. These new developments manifested themselves, for example, in comments made by the Abbé Terrasson during his lengthy 1715 critique of *The Iliad*. In this work, which also offered a defense of dramatic poetry, the cleric stated that poets should be held primarily to the tenets of "civil and human" morality, not to the strictures of Christian ethics:

> I am well aware that many of these virtues [civility, love of the people, a taste for the arts] would be more strongly felt if they had entered the soul by means of Christian instruction. . . . The majority of people, however, are not prepared for this religious education; it is nevertheless in the public interest [*l'intérêt public*] that these men not become barbarians and scoundrels.[3]

---

[2] Louis Bourquin, "La Controverse sur la comédie au XVIIIe siècle et la lettre à d'Alembert sur les spectacles," *Revue d'histoire littéraire de la France* 26 (1919): 43–87, 555–76; 27 (1920): 548–70; 28 (1921): 549–74, remains the primary guide to these developments through 1750, after which see Margaret M. Moffat, *Rousseau et la querelle du théâtre au XVIIIe siècle* (Paris, 1930), 1–36.

[3] Quoted in Bourquin, "La Controverse" (1919): 571.

It followed from this line of reasoning that a critique of dramatic poetry based in Christian morality, such as that vigorously put forward by Bossuet only two decades earlier, failed to address the moral demands of post–louisquatorzian French society; the dramatic arts, and the comic stage in particular, might serve to reform French morals even if they did not meet church standards. Furthermore, Terrasson suggested, Christian leaders should embrace, rather than denounce, the good that would result from the staging of plays that encouraged civilized behavior on the part of spectators. Another cleric, the Abbé de Saint-Pierre, elaborated on the theater's potential to encourage moral reform in his 1730 "Project to Render the Theater More Useful to the State." Saint-Pierre argued that "good" comedy improved the virtues of spectators, thereby serving the "public utility," a goal presumably in accord with the spread of Christian morality. He recommended a series of heavy-handed state interventions to ensure that the theater performed this morally beneficial function; they included a citizen's oversight committee under the direction of the lieutenant general of police, the creation of playwright laureates who would rewrite older plays and censor newer ones, and the establishment of a second national theater in Paris whose cheaper admission prices would encourage poorer sorts to attend the morally purified theater more frequently. A utopian at heart, he forecast that within a generation every provincial town of thirty thousand souls or more would boast an ethically correct theater to which parents would send their children for instruction as though they were going to church to hear a sermon. "The nation would become ever more polite and civilized, even among the people," he wrote, and "society would become sweeter, more tranquil and happier, with each passing day."[4]

As Saint-Pierre's evocation of the "nation" suggests, it was a short jump from these claims for the cleansing potential of a secular, morally enlightened theater to arguments that glorified the aesthetic taste and moral wisdom of a people who gave birth to such a theater. The writers who penned the first full-scale narratives of the French stage in the 1730s and 1740s readily made this connection. Freed of the need to situate French theater history within the moral theology of the Catholic church, they associated the progress of the French stage with the perfection of French morals, or the advancement of polite society within the Bourbon kingdom. Thus, Pierre-François Godard de Beauchamps, a Comédie-Italienne playwright turned theater historian, could write in his 1735 *Inquiries into the History of the French Theater* that his

---

[4] Ibid., 27:559–60. On Saint-Pierre's political ideas, see Thomas E. Kaiser, "The Abbé de Saint-Pierre, Public Opinion, and the Reconstitution of the French Monarchy," *JMH* 55 (December, 1983): 618–43.

goal was not to decide whether the stage was good or bad, but rather, as a "citizen," to view it as a reflection of its time.[5] For Beauchamps, the plays of Molière served as the hinge of French theater history; the great seventeenth-century comic playwright had fomented a "revolution" in the manners of the nation through his negative depiction of hypocrites, misanthropes, and avaricious individuals. His merit in the age of Louis XIV was greater than that of Virgil during the reign of Augustus, "because the Frenchman did more good for his nation than the Roman did honor to his."[6] The better-known *History of the French Theater*, published by the Parfaict brothers in fifteen volumes between 1735 and 1749, also recounted the progressive perfection of the French stage. In this work, Corneille and Racine shared responsibility with Molière for these developments; the example of Corneille in particular had purified "public taste" and obliged the tragic playwright's competitors to elevate the quality of their work.[7]

Thus, by the time Rousseau published the *Letter to d'Alembert on the Theater* in 1758, he was responding not only to the *Encyclopédie* article on Geneva written by d'Alembert, but also to a secular tradition of pro-theatrical writing in France, a position that was firmly implanted in the minds of his readers after several decades in which it had often appeared in print. In one sense, Rousseau ignored the arguments of the pro-theatrical writers of preceding decades, because he contended that the problem was not the role of the public theater in shaping civic morals, but rather the theatricalization of social intercourse itself, the regrettable tendency of the French to model their encounters on the spectator-spectacle relationship encouraged in the theaters.[8] In another sense, however, he reinforced the association between the genres and practices of the Parisian stage and the emerging cultural identity of the French in the eighteenth century. Writers from Terrasson onward had assigned the stage a central place in the fashioning of French national character; Rousseau, for all his hostility to the "effeminized" theatricality of the Parisian *monde*, insisted on the primacy of the theater, metaphorically understood, in the construction of that world. In other words, for Rousseau, theatricalized behavior animated the French variant of civilization on which he had declared war by the late 1750s; d'Alembert's suggestion that Geneva adopt a public theater

[5] Pierre-François Godard de Beauchamps, *Recherches sur les Théâtres de France* . . . (Paris, 1735), 1:162.
[6] Ibid., 1:367.
[7] François et Claude Parfaict, *Histoire du Théâtre François* . . . 15 vols. (Paris, 1735–49).
[8] See David Marshall, "Rousseau and the State of Theater," *Representations* 13 (Winter 1986): 84–114.

modeled after the French example struck Rousseau as the death knell for the virtuous, hard-working Genevan citizens whose interests he thought he was defending.[9] Rousseau's *Letter to d'Alembert* provoked a number of responses in the following two years, many of which turned on the public usefulness of the French theater; although these debates did not resolve the antitheatrical doubts that Rousseau had forcefully resurrected, they did further the association of moral progress (or corruption) in France with the effects generated by the theater.[10]

While these debates regarding the secular merits of the theater unfolded, the monarchy continued its oversight of the privileged stages' repertory and personnel, and its policing of theaters. Since 1715, though, outside of court performances and occasional *gratis* performances in the Parisian public theaters to celebrate royal births or military victories, the King's government had not turned its explicit attention to the exploitation of the public theater for purposes that we would call propagandistic. In the mid-1760s, however, in the wake of substantial colonial losses to the British after the Seven Years War, the royal ministers seized on the theater as one of several forums through which the monarchy might reingratiate itself with the King's subjects. In the immediate aftermath of the peace in 1763, the Duc de Choiseul, head of the King's government at the time, asked the comic writer and librettist Charles-Simon Favart to compose a comic opera that would commemorate the peace.[11] The play, *The Englishman at Bordeaux*, romantically linked a French brother and sister with their English counterparts. The peace between England and France resolved the love complications and permitted the two couples to marry, after which the play concluded with "a dance of many nations, even the negroes," and several couplets. It was favorably received at the Comédie-Française and at court and performed approximately thirty times in the first half of 1763. In spite of the play's popularity, however, it was unclear whether it generated the patriotic sentiment that the government had desired; one commentator noted that several parterre voices had cried out "Vive le Roi!" during the first performance but that the cry had not been generally adopted by the audience.[12]

Two years later, however, a nonlyric play on a theme from France's medieval history excited patriotic enthusiasm among theatergoers in Paris

[9] See note 32 in chapter 5.
[10] Moffat, *Rousseau et la querelle*, 112–78, especially her summary on 173–78.
[11] MS, I:188–91, 194; Collé, *Journal et mémoires sur les hommes de lettres*, 2:292–93, 310; Boes, *La Lanterne magique*, 94–95.
[12] MS, I:190.

and throughout the Francophone world.[13] No evidence exists to suggest that any high government figure commissioned Pierre-Laurent Buirette de Belloy, an itinerant actor and playwright, to write a play based on the English siege of Calais during the fourteenth century; however, once the King's ministers observed the patriotic fervor that swept Parisian audiences who attended the *Siege of Calais*, they took a number of steps to assure the performance of the play throughout the kingdom. Belloy's play emphasized the courage of the mayor of Calais, his son, and four other hostages, who were prepared to sacrifice their lives for the preservation of the town. Ultimately, the English King acknowledged their heroism, released them, and ended the siege. Belloy filled his play with endless patriotic speeches designed to boost the flagging national spirit of the French after the disastrous Seven Years War. In the first act, for example, one character chides:

> Misfortune to nations who, ceding to the storm,
> Allow their setbacks to debase their courage,
> And do not dare to brave the fate that challenges them
> Until, finally, they cease to believe in themselves.

Further along in the fourth act one finds:

> The imperious example of the Heros of Calais . . .
> Reaching to the depths of hearts compassionate and confused
> Will spark a search for honor, and awaken our virtues.[14]

Some theater spectators, left apathetic in the wake of a war that they believed the King's ministers had mishandled, rallied to these evocations of past French heroism. Immediately after the enthusiastic reception granted the play's premiere, Bachaumont noted that the work was "a sermon for the monarchy which the government must protect, spread, and make understood by the entire nation."[15] The King's ministers, rapidly seizing on this gift handed to them to regain the favor of the populace, acted on a number of fronts. A little more than a week after the

---

[13] Boes, *La Lanterne magique*, 95–103; Lennart Breitholz, *Le Théâtre historique en France jusqu'à la Révolution* (Uppsala, 1952), 192 ff.; Margaret M. Moffat, "'Le Siège de Calais' et l'opinion publique en 1765," *Revue d'histoire littéraire de la France* 39 (1932): 339–54; and Clarence D. Brenner, *L'Histoire nationale dans la tragédie française du XVIIIe siècle* (Berkeley, 1929), 251–66.

[14] Both quotes cited in Moffat, "Le Siège de Calais," 348.

[15] MS, 2:157.

play's Parisian debut, Louis XV and the court witnessed a performance at Versailles; afterward, in a widely publicized proclamation, the King granted Belloy a generous pension and gave him a medal that, though created in 1758 to honor successful dramatists, had not previously been awarded. A month after the premiere, the King ordered the Comédie-Française to give a free performance of the play, during which the attentive audience cried out, "Vive le Roi and M. de Belloy!" By this time, the enthusiasm for the play had spread to the provinces, where the play was performed in many of the larger towns. According to his 1779 biographer, Belloy received enthusiastic letters from many military garrisons where the play was staged, and his play was printed and distributed to each company with the inscription "to inspire our current soldiers with the sentiments possessed by their ancestors."[16] By midsummer, the military governor of the Caribbean colony on Saint-Domingue had printed and distributed copies of the play at his own expense; the title page claimed that the *Siege of Calais* was the first French play printed in the Americas. The same year, the town council of Calais voted to make Belloy a full citizen, in addition to placing a bust of the playwright in the town hall. The next year, the official *Journal des Sçavans*, which had judiciously waited to review the play so that it would reflect the true judgment of the public, announced that it considered the play to be the "first French national tragedy."[17]

The Choiseul ministry's response to the enthusiasm for Belloy's play marked a new stage in the growing association between the stage and national identity. Previously, following a pattern established under Louis XIV, the Crown used the dramatic arts as a means to represent the glory of the reigning monarch, usually as a part of court ritual. The patriotism provoked by the *Siege of Calais* created an opportunity for the monarchy to stage national sentiment in urban spaces throughout the kingdom and beyond. Not all observers were optimistic about the new uses of the theater, however. Grimm, for example, complained that even though "idiots say that this tragedy is the work of the nation," the play was so poorly written that it was misplaced, puerile, and far from the true grandeur necessary for the state." Later, he noted that those who dared to speak with little enthusiasm of the play were considered bad citizens, "or, worse,

---

[16] Gabriel Henri Gaillard, ed. *Oeuvres complettes de M. de Belloy, de l'Académie françoise, citoyen de Calais*, 6 vols. (Paris, 1779); 2:340. Another corporal, stationed in Metz, wrote on behalf of his eight squadrons, who had heard a reading of the play, to express that his soldiers "shared with the entire Nation the sentiments of gratitude you are due." Ibid., 2:342.
[17] *Journal des Sçavans*, March 1766, 175.

philosophes," and that future "national plays" already being commissioned were bound to fail miserably.[18]

Thus, the political and moral uses of the theater had become weightier yet also more unsettled questions by the end of the 1760s than at any time since the reign of Louis XIV. Rousseau's diatribe had provided a blueprint for antitheatricalists to attack the public theater on secular terms; the government's use of the patriotic fervor inspired by the *Siege of Calais* threatened to provoke its own backlash that might well discredit the privileged stage as a mere organ of propaganda for the regime. During the Maupeou years, the arguments of historians, critics, and government ministers and censors regarding the historical trajectory of the French theater came under further scrutiny, just as the Crown's claims regarding the historical legitimacy of ministerial government suffered damage when confronted by patriot propaganda. Of course, the triumphalist narrative of French theatrical history, which had emerged in the 1730s and was reiterated in subsequent decades, still found its way into print in the 1770s; indeed, Voltaire had forcefully restated this position in the 1770 preface to his *Sophonisbe* when he wrote that "of all the arts cultivated in France, the theater is the one, by common consent of all foreigners, which most honors our fatherland. The Italians are still our masters in music and painting, and the English in philosophy, but in the art of Sophocles we have no rivals."[19]

One prominent example of the continuing presence of French theatrical chauvinism was a 1777 essay published by the lawyer and man of letters Nicolas-Toussaint le Moyne des Essarts, *Les Trois théâtres de Paris*.[20] Des Essarts began his professional life as a barrister, but by the late 1770s he was also an author who wrote respectable works for establishment figures in government and the literary world. He intended his *Trois théâtres*, which was a narrative compilation of royal edicts, ordinances, and administrative precedents regarding the three privileged theaters, to complement already existing theater histories that he thought had neglected the evolution of these regulations. In a sense, he wished to claim that the policing of the theaters, theoretically outlined by his predecessor de la Mare at the beginning of the century, had succeeded by its end in integrating the public theater into the well-policed world of the capital. Des Essarts' introduction to this work, his "General Reflections on the Theater," stated the case for the merits of the French theater, as presented in the privileged playhouses of Paris, in unmistakable terms. First, following Voltaire's lead,

---

[18] CL, 4:182, 223–24.
[19] Voltaire, *Oeuvres completes* (Kehl, 1785), 5:418–19.
[20] Nicolas Toussaint le Moyne, dit des Essarts. *Les Trois théâtres de Paris . . .* (Paris, 1777).

he listed the advantages of the French stage over its European competitors, a greatness that he believed even foreigners were forced to acknowledge:

> It is in France where one finds the most orderly and the most decent theaters. The immortal plays of Corneille, Racine, Voltaire, Crébillon, etc., have granted the French theater the greatest imaginable superiority over those of other nations. This is why foreigners flock to our theaters to admire the productions of these geniuses who have enriched the French stage, and it is why, even in their own countries, they pay secret hommage to this aspect of our national glory.[21]

Des Essarts' claims marked just how important the theater had become to French national identity since the time of Bossuet's denunciation of the stage at the end of the previous century. Beyond his admittedly chauvinistic sentiments, however, he also argued that the French stage deserved its lofty reputation because its actors were now morally pure and its plays provided the nation with lessons of civic virtue:

> Never have our theaters been more frequented nor more purified than they are today. These stages no longer offer vulgar farces or deformed plays, and the actors are no longer buffoons who cater to the common tastes of the people. Our plays now unite pleasure with virtue and morality, and our performers combine talent with honesty and decency, so that one must admit there is hardly a more agreeable form of relaxation for a civilized nation.[22]

In other words, in des Essarts' view, the French stage under the tutelage of royal administrators and the genius of modern French playwrights had shed the questionable characteristics that had led to its religious and civil condemnation in previous centuries; while others might express Rousseauian doubts about the stage, he believed that in the age of the Enlightenment, the theater exemplified French civilization and cultural superiority.

This official view of the contribution of French theater to French national identity was not, however, without its challengers.[23] In the early and mid-1770s, during and just after the Maupeou crisis, a younger gen-

---

[21] Des Essarts, *Trois théâtres*, 1.

[22] Ibid., 2.

[23] Gelbart, *Feminine and Opposition Journalism*, 207–88, tells the story of the rise and fall of what she terms "frondeur" theater criticism in the 1770s and early 1780s. Gregory S. Brown, "A Field of Honor: The Cultural Politics of Playwrighting in Eighteenth-Century France" (Ph.D. diss., Columbia University, 1997), 168–306, situates these authors' actions among the strategies used by dramatic writers for social advancement in the 1770s.

eration of playwrights, spurned by the play selection committee at the Comédie-Française, began to air dissenting views in more public forums. The most visible of these men was Mercier, an admirer of republicanism and author of a number of *drames,* or moralizing comedies, set in contemporary France and peopled with nonaristocratic characters. Mercier's plays were performed throughout the French provinces in the 1760s and early 1770s, but their social and political messages scared off the Comédie-Française and its courtly overseers. In 1773, in the midst of the Maupeou crisis, Mercier published a long, heated attack on the privileges of the Comédie-Française, titled *Du Théâtre, ou Nouvel essai sur l'art dramatique.* This work, printed in Amsterdam and smuggled into France, condemned the stupidity of a system, established almost a century earlier, which prevented Parisian theater troupes from staging works necessary for the education of French citizens. He criticized both actors and the government for subverting the civic function that the stage should naturally play in the affairs of a healthy polity; Mercier's language and sympathies were in line with other expressions of patriot disgust vented during this period.[24]

This moment of public protest against the court and the Comédie-Française was short lived, however; Charles-Georges Coqueley de Chaussepierre, a censor, colleague of des Essarts, and one of several attorneys who advised the Comédie-Française, used his government connections in 1777 and 1778 to have himself appointed as the censor of these papers. He then shut them down or delivered them into the hands of the publishing titan Charles-Joseph Panckoucke.[25] In spite of Nina Gelbart's characterization of Mercier and his radical cohort as "*frondeur* journalists," the coherency of their position was questionable; while they were united by their dislike for the Comédie-Française, which they believed muffled the political vitality of the theater and stifled their own dramaturgical voices, they did not necessarily agree on an appropriate remedy for the French stage. The incoherence of their position was evident in the group's collapse and dispersal in the wake of Coqueley's attack; later in the decade, a very different kind of organization, the Société des auteurs dramatiques, formed under the impetus of Beaumarchais to pursue the interests of playwrights.[26]

[24] See, however, the critique of *Du Théâtre* in CL, 10:463, which dismisses the author's "youthful passions," and suggests that the true purpose of Mercier's tract is to argue for the merits of his "insipid" *drames* over the classic works of Corneille, Racine, and Molière.

[25] Gelbart, *Feminist and Opposition Journalism,* 219–47, richly details the development of this periodical network and its subsequent dismantling by Coquelay.

[26] On the shifting alliances of playwrights from the 1750s to the early years of the Revolution, and in particular on the history of the Société des auteurs dramatiques founded by Beaumarchais in 1777, see Brown, "A Field of Honor," 308–529.

Nevertheless, the print appearance of the charges levied by Mercier and his discontented, radicalized cohorts in 1775 and 1776 belied the rosy picture painted by Comédie-Française supporters such as des Essarts the following year. Actual abuses that had persisted at the theater for decades, combined with the voices of radical critics forged during the Maupeou crisis, called the triumphalist narrative of French stage history into question. The contentious claims of Mercier and other radical journalists injected the political discontent of the Maupeou period into evaluations of the Comédie-Française in particular and French theater in general. Henceforth, it would be difficult to read apologists such as des Essarts without knowing that patriot commentators would interpret his defense of the French stage as a justification of absolutist tyranny in the cultural realm; this final politicization of the "theater question," in turn, was only conceivable in a climate in which patriot propaganda had questioned the workings of the fundamental political institutions of the kingdom.[27]

These discussions of French theater history, however, rarely turned to direct examination of the activities of parterre spectators, the most socially heterogeneous and most vocal group in the theater. The parterre might appear to be an obvious metaphor for the "nation" or the "people," yet writers did not often make use of it before 1770. The reason lies in part with the relegation of the parterre to the realm of the anecdotal by French theater historians.

The Anecdotal History of the Parterre

Only one theater historian, Beauchamps, in 1735, had attempted to incorporate a discussion of parterre spectators into his interpretation of the theatrical past.[28] In a section of his work titled "Discourse on the Comédie-Française," Beauchamps followed a panegyric of Molière with an equivocal evocation of the "parterre françois," in which he concluded that "the parterre is an undefinable being; but its contradictions are familiar from our ways of thinking and our morals." Ultimately for Beauchamps, the "parterre" exhibited both the strengths and weaknesses of the French; if it was "undefinable," he implied, this was because the French themselves, in their contradictions, escaped easy categorization. But it may also be that

---

[27] On the political culture of the Maupeou period, see Shanti M. Singham, "A Conspiracy of Twenty Million Frenchmen: Public Opinion, Patriotism, and the Assault on Absolutism during the Maupeou Years, 1770–1775" (Ph.D. diss., Princeton University, 1991).

[28] Beauchamps, *Recherches*, 1:369–76.

the parterre appeared undefinable in the 1730s because the categories necessary to make the more politicized analogies found later in the century did not yet exist; the "many-headed" monster of Regnard's 1692 Comédie-Italienne farce had not yet given way to the solid respectability of the "nation." The anecdotal characterizations of the parterre, which began with Beauchamps and the Parfaicts, began to offer new possibilities in the decades that followed.

Although historians and commentators over the next thirty years chose not to offer interpretations of parterre comportment that called on tropes of French national character, they continued the work of compilation begun by Beauchamps and others in the 1730s. Theater anecdotes appeared with increasing regularity in the dictionaries, tables, and other print compendia published from 1735 onward. This steady increase in theater anecdotes paralleled the popularity of the anecdotal genre at large in eighteenth-century France; periodical editors grew increasingly fond of "anecdotes" or "fait divers" sections, and publishers churned out compendiums of anecdotes related to a variety of topics. In the eighteenth-century French dictionaries, including the *Encyclopédie*, lexicographers defined *anecdotes* as *choses inconnues* or *choses non publiées*. Implicitly, then, anecdotes were bits of information that had remained outside the published realm until the moment when a writer or compiler chose to make them public; or, as Voltaire commented in his *Siècle de Louis XIV*, "anecdotes are a narrow field where one gleans after the vast harvest of History."[29] But the newness of the anecdote's publicity, that which made it interesting or valuable, also called into question its plausibility. The fact that the anecdote was not widely known rendered it less credible; the possibility always existed that an anecdote's author might have fabricated it. The anecdote, therefore, poised between fact and fiction, between publicity and obscurity, became the repository of the semiofficial and the slightly illicit. Similar to the *on dit* of eighteenth-century police spies, the anecdote emerged from a hazy world of subjectivity and potential embellishment. This possibility of unwarranted exaggeration or outright falsehood made the anecdote at once more compelling and more questionable. The vogue for theatrical anecdotes culminated in the 1775 publication of the *Anecdotes dramatiques*, a three-volume work edited by the Abbé de La Porte and Jean-Marie Bernard Clément.

Most interpreters of the French theatrical past had been content to avoid a discussion of the actions of parterre spectators, leaving the topic in

---

[29] Voltaire, *Le Siècle de Louis XIV*, in *Oeuvres complètes de Voltaire* (Paris, 1878), 14:421.

the ambiguous realm of the anecdotal. The Abbé de La Porte, however, had taken a different approach. The annual theatrical almanac *Les Spectacles de Paris*, which he had edited since 1751, steadily expanded its anecdotal offerings, in part as a way to increase the historical value of the almanac. La Porte had stressed the merits of this approach to theater history a dozen years earlier in the 1762 edition of his theatrical almanac when he had written, "This collection assembles and observes with care . . . all the happenings which might contribute one day towards a complete history of our theaters." The almanac's publisher kept back issues in stock throughout the latter half of the century, and the Parisian *Affiches* noted in 1769 that "amateur theater lovers collect this work as a way of recording the history of our theater."[30]

In 1775, La Porte and his collaborator, the younger Burgundian tutor and literary critic Clément, prefaced their three volumes of theatrical anecdotes with a brief statement that, inter alia, justified their enterprise through analogies between the "Nation" and the public theater audience:

> One must admit that since there is no People more passionate about the pleasures of the theater than the French, there are no others about whom one can assemble more tales as unique and agreeable on this topic. . . . Since it is at the Theater that a Nation makes itself best known, and discovers its wit without effort, it is perhaps in its dramatic anecdotes, more than in any other history, where one can see the joking character and the effortless wit of the French in all their glory.[31]

Here, then, was a third approach to national identity as constructed within the walls of the playhouse. Rather than emphasizing authorial genius, the performance of civility, or the absence of these characteristics owing to administrative tyranny, the editors of the *Anecdotes dramatiques* restored the agency of audience members by claiming that witty interventions of theater spectators provided the surest guide to national character. This formulation promised a greater role for parterre spectators in the history of the French stage. Beyond this brief preface, however, the editors made no overt efforts to assist their readers in abstracting historical lessons from their three voluminous tomes, each of which approached six hundred pages of small, cramped

---

[30] La Porte, *Les Spectacles de Paris* (1762), unpaginated *avertissement; Affiches, annonces, et avis divers*, 11 January 1769, 6; see the publisher Veuve Duchesne's 1767 catalogue, 1, 22, which lists a price of 1 livre, 4 *sous* for each year's edition.
[31] AD, 1:iii.

type.[32] In what ways, then, did these anecdotes constitute a history of French wit, as the editors promised in their preface? And did this laughter, generated largely at the expense of the institutions, playwrights, and performers of the state-administered stage, carry political implications as well?

La Porte and Clément, the editors of the *Anecdotes dramatiques*, did not contribute directly to any of the radical theater journals of the mid-1770s; but they had good reason to side with what might loosely be termed the anti–Comédie-Française faction. Both were anti-Voltaireans in good standing, a stance that, after the Maupeou crisis, implied an oppositional political position owing to Voltaire's staunch pamphleteering on behalf of the Maupeou reforms. La Porte, an ex-Jesuit and former collaborator of Voltaire's long-standing nemesis Fréron, had been derisively labeled "the most active used clothes peddler in French literature" by the philosophes for his endless compilations and digests of the works of others.[33] Clément, a youthful newcomer to the Parisian literary scene in the 1770s, achieved notoriety during the Maupeou years for his nine letters to Voltaire in which he ravaged the elderly poet's literary output over the course of the century.[34] Although the *Anecdotes* give Voltaire credit for the fecundity and innovation of his dramatic output, particularly in the brief biographical notice found under his name in the third volume, many of the anecdotes associated with his plays emphasize audience disapproval of Voltaire's works when initially performed, or detail Voltaire's machinations to ensure the favorable reception of his dramatic work.

[32] Although the work was published in 1775, its approbation was dated September 1771, and its privilege, January 1772. The discrepancy between the dates of state approval and the actual publication date presumably accounts for the failure to incorporate all of the work's anecdotes into one alphabetical list of plays. All of the first volume and half the second contained an alphabetical list of plays followed by anecdotes that related to them in some fashion; some of the plays were listed without anecdote. The editors devoted the next two hundred pages of the second volume to a second alphabetical list, called a *supplément*, which added plays and anecdotes not included in the main list. Some of these plays and anecdotes had transpired since the original composition of the *Anecdotes* in the early '70s; others may have been deemed more acceptable in the post-Maupeou era. The second volume finished with anecdotes related to foreign stages from classical antiquity to the contemporary world, including *anecdotes asiatiques* and more *anecdotes françoises*. All but one hundred pages of the final volume catalogued anecdotes related to actors or authors, rather than plays and their performances. The volume concluded with *additions*, another thirty-page alphabetical list of plays and their anecdotes not previously included, and a reprinting of the regulations and personnel of the three privileged troupes as of 1775.

[33] Jean-François de la Harpe, a highly successful disciple of Voltaire within the world of letters, commented that La Porte was "le fripier le plus actif de notre littérature." See also the mock eulogy of La Porte in MF, January 1780, 139–42.

[34] Clément, *Lettres à M. de Voltaire*, 3 vols. (La Haye, 1773–76).

The first paragraphs of the work's preface provided further evidence of the editors' literary and political sympathies for discerning readers. There, the editors stated that the idea for the work, as well as many of the anecdotes, came from Voltaire's long-standing rival and Clément's countryman, the Burgundian dramatist and poet Alexis Piron, who had passed away in January 1773. La Porte and Clément's preface also mentions a second, anonymous individual, an avid theatergoer, who had provided material collected over several decades of involvement with the Parisian theaters; this secret collaborator was Charles Collé, whose plays had repeatedly been rejected by the Comédie-Française.[35] Thus La Porte and Clément proclaimed at the outset of the work that their inspiration and their information came from sources indifferent, if not hostile, to the Comédie-Française and that the anecdotes collected would not serve the cause of the privileged troupe and its courtly overseers. Favorable biographical notices for authors such as Mercier, Palissot, and Cailhava de l'Estendoux, who were publicly at odds with the Comédie-Française in the 1770s, reinforced the editors' anti–Comédie-Française sympathies.[36] At the same time, it is difficult to characterize the *Anecdotes* itself as a *frondeur* publication. The editors of the *Anecdotes* were at times lukewarm in their praise of some of the radical theater critics, and their biographical note on Beaumarchais, already celebrated for *The Barber of Seville* and his legal memoires against the financier Goezmann, damned Beaumarchais's theatrical innovations with ironic praise. And although the editors appended sympathetic anecdotes to Mercier's *drames*, they included stories and editorial asides elsewhere that suggested a strong antipathy to the new genre theorized by Diderot and practiced by Mercier and other radical theater critics.[37]

Not surprisingly, therefore, it is difficult to discern a coherent representation of the parterre from the many anecdotes in which it is mentioned. Perhaps it is more accurate to say that several different "parterres" occupy the pages of the *Anecdotes*. For example, a strain of anecdotes in which parterre members display examples of their devastating wit is included. When a much-maligned actor upbraids the audience by crying, "Ungrateful parterre, what have I done to you?" jokers at the box office the next day ask not

---

[35] Collé, *Journal et mémoires sur les hommes de lettres*, 3:275–76; a good number of the anecdotes in La Porte and Clément's compilation appear word for word as Collé first penned them in his journal.

[36] AD, 3:81 (Cailhava); AD, 3:334–35 (Mercier); and AD, 3:371–74 (Pallissot).

[37] See AD, 1:378, which praised Jean-Baptiste Rousseau's 1696 comedy *Le Flatteur*, at the expense of the *drame*.

for parterre tickets but rather for "ungratefuls."[38] When a new Harlequin debuts to hoots and derision, he tells the spectators that he will play the role again the next day, then burn his costume and retire if he does not find favor with the audience. At the following performance, parterre members throw boxes of matches on the stage when he appears.[39] And when a character in the Chevalier de La Morlière's rapidly disintegrating 1754 one-act *La Créole* relates to another the events of a feast he has just attended and then sums up by saying, "All of this isn't worth a damn," parterre spectators chant the line in chorus until the actors halt the performance.[40]

Other anecdotes give the impression that parterre spectators willingly cede to the authority of actors whom they admire. Michel Baron, a youthful contemporary of Molière who returned to the stage in the early eighteenth century after a thirty-year retirement, serves as the source for several of these stories. In one instance, he is playing the lead role, an adolescent, in Racine's *Britannicus*. The audience, struck by the contrast between the character and the eighty-year-old actor playing the role, begins to disrupt the performance with laughter. According to the anecdote, Baron interrupts the performance, advances to the edge of the stage, then crosses his arms and stares at the pit for a moment before heaving a profound sigh and announcing, "Ungrateful parterre, which I educated in my youth!" The audience reportedly listened to the rest of the play in respectful silence.[41] The tragic actress Duclos also supposedly chastised the parterre during the premiere performance of Antoine Houdart de La Motte's *Inès de Castro* in 1723. The presence of child actors in the tragedy's climactic scene, an innovation at that time on the French stage, provoked several *plaisanteries* from parterre audience members. Irritated by this response, Duclos, playing the title character, interrupted the scene in indignation to tell the parterre, "Go ahead and laugh, foolish Parterre, at the most beautiful moment in the play!" According to the *Anecdotes*, she then resumed her character, the parterre applauded the child actors, and the play was a huge success.[42]

The parterres of the *Anecdotes dramatiques* were therefore witty, yet also submissive, and unpleasantly aggressive, but also inconstant. These conflicting representations of the parterre, recorded alongside each other in this huge, at times poorly edited compilation of anecdotes, indicate the

---

[38] AD, 1:58. This episode supposedly occurred in Lyon in 1673.
[39] AD, 1:261, supposedly in Brussels at some unspecified time.
[40] AD, 1:237.
[41] AD, 1: 160–61; see similar Baron anecdotes at AD, 1:202–3; and AD, 2:137.
[42] AD, 1:447.

difficulty of distilling the political sympathies of the parterre from the *Anecdotes*.[43] Often in the *Anecdotes*, parterre spectators confirm their collective support for the monarchy; evocations of Louis XVI and Marie-Antoinette in 1774–1775 provide evidence of the effort to craft an anecdotal parterre that is sympathetic to the Crown. The *Anecdotes* report, for example, that when the royal couple were still Dauphin and Dauphine in the early 1770s, they requested that the Comédie-Française stage the *Siège de Calais* for their first appearance at the privileged theater. The ensuing performance reportedly became an opportunity for audience members to express their support for the future King and Queen:

> There were moments in the performance when a sort of dialogue seemed to form between the future King and the Nation. All the French hearts repeated energetic expressions of love, zeal, and fidelity for the Prince which the author had put in the mouth of the Calais heros.

The Dauphin, in turn, was supposedly the first to applaud lines from the play that reminded him of his duty toward the people.[44] Anecdotes that postdate the death of the old King also suggest the love of parterre spectators for their new sovereigns; when the theaters reopened in 1774 after the death of Louis XV, at the Comédie-Italienne an *opéra-comique* that included the lines "Vive le Roi!" caused the parterre to sing these words with an enthusiasm that was repeated when an actor onstage followed with the cry "Vive la Reine!" At the Comédie-Française the same night, the parterre raucously associated the tag line "Show Héraclius to the people who await him," with the advent of the new reign.[45]

Thus, La Porte and Clément's sprawling compendium of theatrical anecdotes offered several strategies to reduce the heterogeneity of parterre spectators to a unitary representation endowed with one or two prominent characteristics. These representations, being anecdotal, had a tenuous relation to the past; they did not express historical fact as much as they captured the desires of a present, that of the first half of the 1770s. Consider one final, striking entry from the *Anecdotes dramatiques*:

> The Great Condé was forced to lift his siege of the Spanish town of Lerida during the campaign of Catalonia [in 1647]. Not long afterwards, this

---

[43] The *Année littéraire* (1775), tome 7, 73–93, esp. 93, for example, noted the unfortunate repetition of several anecdotes at different points throughout the volume; the reviewer might have noted dozens more examples of shoddy editorial work.
[44] AD, 2:177–78.
[45] AD, 3:493–94. See also AD, 3:520.

Prince found himself at the premiere of a play whose author he protected, and against whom the cabal continually agitated. The Prince, indignant that his presence did not command more respect from the audience, arose in his loge and pointed to a man in the parterre who seemed to be making more noise than anyone else. "Seize that man there for me!" commanded the Prince. The man turned defiantly towards Condé and responded: "You will never seize me; I am called Lerida!" And no sooner had he spoken these words than he disappeared in the crowded parterre, lost from view, and escaped the Prince. It is said that the Great Condé, once his anger had passed, admired this firm, witty retort so much that he tried to discover the identity of the anonymous spectator, promising to grant him many favors. But the spectator, who had known how to speak so well, knew how to maintain his silence even better; he has remained forever incognito.[46]

The incident purportedly memorialized in this anecdote occurred in the distant past, just before the outbreak of the Fronde in the mid-seventeenth century. Yet it also offered a potentially devastating comment on the post-Maupeou, post–Louis XV political situation. The story might have appealed to readers for a number of reasons: the dramatic confrontation of the great military hero with the anonymous parterre spectator, the spirited and critical *bon mot* of the audience member, or the reported admiration of the Prince, bested in this public encounter by a social inferior. All these elements resonated with a readership who had just lived through a successful challenge to perceived royal despotism. But the anecdote is also noteworthy for its representation of the parterre as a disorderly mass of individuals who harbored within their midst the anonymous, impertinent, yet well-founded voice of criticism. The devastating retort of the parterre spectator, and the Prince's unsuccessful efforts to learn his identity, suggested that the penetrating insight of the people regarding affairs of state was beyond the control and manipulation of France's aristocratic elites. Assembled parterre spectators, in this anecdote, constituted an unassailable repository for the political wisdom of the nation.

Two years after the publication of the *Anecdotes dramatiques*, many playwrights, men of letters, and theatrical spectators moved beyond the realm of the anecdotal to a direct discussion of the political implications of parterre practices. This debate was occasioned by a proposal to install benches in the parterres of the capital's privileged theaters, a seemingly inconsequential suggestion that was freighted with meaning.

[46] AD, 2:578.

Debates over Seating the Parterre

The idea of seating the parterre was not new in the 1770s. More than a century earlier, in his 1657 proposal *Pour le rétablissement du théâtre françois*, the dramatic theorist Aubignac had proposed to remedy theater disorders by installing fixed seating in the pit.[47] Voltaire, whose plays at times fell victim to unruly audiences, echoed these sentiments in his "Dissertation sur la tragédie ancienne et moderne," which served as a preface to the print version of his 1748 tragedy, *Sémiramis*.[48] In the course of stating his case for the excellence of French tragedy in general (and his tragedy in particular), he decried the "poor taste" and "lack of dignity" inherent in the "tennis courts" where the French viewed their masterpieces. Certainly, he thought, the genius of Corneille and Racine deserved better than to be played in front of "those who stand in what is known as the parterre, where the spectators are cramped and indecently jostled, and where they sometimes hurl themselves precipitously against each other, as though participating in a popular riot" (*sédition populaire*).[49]

Thus, Voltaire identified the parterre as a space dominated by a popular culture incompatible with the high-culture products of the privileged Comédie-Française. In his view, the plays of Corneille and Racine belonged to an elitist milieu that could only be sullied by its commerce with the urban masses and their popular riots. After the elimination of stage seating in 1759 and 1760, a number of calls for reform in the parterre appeared in the next decade and a half.[50] The architectural discourse of the period exhibited this tendency; in both their texts and their drawings, the era's most prominent theater architects took up Voltaire's challenge to eliminate the taint of "popular riot" from the pit. In his courses on architecture, offered in the 1750s and published in 1771, Jacques-François Blondel recommended that the parterre be replaced in all French theaters by a series of graded benches. This innovation would "eliminate tumult and procure the tranquility of our playhouses, which they would perhaps enjoy only imperfectly without these precautions."[51] Ledoux, a student of Blondel, imple-

---

[47] L'Abbé d'Aubignac, *Pour le rétablissement du Théâtre François*, reprinted in Pierre Martino, ed., *La Pratique du théâtre* (Paris, 1927), 397. I discuss the seating debates in greater detail in Jeffrey S. Ravel, "Seating the Public: Spheres and Loathing in the Paris Theaters, 1777–1788," *FHS* 18 (Spring 1993): 173–210.

[48] Voltaire, "Dissertation sur la tragédie ancienne et moderne," in *Oeuvres complètes de Voltaire* (Paris, 1877), 4:487–503.

[49] Voltaire, "Dissertation," 499.

[50] For example, see Bricaire de la Dixmairie, *Lettre sur l'état présent de nos spectacles* (Amsterdam, 1765); and CL, 7:450–51.

[51] Jacques-François Blondel, *Cours d'architecture . . .* (Paris, 1771), 2:266.

mented these precepts in the seated parterre of the Besançon public theater, which he designed at this time. In a 1775 letter to the Burgundian *intendant* who oversaw the project, Ledoux complained that only in the pits of French theaters was the "poorest part of humanity" condemned to be on its feet for two hours. In his theater, however, purged of a standing parterre, Ledoux said, "the cabal will end, and we will judge authors more rationally once we have destroyed what is incorrectly called the enthusiasm of the parterre."[52] Both master and student thus sought to "perfect" French theater through architectural modifications that would inhibit unseemly parterre behavior.

The same concerns were at work in a 1771 engraving of the proposed interior for the new Comédie-Française theater in Paris by the building's eventual architect, Charles de Wailly (figure 11). This drawing, destined for public display at the Salon of 1771, suggested the new importance of the theater as civic monument and harbinger of urban renewal in the late-eighteenth-century metropolis.[53] It also foretold the coming attempts at parterre regulation. Inside the hall, the lateral view adopted by de Wailly presented a ground level entirely filled with benches. The segment closest to the stage, which housed the orchestra, and the next section, the parquet, had contained benches in the old theater since the remodeling of 1759. But the largest section of the floor area, the parterre, contained fifteen rows of benches in this imaginary rendering, leaving no room for standing spectators. In place of the overflowing crowds that frequently stood in the parterre, de Wailly populated his drawing of the seated pit with half a dozen male figures who calmly conversed or watched the play. He removed the multitude who previously occupied the pit to the third balcony, out of the view of spectators who purchased expensive first and second balcony seats. The displacement of standing parterre spectators by largely empty benches created a void at the center of the social space shaped by de Wailly's structure; the bustle of the balconies contrasted vividly with the absence of human activity in the pit. The architect offered his patrons and the salon public a sanitized image of the social world of the theater, one where the tumult of the standing parterre would be hidden from sight in the third balcony and the *paradis*. In this architectural vision,

---

[52] Quoted in Jacques Rittaud-Hutinet, *La Vision d'un futur: Ledoux et ses théâtres* (Lyon, 1982), 132–33.

[53] Michel Gallet, "Un Projet de Charles de Wailly pour la Comédie-Française," *Bulletin du Musée Carnavalet* 1 (June 1965): 3–18; and Monika Steinhauser and Daniel Rabreau, "Le Théâtre de l'Odéon de Charles de Wailly et Marie-Joseph Peyre, 1767–1782," *Revue de l'art* 19 (1973): 8–49. On the sociology of eighteenth-century French theatrical architecture, see Rougemont, *La Vie théâtrale*, 155–72.

INTÉRIEUR DE LA NOUVELLE SALLE DE COMÉDIE FRANÇAISE DE L'ANCIEN PROJET.

which assumed the same need for discipline found in the texts of Blondel and Ledoux, parterre denizens would no longer be capable of disrupting the evening's events. Writers and spectators who began to argue in earnest for a seated parterre in 1777 shared the sympathies of these architects.

The question first became imperative thanks to a July 1777 article by Jean-François de La Harpe; the piece, a review of Cailhava's play *L'Egoïsme*, appeared in a recently purged periodical called *Journal de politique et de littérature*.[54] La Harpe, one of the second-generation philosophes who consolidated the institutional power and social prestige accumulated by Voltaire, Rousseau, Diderot, and their contemporaries, was an unpopular literary critic who found himself constantly attacked and satirized in print.[55] In his 1777 critique of Cailhava's play, he criticized what he perceived as an unjustly negative reaction the first night and then an overly positive response the second night when the parterre was supposedly filled with men paid to applaud the play. He went further than simply castigating the parterre, however, in this ringing call to action:

It is high time to end the shameful indecency of our tumultuous performances, which have been abandoned to the jeering cabal while decent sorts are silent. We must restore the necessary and appropriate order which should reign in a theater as refined as ours. Those persons charged with the oversight of its maintenance and progress know that there is only one way to prevent the absolute decadence of the theater: this is to seat the parterre. The time has now come for this revolution.[56]

La Harpe's text indicates his sympathies: all the troubles in Paris's privileged theaters, including the reign of the cabal, the decline in manners and taste, and the failure to support and nourish "talented" playwrights, could

---

[54] *Journal de politique et de littérature* (July 1777): 307–8. In August 1776, Panckouke, the paper's owner, had replaced its former editor, the radical barrister Linguet, with La Harpe; see Christopher Todd, *Voltaire's Disciple: Jean-François de La Harpe* (London: 1972), 25–26. On Cailhava, see Brown, "A Field of Honor," 646.

[55] On La Harpe in these years, see Todd, *Voltaire's Disciple*, 22–41; and Alexandre Jovicevich, *Jean-François de La Harpe, adepte et renégat des lumières* (South Orange, NJ: 1973), 91–130.

[56] *Journal de politique et de littérature*, 307.

Fig. 11. ◄ Charles de Wailly, *Early Design for the Interior of the New Comédie-Française Playhouse*, 1771. (Courtesy of the Photothèque des musées de la ville de Paris.)

be cured by the simple expedient of seating the parterre. In the heat of his journalistic passion, La Harpe avidly refuted theater enthusiasts who predicted doom if benches were installed in the parterre. To those who objected that a seated parterre would be less involved, and therefore less passionate, La Harpe invoked the experience of the Concert Spirituel and, of course, the assemblies of the French Academy; in both cases, he asserted, a seated audience responded no less intently for its added comfort. To those who believed that the actors would suffer at the box office, he pointed out that those now in the parterre would simply move to the cheaper *paradis*, or top balcony, and that a whole new class of spectator, presently discouraged from theater attendance by the chaos of the parterre, would eagerly buy pit tickets if order were returned to the theater.

La Harpe's comments drew immediate and often contentious response, as well as support from others who sided with him.[57] But the most forceful defense of the standing parterre before the 1782 installation of benches at the Comédie-Française appeared in the *Supplément* to d'Alembert and Diderot's *Encyclopédie*. In a 1777 revision of the article "Parterre," the playwright, moralist, and critic Jean-François Marmontel analyzed the pit in ways that differed markedly from those who sought to discipline its members and weed out the remnants of popular culture.[58] The fundamental contrast between those who wished to seat the parterre and Marmontel lay in the latter's belief that an audience on its feet was more vigorous, and therefore more just in its judgments, than a seated, indolent audience.[59] Parterre patrons, he wrote in the *Supplément*, were the least rich, the least refined, and the least mannered in their morals. But they were also the least altered, the least pretentious, and the least corrupted by the decadence of the times.[60] These men were veteran theatergoers, and their long experience of the stage had provided them with an instinctive sense of comparison and good taste. In Marmontel's view, the parterre's lack of social polish became a merit; the "instinct" of the parterre served it well in its on-the-spot evaluations of plays.

---

[57] See Ravel, "Seating the Public" 191 n. 46, for positive and negative responses to La Harpe's polemic.

[58] Jean-François Marmontel, "Parterre," in *Supplément à l'Encyclopédie, ou Dictionnaire raisonné des sciences, des arts et des métiers* (Amsterdam, 1777), 4:241–42. Republished with slight revisions in Marmontel's *Eléments de littérature* (1787; reprint, Paris, 1867), 3:83–88.

[59] On Marmontel, see Frank A. Kafker and Serena L. Kafker, *The Encyclopedists as Individuals: A Biographical Dictionary of the Authors of the Encyclopedia*, published as *SVEC* 257 (1988): 248–54; and the first chapter of Michael Cardy, *The Literary Doctrines of Jean-François Marmontel*, published as *SVEC* 210 (1982).

[60] Marmontel, "Parterre," 241.

Nevertheless, Marmontel believed, the parterre's innate incorruptibility, by itself, was insufficient to appreciate fully the beauties and the moral lessons of the stage. That the parterre managed to seize the full impact of the theatrical experience was owing to the judgment of a small number of highly enlightened men also found in the pit. "The multitude listens to these men, and it does not have the vanity to be humiliated by their lessons."[61] Marmontel attributed this vanity to the effeminizing influence of the loges; having no women in the pit, the taste of the parterre might be less delicate, but it was also "less capricious, and above all more masculine (*mâle*), and more firm." The pit, then, was the perfect masculine mixture of instinct and reason:

> The parterre is . . . habitually composed of men without culture and without pretention, whose native sensibility delivers them over to the impressions they receive from the spectacle. What's more, these men seem to form but one spirit and one soul with those more enlightened spectators who teach them to think and to feel.[62]

A handful of philosophes and the male masses worked together in the tribunal of the parterre to pass unanimous, unerring judgment on the plays onstage. The standing parterre thus provided, in Marmontel's sense, the ultimate synthesis of philosophe and people, human learning and natural instinct that guaranteed proper taste and the flowering of civilization.

For the theater to fulfill its didactic potential, Marmontel argued, it was necessary for the parterre to remain standing. "When one stands in the parterre," he wrote, "everything is apprehended with more warmth; anxiety, surprise, feelings of ridicule and pathos, are all more alive and more rapidly felt."[63] The seated spectator, on the other hand, is more at ease but colder, more reflective, less susceptible to illusion, and less disposed to movements of "drunkeness and transport." Furthermore, he argued along the same lines as Condillac and Diderot, the press of people multiplies the individual's emotional output; the crowd of spectators was like five hundred mirrors reflecting light (*lumière*) off each other, or five hundred echos reverberating around the playhouse. Marmontel supported these visual and audio metaphors with another borrowed from the electrical experiments of eighteenth-century scientists:

[61] Ibid.
[62] Ibid.
[63] Ibid.

It is above all in the parterre, and in the standing parterre, that this type of electricity is sudden, forceful and rapid. This effect is caused by the more arduous situation of the [standing] spectator, who is kept in motion by a constant disturbance and perpetual pushing.[64]

In this atomistic universe, transferred to the floor of the theater, the constant friction of the spectators facilitated the circulation of some form of emotional energy. This "electricity," in turn, was the component essential to the creation of a unified voice that passed judgment on spectacle through a serendipitous mixture of reason and instinct.[65] Were one to seat the parterre, the formidable balance of these two factors would be undone.

At the end of his article, Marmontel sketched out the harmful effects of a seated parterre in language that drew from the political discourse of the post-Maupeou world. Without the free communication of emotion and opinion that existed in the standing parterre, spectators would never reach a common decision; the caprice, vanity, and fantasy that ruled the loges would also overtake the pit, with grave consequences:

[I]f the parterre, such as it is, does not reduce public opinion to a single voice, there would most often be as many diverse judgments as there were loges in the playhouse. The success of a play would be neither unanimous nor firmly decided for a long while.[66]

This fear of divisiveness, an anxiety fundamental to the political culture of the Old Regime, led Marmontel to use language that underlined his sense of the political significance of parterre activity. Once seated, he feared, the "democracy" of the parterre would degenerate into an "aristocracy," resulting in less liberty, less ingenuity, less warmth, less frankness, and less integrity. It is from a free parterre that applause arose, wrote Marmontel, and applause was, inter alia, "the public sanction of private judgments." In a spectacle without applause, as in a polity without representation, the spectators' souls were isolated and their opinions insignificant.

[64] Ibid.
[65] Although Marmontel's article predates the Mesmerist fad of the 1780s, "electricity" was only one of many invisible forces that scientists and pseudo-scientists explored in the late 1770s; see Robert Darnton, *Mesmerism and the End of Enlightenment in France* (Cambridge, MA, 1968), 14–16, 28–29. The physical space of the theater was one site for the investigation of these forces; Lavoisier, for example, analyzed the chemical composition of theater air in the experiments that led to his scientific breakthroughs.
[66] Marmontel, "Parterre," 242.

Marmontel's argument, then, brings into focus several major issues in the debate to seat the parterre. Authors on both sides of the seating question adapted an Enlightenment debate over the merit of popular culture versus elite culture to the question of theater architecture. La Harpe had advocated a separation of these two worlds, a separation that would be reflected in the two-tiered system of privileged and boulevard theater. Marmontel's appeal to the "common sense" of the standing parterre spectator, however, echoed a Rousseauian veneration for the judgment of simple people uncorrupted by the artificiality of eighteenth-century society; unlike Jean-Jacques, however, Marmontel located these natural virtues in the parterre of the public theaters.[67] For La Harpe, a theater public existed primarily in its ability to construct through its gaze both the spectacle and the well-disciplined society that watched. This "public" was a collective entity that hovered somewhere above or beyond the physical presence of the parterre spectators; the public gaze ought to be used to contain the bodily excesses of the pit. In contrast, Marmontel implied that the men standing in the parterre constituted the public. The standing spectator paid attention to the stage, Marmontel believed, because he came to watch the play. This process was mutually reinforcing, because it was much easier for emotional impressions to reach the soul when one was standing in a crowded pit. The body thus became a conduit between the passions evoked on the stage and the individual soul at which they were aimed. Stated differently, the body served as the link between philosophical ideas and virtuous political behavior by the masses. Benches in the pit, in Marmontel's formulation, would impede audience democracy.

Politicized characterizations of the parterre were not confined to the writings of the philosophes in 1777, as correspondence in the daily *Journal de Paris* from late August to early October of that year indicates. On 23 August, approximately a month after La Harpe's review had appeared in print, the editors of the *Journal de Paris* printed a letter from an individual identified as Roier de Carinsi.[68] "Roier" noted the proposals circulating in Paris to seat the parterre and raise prices at the Comédie-Française, but he claimed that it would not be necessary to oblige the city's youths and its many other less fortunate citizens to increase their expenditures or forego the theater altogether. Yes, the *flux et reflux* in the parterre was undesirable and "unnatural," but he had a proposal for the configuration of the parterre that would alleviate crowding without the installation of benches. Although

---

[67] Marmontel, *L'Art du théâtre* (Paris, 1761), is a rebuttal to Rousseau's *Letter to d'Alembert*.
[68] *Journal de Paris*, 23 August 1777, 1–2.

he did not divulge the details of his proposal, he did promise that if the Comédie-Française agreed to perform a play he had written within the next three months, he would earmark his royalties, as well as any proceeds from the sale of the printed version of his play, to a redesigned parterre.

Roier's letter drew a response in the same journal approximately two weeks later from a writer identified as Binel, who wanted to relate a recent conversation to the readers.[69] He claimed in his letter that he had encountered an *honnête bourgeois de Paris* who was "scandalized" by Roier's proposals. According to Binel, this man had faithfully attended the Comédie-Italienne every day of his life for the last fifty years; approximately twenty years previously, the Italian actors, moved by his faithful attendance, had offered him free entry to their theater, which he had refused. This pillar of probity and goodwill had not taken kindly to Roier's proposals, in part because he suspected that they were self-serving tactics to have his play performed on the stage of the Comédie-Française.[70] More important, however, he feared that Roier's innovations would prove harmful to the freedoms of parterre spectators:

> By removing pulsations from the parterre, one would deprive the first estate of spectators of the liberty which is so natural to Man, that of coming and going, entering and exiting, following the performance or not. In a word, one would remove the pit's ability to judge, and with it its pleasures, so that the parterre would be reduced to a dull atony.[71]

After a few more exchanges in which both Binel and his interlocutor questioned the merit of Roier's proposal, his play, and his ability to write French prose, the two parted company; it was 5:30, and Harlequin awaited the avid follower of the Comédie-Italienne.

Readers of the *Journal de Paris* had to wait another ten days for Roier's riposte, in which he identified Binel as his neighbor and denied that he wished to constrain the liberties of the parterre.[72] On the contrary, he suspected that a medical term such as "atony," which Binel's acquaintance had used, betrayed his true motives; the man must have been a doctor who wished to see parterre spectators continue to break their arms and legs so that his practice would thrive. But Roier was not content to let the matter

[69] Ibid., 2 September 1777, 2.
[70] On the difficulty of getting one's play accepted and performed at the Comédie-Française in the second half of the eighteenth century, see Brown, "A Field of Honor," 98–167.
[71] *Journal de Paris*, 2 September 1777, 2.
[72] Ibid., 12 September 1777, 2–3.

rest there. Four days later, the *Journal de Paris* published another of his letters in which he reported a lengthy conversation he claimed to have overheard in the parterre of the Comédie-Française.[73] His parterre neighbors, although exhausted by their efforts to obtain tickets and wearied by the crush of the pit, had begun to discuss his proposals in unflattering terms. Listening anonymously, he heard "a little, sunburnt man with an intent stare" suggest that his proposal in the paper was nothing but the humble preface to his play, which he hoped to convince the "public" to applaud as the work of a responsible citizen and patriot rather than the machinations of a self-interested author. Another spectator replied that he would wager thirty amphitheater tickets that Roier did not have a play ready to submit to the actors. The latter, unable to maintain his silence, identified himself and was about to accept the wager when a man standing next to him whispered in his ear that his challenger was a hairdresser who received the tickets free and therefore risked nothing in the exchange. Going over this conversation at home after the play, Roier admitted that, with his proposal, he had made a fool of himself when he had intended to do good. His fellow parterre spectators doubted his intentions, and the Comédie-Française actors had not responded to his public offer. He therefore determined to publish his play at his own expense, before the Comédie-Française considered performing it; he would then use the proceeds from the sale of his play to finance his reforms in the pit.

The "Roier exchange" had two more sequels in the pages of the *Journal de Paris*. Almost two weeks after Roier reported the parterre conversation he had overheard, an anonymous correspondent who signed his letter the "Hermit of Samoyed" wrote to renew the charge that Roier was playing on patriotic sympathies to get his comedy performed on France's leading public stage.[74] He also proposed that parterre congestion could be eased by installing benches, quadrupling the price of parterre tickets, and permitting poorer spectators to enter the pit after the first act for half that price. Roier responded that after watching the confusion and discomfort of parterre spectators at the Comédie-Française on 4 October, when, he would wager, almost forty people were seriously injured in a scene that the soldiers were powerless to stop, he would end the mysterious nature of his proposals.[75] The remainder of his letter only provided details for a new scheme to prevent crowding at the ticket window, however; he still did not

[73] Ibid., 16 September 1777, 2–3.
[74] Ibid., 28 September 1777, 1–2.
[75] Ibid., 9 October 1777, 2–3.

disclose his plan to reconfigure the parterre. The exchanges in the Parisian daily end with this letter from Roier, who appears never to have published his promised play or had it performed at the Comédie-Française.

The colloquy between Roier and his correspondents took place at a different rhetorical level and in front of a different reading audience than the viewpoints put forth by La Harpe and Marmontel. No reason exists to believe, in fact, that any of the claims made by Roier and his print adversaries had any grounding in fact; their arguments may well have had more to do with the popular assumptions expressed in the *Anecdotes dramatiques* than with the reasoned debate of the intelligentsia. But although their exchange was amusing, it borrowed from the same political vocabulary as that used by the philosophes; the language of citizenship, patriotism, and liberty found its way into popular journalism's representation of street encounters and snatches of conversation overheard in the parterre. These letters in the *Journal de Paris* in the second half of 1777 suggest that the debate over seating prompted a wide spectrum of the literate, theatergoing population to analyze the problem in overtly political terms.

The End of the Theatrical Old Regime

The discourse of the politicized parterre continued in the aftermath of the Comédie-Française's decision to install benches in the parterre area of its new theater, which opened on 9 April 1782. The chaotic events inside and outside the Comédie-Française that evening, however, hinted that the parterre reforms were not effective. The actors admitted so many people that fights inevitably broke out among spectators, and observers reported that it was impossible to hear the performance. One *nouvelliste* noted, "One got there, one was smothered in spite of the rows of benches, and the tumult was continuous during the first play."[76] Three months later, Henri Meister commented on a particularly disruptive parterre performance in the *Correspondance litteraire*:

> [T]he parterre was calmly seated and even quite at ease, the benches being only half-full. Still, one can defy all the standing parterres ever assembled to demonstrate their sentiments with more energy or more violence than the pit did on that day. This observation does not seem unworthy of note;

---

[76] MS, 20:13; Bailey Stone, *The Parlement of Paris, 1774–1789* (Chapel Hill, 1981) 102–4; and CS, 12:404.

many people have presumed, not without some semblance of reason, that a seated parterre would enjoy much less liberty than a standing one.[77]

Thus, the initial results of the seating experiment failed to create the picture of tranquility confidently drawn by de Wailly in his engraving a decade earlier; Meister, at least, thought that the benches did not break the "electrical circuit" of the parterre.

While the partisans of parterre seating grappled with the meaning of the pit's continued disorder, those who opposed the benches expressed their misgivings about the new Comédie-Française parterre for the remainder of 1782 and well into 1783. In a 1783 *Tableau de Paris* article entitled "Théâtre National," Mercier wrote that the formerly vigorous parterre had fallen into lethargy.[78] "Now that the benches do not permit heads to touch and intermingle, the electricity is broken." He bewailed the loss of a "general effervescence" and an incredible enthusiasm that had previously made the theater interesting. "Today calm, silence and chilly disapproval have replaced the tumult," he concluded in despair. On the whole, the seating experiment at the Comédie-Française failed to satisfy almost everyone concerned. Perhaps taking note of the ambivalent results obtained by their competitors, the Comédie-Italienne did not install benches in the pit of its new theater on the boulevard, which opened a year later in April 1783. The next year, however, a new editorial in the *Mercure* attacked the absence of benches in the Italians' playhouse in the charged language of the day: "This standing parterre is, beyond a doubt, a barbarous relic of the past, of those centuries of feudalism, where the great and the rich, persuaded that they were everything, and that the people were nothing, believed they had done enough by permitting the people standing access to their pleasures."[79] Far from the productive republic of theater patrons envisioned by those in favor of the standing parterre, the writer claimed that a parterre forced to stand could only oppress the people. The only sure way to increase the happiness of the "nation," he went on to add, was to seat the parterre.[80]

Writers, performers, and spectators failed, in the last years of the Old Regime, to resolve the issues occasioned by the seating of the parterre. As late as January 1788, when the Comédie-Italienne finally seated its parterre

[77] CL, 13:157–58.
[78] Mercier, *Tableau de Paris*, 7:102–10.
[79] MF, 3 April 1784, 4.
[80] MF, 3 April 1784, 6; see also the anonymous printed riposte, *Réponse à l'anonyme auteur de la dissertation sur les Parterres debout ou assis insérée dans le Mercure de France du 3 avril 1784, n. 14* (Paris, 1784).

in the wake of the December 1787 riot, described in chapter 5, one could still find advocates both for and against the benches. Each side continued to associate the parterre with the French nation and revile the "despotic" implications of their opponents' positions.[81] Nor did the experience of 1789 clarify the issues in the minds of theatergoers. Two days after the night of 4 August, the heady evening when the National Assembly "abolished feudalism," a group of citizens presented themselves at the Comédie-Italienne to demand that the troupe remove the benches installed a year and a half earlier and lower the price of parterre admission, presumably so more citizens would have access to the playhouse. The actors, who capitulated to the request, soon found themselves under attack by an equally fervent revolutionary. An anonymous citizen and law clerk, who had absented himself from the capital on unspecified revolutionary business in the beginning of August, returned to the parterre of the Comédie-Italienne one night to find the benches gone. How could the revolutionary government, he wrote in a pamphlet published that month or the next, have permitted the reestablishment of the standing parterre, an "old vestige of vassalage," at the very moment when it wished "to make disappear all the shameful distinctions that swallowed up humanity, and that led the kingdom to its ruin?"[82]

It would be another year and a half before the National Assembly turned its attention to the abuses of theatrical privilege. The seven articles adopted by the assembly on 13 January 1791 abolished censorship, permitted any citizen to open a public theater, granted greater intellectual property rights to dramatic authors, and placed local officials in charge of limited theater policing. These provisions were all challenged during the next several years; the new theatrical regime, like its political counterpart, emerged fitfully from the clashes between political factions in the assembly, the streets of Paris, and the nation at large, only to be submerged in the wave of Napoleonic authoritarianism at the beginning of the new century.[83] But if the revolutionaries did not fix a new legislative framework for French public theater between 1789 and 1799, they did decisively destroy the old one. After January 1791, the theatrical Old Regime, as cre-

---

[81] See Ravel, "Seating the Public," 207–10.

[82] U.S. Library of Congress, MLA Deposit 807F, *Registres journaliers de la Comédie-Italienne* 87, 6 August 1789; AN, O¹500, f. 423; *Pétition d'un membre de la Basoche aux très-honorables Membres des Assemblées du Palais-Royal* (Paris, 1789).

[83] For an overview of the legislative history of the French theater during the Revolutionary and Napoleonic periods, see F. W. J. Hemmings, *Theatre and State in France, 1760–1905* (Cambridge, 1994), 64–91, 101–12.

ated by Louis XIV in 1680 and preserved by his successors until the Revolution, became untenable.

At one level, the reforms articulated in the January 1791 law served the commercial interests of playwrights.[84] With the advent of the Revolution, and the abolition of so-called feudal privileges in August 1789, the authors, who had presented the proposal that eventually became law, at last saw an opportunity to gain greater control over their "intellectual property" and the performance conditions of their plays. But the reforms approved by the assembly in January 1791 also altered all other aspects of theatrical production and consumption. The first article, which guaranteed all citizens the right to open public theaters in which they might stage any dramatic genre, subject to municipal approval, effectively ended the monopolies on tragedy and lyric drama enjoyed by the Comédie-Française, the Comédie-Italienne, and the Opera. Article 6 mandated that censorship would be abolished or drastically curtailed, subject to further deliberations; and article 7 prohibited the national army from policing the theaters. These last two provisions terminated the monarchy's century-long efforts to control the content of plays and the behavior of public theater audiences. The playwrights, legislators, and others who backed the law of 13 January 1791 wished to eliminate all surviving Old Regime ideological, economic, and military constraints on the theater.

They made their intent particularly clear in the assembly debate that day on article 7 of the law.[85] The article provided that only a *garde extérieure*, not to be composed of government soldiers, be allowed outside the kingdom's playhouses. A few civil officers would be the only officials permitted inside the theaters, and the exterior troops would enter the playhouse only on invitation by a civil officer who had determined that public security (*sûreté publique*) had been compromised. In other words, the law proposed a complete break with all pre-1789 methods of policing the parterre. During the discussion after presentation of the law, a representative named Lavie questioned the wisdom of the article. A lone civil officer, he thought, would be without means to suppress riotous behavior inside the playhouse, and he might well be prevented from communicating with the guards outside the building. His point was one that countless royal ministers, lieutenant generals of police, exempts, soldiers, and provincial

---

[84] For a preliminary proposal, the final text of the law, and debates concerning both, see M. Mavidal and E. Laurent, eds., *Archives parlementaires de 1787 à 1860. Première série, 1787 à 1799* (Paris, 1885), 18:249–57 and 22:210–16; on the aims of playwrights at this moment, see Brown, "A Field of Honor," 598–603.

[85] Mavidal and Laurent, *Archives parlementaires*, 22: 214–16.

officials throughout the eighteenth century would have supported. In January 1791, however, their position was not in the ascendant. The proceedings of the assembly record that Mirabeau, aristocratic son of an inveterate parterre spectator and no doubt a habitué of the pit himself, closed discussion on the topic of policing with a single, striking declaration: "A public theater bristling with bayonets is a horrifying spectacle that we must reject!"

Afterword

Since the early 1990s, as I have presented my work on the eighteenth-century parterre at academic conferences and other gatherings, I have almost always heard one of two comments during question and answer sessions. Some listeners would mention that the parterre reminded them of today's soccer hooligans, while others would ask whether parterre spectators in the eighteenth century were like rock concert audiences in the late twentieth century. Readers of *The Contested Parterre* may have similar thoughts. On one level, I have found these interventions encouraging; they imply that I have succeeded in revivifying the tumult and the energy of the parterre in the minds of my auditors and readers. On another level, however, I have thought these associations troubling, because violence, death, and the racist and nationalist politics of the far right have manifested themselves at soccer matches and rock concerts throughout the world in the 1980s and '90s. Did my interlocutors see the parterre in the eighteenth century as an irresponsible, hedonistic space where normally rational individuals left all constraints behind? Was my work on the parterre simply another demonstration, following Horkheimer and Adorno, of the way in which eighteenth-century conceptions of secular equality and community, like Rousseau's "General Will," prefigured the evils of twentieth-century totalitarianism?[1]

Certainly, my soundings in the police archives and other eighteenth-century sources have turned up examples of irrational, often ugly, individual and group activity. A public space in which people pushed, thieved, groped, urinated, and defecated is not a model of civic comportment, and not only because we may have grown more prudish in the intervening period. But the evidence I have presented here also suggests a different

---

[1] Max Horkheimer and Theodor W. Adorno, *Dialectic of Enlightenment*, trans. John Cumming (New York, 1972); for an overview of French statements of this connection, see Steven L. Kaplan, *Farewell Revolution: The Historians' Feud, France, 1789/1989* (Ithaca, 1995), 25–49.

contemporary parallel, one evoked by the Czech dissident playwright Vaclav Havel in letters to his wife, Olga, written during political imprisonment in the late 1970s and early '80s. Because a literal-minded prison warden scrutinized his correspondence, Havel masked his criticism of the regime by writing on abstract themes that would not provoke the suspicion of his jailers. In late 1981, he took up the question of the "social nature of the theater," by which he meant the power of live theater to create a sense of community, and an occasion for political resistance, among its adherents.[2] He postulates that there are three "zones" of theatrical sociability, the first being the "immediate social aspect of each individual performance," and the second being the extended group of playgoers who regularly attend a particular theater because they have found there a "spiritual" home. The third zone, which transcends not only the time of a specific performance but also the space of the playhouse walls, reaches out in a "mysterious and complex way" to shape the "self-esteem" of an entire society. For Havel, writing from the prisons of post-1968 Czechoslovakia, theater provides an uncompromised, genuinely democratic method to build a free society. Unique performances lead to groups of committed theatergoers who in turn spread the message in a thousand subtle ways to society at large. Part of Havel's hope lay in the medium of the theater itself; the ubiquitous propaganda machine of the state cannot distort the memory of the ephemeral theatrical moment, because no photos, texts, or moving images exist for the government to alter or destroy. Although this vision of a politicized theater might strike North Americans and Western Europeans in the late twentieth century as hopelessly naive, we should not forget that Havel went on to direct the Velvet Revolution of 1989 from backstage at the Magic Lantern theater in Prague.[3]

I bring up Havel as a counter to the image of soccer fans and rock audiences run amok because his "zones of theatrical sociability" remind us that we need not always be suspicious of profound sentiments stirred up by mass gatherings. The sense of community generated in the theater is not always overtly politicized, although it may have been difficult to avoid political connotations in any public gathering under the cold war Communist regimes of Eastern Europe. But when it occurs, this connection to a larger social entity is almost always a transformative sensation that stays with the spectator long after the house lights have come up. In this book, I

[2] Vaclav Havel, *Letters to Olga, June 1979-September 1982*, trans. Paul Wilson (New York, 1988), 246–93, esp. 260–62.
[3] Timothy Garton Ash, *The Magic Lantern: The Revolution of '89 Witnessed in Warsaw, Budapest, Berlin, and Prague* (New York, 1990), 78–130.

have tried to illuminate the "mysterious and complex" way in which the experience of the parterre enabled the French and French speakers in the eighteenth century to suggest a positive sense of community, political and otherwise, which differed from the models favored by the absolutist monarchy or the social elites who sat on the stage and in the loges. The experience of the pit, as Marmontel and Mercier attested at the end of the Old Regime, could transform a group of pleasure-seeking individualists into a coherent community capable of speaking on behalf of their compatriots. Certainly, this communal transformation did not occur at every performance, but by the end of the century such transformations had cultural, social, and political consequences for the French.

The dynamics of the parterre, then, are central to understanding the passage from the world of kings, courtiers, and absolute sovereignty to our current regime of laws, citizens, and inalienable rights, a transition that took place most surprisingly and unsettlingly in eighteenth-century France. From Alexis de Tocqueville to François Furet, this transition has been the major preoccupation of those who have studied the period. The concept of the public sphere, as defined by Jürgen Habermas, has provided important insight into this problem. But the "enlightened" public was not composed uniquely of reader-citizens, and the revolutionaries at the end of the century did not merely envision a disembodied entity when they spoke of the nation. In an essay on acting, written in the 1770s but unpublished in his lifetime, Denis Diderot stated his own sense of the importance of the parterre, as he adopted the Renaissance trope of the *theatrum mundi* to the changed circumstances of the eighteenth century. Gifted actors might display a certain brilliance in their performances onstage, he suggested in this telling passage, but they are ultimately too occupied with observing and copying human nature to comprehend and act on the meaning of the performance. Only a spectator can fully appreciate and use the intellectual and emotional impact of the scene onstage: "In the great drama, the theater of the world, the one to which I always return, all of the passionate souls are on the stage, but all the men of genius are in the parterre."[4] It is the *hommes de génie*, and not the *âmes chaudes*, whom Diderot would make kings, ministers, military captains, lawyers, and doctors. It is the fully engaged parterre spectator, and not the stage mimic, in whose hands he would place authority.

---

[4] Denis Diderot, *Paradoxe sur le comédien, précédé des Entretiens sur le Fils Naturel* (Paris, 1981), 131.

Appendix: List of Spectators in Paris Parterres by Social Category and Theater, 1717–68

Sources: Bibliothèque de l'Arsenal, Archives de la Bastille; Archives Nationales, "Y" series, papers of the Paris commissioners. Categories are devised to give a general idea of the professions and occupations represented in the parterre. The Service Classes category includes men involved in law, finance, the government bureaucracy and its tax collecting machinery, as well as the ambiguous category "Bourgeois de Paris." The titles, or qualities, that appear below are transcribed as they appear in the police reports.

Military Officers (24)

Comédie-Française (6)

1758   Capitaine au Régiment des gardes Lorraines
1758   Lt. Colonel du Régiment d'Artois
1765   Capitaine d'infanterie
1765   Capitaine au service du Roy de Prusse
1765   Officier reformé
1766   Lieutenant au Régiment, commissaire général cavalerie

Comédie-Italienne (10)

1720   Capitaine reformé, Régiment Royal Roussilon
1743   Lieutenant au Régiment de Berchiny Hussard
1743   Capitaine des Dragons d'Harcourt
1758   Marquis, military officer
1763   Aide-majeur au Régiment Dauphin dragons

1763   Chevalier de l'ordre royale et militaire de St Louis, Capitaine au Régiment de Champagne
1765   Officier chargé de l'inspection de la police dans les maisons de plaisance du Roi
1765   Lieutenant du Roy de la ville de Rue en Picardie
1765   Officier garde de la connétablie de France
1766   Marechal des logis au regt Royal étranger cavalerie en garnison au Poitou

Opera (8)

1758   Sergent majeur au Régiment des gardes françaises
1758   Chevalier de Malte
1758   Capitaine du corps Royal de l'Artillerie
1758   Capitaine en cavalerie
1758   Officier commandant la brigade en Maréchaussée de Lille
1759   Lt. Colonel d'infanterie ayde Maréchal de logis
1759   Baron de Ste Sévère, maître de camp de cavalerie
1765   Capitaine au Régt. du Royal Piedmont cavalerie

Service Classes: Lawyers, Financiers, Bourgeois, Etc. (57)

Comédie-Française (20)

1717   Procureur en parlement
1720   Avocat en parlement
1751   Payeur des rentes
1758   Ecuyer
1758   Bourgeois de Paris
1758   Avocat au parlement
1758   Inspecteur de fourrages de l'armée de Contade
1758   Bourgeois de Paris
1759   Bourgeois de Paris
1760   Ecrivain de la Marine
1760   Marchand bourgeois de Paris
1763   Controlleur des hopitaux en Bourgogne
1763   Ecuyer Lt. général des grenadiers royaux
1765   Ecuyer
1765   Bourgeois de Paris

1765   Procureur en parlement
1766   Subdélégué de l'Intendant de la généralité de Paris
1767   Employé dans le service du Roy
1768   Bourgeois de Paris
1768   Seigneur de Nanteuil

Comédie-Italienne (28)

1749   Ecuyer
1757   Avocat en parlement
1758   Banquier à Paris
1758   Ecuyer, sous-gouverneur des pages de l'Ecurie du Roy
1758   Intéressé dans les affaires du Roy
1758   Huissier à verge au Châtelet
1759   Avocat en parlement
1759   Directeur de correspondance chez le Sieur Chardon, intéressé
dans les affaires du roi.
1761   Avocat en parlement
1761   Procureur en la sénéchaussé en siège présidial d'Angoumois
1761   Procureur au Châtelet de Paris
1761   Bourgeois de Paris
1761   Avocat en parlement
1762   Avocat en parlement
1762   Ecuyer enseigne des vaisseaux du Roy
1762   Chevalier grand tresorier des ordres militaires et hospitaliers
1762   Vérificateur des douanes du Roy de la généralite de Bourges
1762   Receveur général des terres de M le Marquis de Lauraguais
1763   Graveur général des monnoyes de France
1763   Bourgeois de Paris
1764   Négociant
1764   Bourgeois de Paris
1765   Contrôlleur des postes
1765   Bailly civil, criminel et de police du Marquisat du Vilaine la
Juchelle et subdélégué de l'Intendance de Touraine
1766   Ecuyer ordinaire (?) des gardes du corps du Roy, compagnie de
Noailles
1766   Conseiller (?) du Roy, receveur du grenier à sel de Melun
1767   Entrepreneur pour le Roy de l'habillement des troupes,
intéressé dans ses affaires
1768   Avocat en parlement

Opera (8)

1758   Conseiller au parlement de Metz
1758   Intéressé dans les affaires du Roy
1758   Ecuyer, avocat au Parlement
1758   Contrôlleur de la maison du Roy
1758   Receveur general des finances
1759   Prêtaire de la valerce (?) au Régt. du colonel général
1761   Conseiller secrétaire du Roy, maison couronné de France et de
          ses finances
1765   Avocat au parlement

Nonprivileged (1)

1760   Ecuyer conseiller secr. du Roy maison couronné de France et
          de ses finances

Merchants, Master Artisans (43)

Comédie-Française (16)

1735   Joaillier
1743   Maitre fourbisseur
1749   Joaillier
1751   Glasseur de tabatiers
1758   Maître boucher de Paris
1758   Maître fayencier
1765   Maitre Tombineur (?)
1765   Architecte, entrepreneur des bâtiments
1765   Chirurgien des gardes françaises
1765   Chirurgien aide-majeur des armées du roy
1765   Maitre en chirurgie
1765   Maitre joaillier
1765   Marchand
1766   Chirurgien
1767   Médecin
1768   Marchand

Comédie-Italienne (18)

1737   Marchand sous la quay des Gesvres

1749	Architecte de campagne
1749	Relieur
1759	Horloger
1760	Fourrier de la seconde compagnie des mousquetaires noires
1760	Peintre de l'académie de St Luc
1760	Médecin
1761	Marchand orfebvre
1761	Marchand de chevaux
1763	Employé au service de la compagnie des Indes
1763	Ci-devant sous-directeur de la compagnie des Indes
1763	Marchand épicier, bourgeois de Paris
1763	Maître boucher
1763	Chirurgien à Paris
1763	Cuisinier à Paris
1766	Fabricant d'étoffe de soie en province
1766	Négociant à Strasbourg
1766	Négociant à Strasbourg

Opera (5)

1758	Marchand tireur d'or
1758	Maître pâtissier
1759	Architecte
1766	Chirurgien
1768	Ci-devant secrétaire général du gouverneur des isles du vent

Nonprivileged (4)

1744	Marchand de vin
1752	Maître Bourlier
1753	Chef de cuisine
1753	Maître brasseur

Soldiers (9)

Comédie-Française (6)

1736	Ancien soldat
1738	Garde du Roy
1747	Soldat dans le Régiment du Hainault
1750	Dragon dans la compagnie de M Deffosses

1750   Volontaire dans le Régiment de la Reine
1758   Mousquetaire de la première compagnie

Comédie-Italienne (2)

1728   Cadet suisse
1767   Ancien employé de la regt des fourrages de l'armée

Opera (1)

1758   Enseigne de la Colonel au Régt. du Roy, infanterie

Clerks, Domestics (20)

Comédie-Française (9)

1733   Clerc d'un procureur au parlement
1736   Clerc d'un notaire
1741   Clerc d'un procureur des consuls
1743   Logé chez un avocat
1747   Clerc d'un secrétaire de plusieurs avocats
1748   Clerc chez un secrétaire
1750   Clerc d'un procureur au Parlement
1758   Valet de chambre de M l'abbé de Very
1765   Domestique au service de M l'Evêque d'Angoulesme

Comédie-Italienne (7)

1728   Clerc d'un procureur en parlement
1735   Clerc de procureur
1749   Secretaire du Sr Beaulieu
1749   Clerc d'un procureur au parlement
1750   Employé au bureau d'un caissier des domaines
1762   Principal clerc de Me Macques notaire au Châtelet de Paris
1765   Principal clerc d'un notaire au Châtelet de Paris

Opera (1)

1752   Commis des fermes

Nonprivileged (3)

1744   Valet de chambre
1753   Premier page du Prince de Condé
1753   Clerc d'un procureur au Châtelet

Apprentices, Assistants, Sons of Merchants or Artisans (20)

Comédie-Française (11)

1733   Apprenti tapissier
1734   Garçon marchand d'un bijoutier
1737   Fils d'un horloger
1737   Tailleur de pierre; fils d'un architecte
1748   Garçon marchand (mercier)
1749   Garçon sellier, "nègre d'Amérique"
1750   Garçon marchand (de boutique)
1750   Garçon apothicaire
1751   Travaille chez un horloger
1751   Garçon tailleur
1751   Garçon bijoutier

Comédie-Italienne (9)

1738   Fils d'un maître tailleur, peintre
1749   Fils d'un imprimeur de l'Imprimerie royale
1749   Laboureur
1749   Garçon chapelier
1749   Garçon chapelier
1749   Garçon mercier
1751   Garçon marchand
1762   Employé dans les vivres
1768   Tailleur de pierre

Students, Other Young Men (19)

Comédie-Française (17)

1733   "Jeune Gens"

1733   "Jeune gens"
1734   Etudiant, fils d'un procureur en parlement
1736   Etudiant; fils du secretaire du premier chirurgien
1736   Etudiant en droit
1741   Pensionnaire, étudiant
1741   "Jeunes gens"; frère d'un procureur au Parlement
1743   Etudiant en droit; de la province
1744   Etudiant en droit, "hack-writer"
1747   Fils du directeur de la monnoye de Bayonne
1750   Etudiant en pharmacie
1751   Fils d'un Lieutenant Général de province
1751   Etudiant en droit, fils d'un marchand quinquaillier
1758   "Homme de lettres"
1758   Fils d'un peintre qui est membre de l'Académie royale
1758   Etudiant en droit
1759   Etudiant en droit, clerc d'un procureur

Comédie-Italienne (1)

1766   Affiliated with the côllege de Navarre

Nonprivileged (1)

1732   Etudiant en médecin

Provincials (8)

Comédie-Française (2)

1735   De Languedoc, à Paris pour des affaires
1742   Natif de Marseille

Comédie-Italienne (5)

1730   A Paris pour des affaires
1731   De province
1749   Jeune homme de province
1749   Provincial, learning to write, father an architect
1765   Bourgeois de ? (not Paris)

Nonprivileged (1)

1736   Genevois, orfèvre

Unemployed, Unknown, Other (7)

Comédie-Française (3)

1734   Sans emploi
1748   Voulant entrer dans les fermes
1765   Prêtre

Comédie-Italienne (2)

1730   Cy-devant commis
1730   Abbé

Opera (1)

1728   (Not recorded)

Nonprivileged (1)

1752   Sans emploi

Bibliography

Archival Sources

Archives départementales de Maine-et-Loire. 49 3.E.9. Théâtre d'Angers. Affaire du Capitaine Renty et Bancelin, 1775.

Archives Municipales de Bordeaux. BB 179. FF 70. GG 1004.

Archives Nationales. Paris. Series AD^{VIII}, 6–10. Series O^1, 18–126, 613–20, 846–47, 848. Series Y, 10719–17623.

Bibliothèque de l'Arsenal. Paris. Archives de la Bastille, ms 10,001–12,727. See the preliminary essay in Frantz Funck-Brentano, *Catalogue des manuscrits à la Bibliothèque de l'Arsenal*, vol. 9. (Paris: E. Plon, 1892). Fonds Rondel. See Robert Dawson, "Theatre and Research in the Arsenal: the Rondel 'Inventaire,'" *Studies on Voltaire and the Eighteenth Century* 260 (1989): 465–512.

Bibliothèque de l'Opéra. *Réserve* 625 (1–2). Papers of Thomas-Simon Gueullette regarding the Comédie-Italienne. Some of the material has been published under Gueullette's name as *Notes et souvenirs sur le Théâtre-Italien au XVIIIe siècle* (Paris: Droz, 1938).

Bibliothèque Historique de la Ville de Paris. NF35380. Various printed ordinances related to the theater. 138 450. Various printed ordinances related to the theater.

Bibliothèque Nationale, Salle des Manuscrits. MS 6680–87. Siméon-Prosper Hardy. *Mes Loisirs, ou Journal d'Evenements, tels qu'ils parviennent à ma connaisance.* 1764–1789. MS 21625. Various ordinances and other documents related to spectacle.

Cornell University. Carl A. Kroch Library. Maurepas Collection. Nine boxes of documents related to the ministry of Jean Frédéric Phélypeaux, Comte de Maurepas, in the 1740s. Primarily concerned with his duties as Minister of the Marine, but also contains documents related to the policing of the Paris theaters; supplements Boislisle, *Lettres de M de Marville Lieutenant Général de Police au Ministre Maurepas, 1742–1747.*

Service Historique des Armées de la Terre. Chateau de Vincennes. Series Y^a, 272–74.

U.S. Library of Congress. MLA Deposit 523F, 561F, 808F. *Registres journaliers de la Comédie-Française, 1680–1774.* Microfilm copies of the registers kept at the *Bibliothèque de la Comédie-Française* in Paris. MLA Deposit 807F. *Régistres journaliers de l'Opéra-Comique, 1717–1825.* Microfilm copies of the Comédie-Italienne registers kept in the *Bibliothèque de l'Opéra* in Paris.

Selected Print Sources

Argenson, Réné de Voyer, Comte d'. *Notes de Réné d'Argenson, lieutenant générale de police, intéressantes pour l'histoire des moeurs et de la police de Paris à la fin du règne de Louis XIV.* Paris: F. Henry, 1866.

———. *Rapports de police de Réné d'Argenson (1697–1715), publiés d'après les manuscrits conservés à la Bibliothèque Nationale.* Edited by Paul Cottin. Paris: Plon & Nourrit, 1891.

Aubignac, François Hédelin, Abbé d'. *Projet pour le rétablissement du Théâtre François.* In *La Pratique du Théâtre*, edited by Pierre Martino, 387–97. Paris: Champion, 1927.

Bachaumont, Louis Petit de. *Mémoires secrets pour servir à l'histoire de la république des lettres en France.* 36 vols. London: Adamson, 1777–89.

Boindin, Nicolas. *Lettres historiques sur tous les spectacles de Paris.* Paris: P. Prault, 1719.

Boislisle, Arthur Michel de. *Lettres de M de Marville Lieutenant Général de Police au Ministre Maurepas, 1742–1747.* 3 vols. Paris: Société de l'histoire de Paris, 1896.

Boysse, Ernest, ed. *Journal de Papillon de la Ferté, intendant et controlleur de l'argenterie, menus-plaisirs et affaires du Roi, 1756–1780.* Paris: Paul Ollendorf, 1887.

Campardon, Emile. *L'Académie royale de musique au XVIIIe siècle.* 2 vols. Paris: Berger-Levrault, 1880.

———. *Les Comédiens du roi de la troupe française pendant les deux derniers siècles.* Paris: H. Champion, 1879.

———. *Les Comédiens du roi de la troupe italienne.* 2 vols. Paris: Berger-Levrault, 1880.

———. *Les Spectacles de la foire.* 2 vols. Paris: Berger-Levrault, 1877.

Casanova, Jacques. *The Memoirs of Jacques Casanova.* Edited by Leonard Louis Levinson. New York: Collier Books, 1958.

Chappuzeau, Samuel. *Le Théâtre François.* Paris: Guignard, 1674.

Collé, Charles. *Journal et mémoires sur les hommes de lettres, les ouvrages dramatiques et les événements les plus mémorables du regne de Louis XV (1748–1772).* Edited by H. Bonhomme. 3 vols. Paris: Didot, 1868.

Coup d'oeil sur le théâtre français depuis son émigration à la nouvelle salle, "Aux dépens de MM. les comédiens français." N.p., 1783.

Encyclopédie, ou Dictionnaire raisonné des sciences, des arts et des métiers. 17 vols. Paris: Briasson, 1751–65.

Fleury, Joseph-Abraham Bénard. *Mémoires de Fleury de la Comédie-Française, 1757–1820. Procédés d'une introduction.* Edited by Jean B. P. Lafitte. Paris: Dupont, 1836.

Gherardi, Evaristo, ed. *Théâtre Italien ou Recueil de toutes les scènes françoises qui ont été jouées sur le Théâtre-Italien de l'Hôtel de Bourgogne.* 6 vols. Paris: Briasson, 1700.

Grimm, Friedrich Melchior, et al. *Correspondance littéraire, philosophique et critique.* 16 vols. Paris: Garnier frères, 1877–82.

Journal de Paris, 1777–89.

Journal de politique et de littérature, 1777.

Journal des Théâtres ou Le Nouveau Spectateur, servant de Répertoire universel des spectacles 1776–1778.

Jurgens, Madeleine, and Elizabeth Maxfield-Miller, eds. *Cent ans de recherches sur Molière, sur sa famille et sur les comédiens de sa troupe.* Paris: Imprimé nationale, 1963.

La Bretonne, Rétif de. *Les Nuits de Paris.* Paris: Folio, 1987.

La Porte, Abbé Jean-Barthélemy de, ed. *Les Spectacles de Paris.* Paris, 1751–89.

La Porte, Abbé Jean-Barthélemy de, and Jean-Marie-Bernard Clement. *Anecdotes dramatiques contenant 1) Toutes les pièces de théâtre . . . qui ont été jouées . . . depuis l'origine des spectacles en France jusqu'à l'année 1775 . . . 2) Tous les ouvrages dramatiques qui n'ont été representés sur aucun théâtre, mais qui sont imprimés . . . 3) un receuil de tout ce qu'on a pu rassembler d'anecdotes. . . .* 3 vols. Paris: Veuve Duchesne, 1775.

Lettre à M. La Harpe, de l'Académie Française, sur l'Egoïsme, comédie nouvelle en cinq actes & en vers, de M. Cailhava, N.p., n.d.

Marmontel, Jean-François. "Parterre." In *Supplément à L'Encyclopédie, ou Dictionnaire raisonné des sciences, des arts et des métiers*, 4:241–42. Amsterdam, 1777.

Mercier, Louis-Sébastien. *Tableau de Paris.* 12 vols. Amsterdam: Faulche, 1783–89.

———. *Du Théâtre, ou Nouvel essai sur l'art dramatique.* Amsterdam: E. van Harrevelt, 1773.

Mercure de France, 1724–89.

Métra, François, et al. *Correspondance secrète, politique et littéraire, ou mémoires pour servir à l'histoire des cours, des sociétés, et de la littérature en France, depuis la mort de Louis XV.* 12 vols. London: Adamson, 1787–88.

Mirabeau, Marquis de. "Journal de la jeunesse du Marquis de Mirabeau." *Revue rétrospective* 4 (1834): 362–90; and *Revue rétrospective* 5 (1835): 5–24.

Nemeitz, J. C. *Séjour de Paris, c'est-à-dire instructions fidèles pour les voyageurs de condition, comment ils se doivent conduire, s'ils veulent faire un bon usage de leur temps et argent durant leur séjour à Paris.* French translation in *La Vie privée d'autrefois*, vol. 21, edited by Alfred Franklin. Paris: Plon & Nourrit, 1897.

Parterre justifié, ou précis historique et réflexions sur la représentation du 26 décembre 1787, Le. London, 1788.

Recueil de planches sur les sciences, les arts libéraux, et les arts méchaniques, avec leur explication. 11 vols. Paris, 1772.

Réponse à l'anonyme auteur de la dissertation sur les Parterres debout ou assis insérée dans le Mercure de France du 3 avril 1784, n. 14. Paris, 1784.

Rousseau, Jean-Jacques. *Politics and the Arts: Letter to M. D'Alembert on the Theatre.* Translated from the French by Allan Bloom. Ithaca: Cornell University Press, 1968.

Sterne, Laurence. *A Sentimental Journey Through France and Italy.* New York: Oxford University Press, 1968.

Supplément à l'Encyclopédie, ou dictionnaire raisonné des sciences, des arts, et des métiers. 4 vols. Amsterdam, 1776–77.

Tralage, Jean Nicolas du. *Notes et documents sur l'histoire des théâtres de Paris au XVIIe siècle.* Edited by P. L. Jacob. Paris: Libraire des bibliophiles, 1880.

Voltaire, (François-Marie Arouet). *Correspondence and Related Documents*. Edited by Theodore Besterman. 51 vols. Oxford: Voltaire Foundation, 1968–77.

Selected Secondary Works

Alasseur, Claude. *La Comédie-Française au XVIIIe siècle: étude économique.* Paris: Mouton, 1967.

Apostolidès, Jean-Marie. *Le Prince sacrifié. Théâtre et politique au temps de Louis XIV.* Paris: Editions de minuit, 1985.

Auerbach, Erich. "La Cour et la Ville." In *Scenes from the Drama of European Literature*, 133–79. New York: Meridian Books, 1959.

Baker, Keith Michael. *Inventing the French Revolution: Essays on French Political Culture in the Eighteenth Century.* Cambridge: Cambridge University Press, 1990.

Barish, Jonas. *The Anti-Theatrical Prejudice.* Berkeley: University of California Press, 1981.

Bell, David Avrom. *Lawyers and Citizens: The Making of a Political Elite in Old Regime France.* New York: Oxford University Press, 1994.

Benabou, Erica-Marie. *La Prostitution et la police des moeurs au XVIIIe siècle.* Paris: Perrin, 1987.

Bercé, Yves-Marie. *Fête et révolte: des mentalités populaires du XVIe au XVIIIe siècle.* Paris: Hachette, 1976.

Berlanstein, Lenard. "Women and Power in Eighteenth Century France: Actresses at the Comédie-Française," *Feminist Studies* 20 (1994): 475–506.

Boes, Anne. *La Lanterne magique de l'histoire: essai sur le théâtre historique en France de 1750 à 1789.* Oxford: Voltaire Foundation, 1982.

Bonnassiès, Jules. *La Comédie-Française: histoire administrative (1658–1757).* Paris: Didier et Cie., 1874.

————. *Les Spectacles forains et la Comédie-Française d'après des documents inédits.* Paris: E. Dentu, 1875.

Bourquin, Louis. "La Controverse sur la comédie au XVIIIe siècle et la lettre à d'Alembert sur les spectacles." *Revue d'histoire littéraire de la France* 26 (1919): 43–87, 555–76; 27 (1920): 548–70; 28 (1921): 549–74.

Brennan, Thomas. *Public Drinking and Popular Culture in Eighteenth-Century Paris.* Princeton: Princeton University Press, 1988.

Brenner, Clarence D. *A Bibliographical List of Plays in the French Language, 1700–1789.* Berkeley, 1947.

————. *The Théâtre Italien. Its Repertory, 1716–1793, with a Historical Introduction*, published as *University of California Publications in Modern Philology* 63 (1961).

Brown, Gregory S. "A Field of Honor: The Cultural Politics of Playwrighting in Eighteenth-Century France." Ph.D. diss., Columbia University, 1997.

————. "Dramatic Authorship and the Honor of Men of Letters in Eighteenth-Century France." *Studies in Eighteenth-Century Culture* 27 (1998): 259–82.

Chagniot, Jean. *Paris et l'armée au XVIIIe siècle. Etude politique et sociale.* Paris: Economica, 1985.

Chartier, Roger. *The Cultural Origins of the French Revolution.* Trans. Lydia G. Cochrane. Durham: Duke University Press, 1991.

———. *The Cultural Uses of Print in Early Modern France.* Trans. Lydia G. Cochrane. Princeton: Princeton University Press, 1987.

———. "From Court Festivity to City Spectators." In *Forms and Meanings: Texts, Performances, and Audiences from Codex to Computer,* 43–82. Philadelphia: University of Pennsylvania Press, 1995.

Crow, Thomas E. *Painters and Public Life in Eighteenth-Century Paris.* New Haven: Yale University Press, 1985.

Darnton, Robert. *The Forbidden Best-Sellers of Pre-Revolutionary France.* New York: Norton, 1995.

———. *The Great Cat Massacre and Other Episodes in French Cultural History.* New York: Random House, 1984.

———. *The Literary Underground of the Old Regime.* Cambridge: Harvard University Press, 1982.

Deierkauf-Holsboer, Wilma. *Le Théâtre de l'Hôtel de Bourgogne, 1548–1635.* Paris: A. G. Nizet, 1968.

Duvignaud, Jean. *Sociologie du théâtre: Essai sur les ombres collectives.* Paris: Presses Universitaires de France, 1965.

Farge, Arlette. *Fragile Lives: Violence, Power, and Solidarity in Eighteenth-Century Paris.* Trans. Carol Shelton. Cambridge: Harvard University Press, 1993.

———. *Subversive Words: Public Opinion in Eighteenth-Century France.* Trans. Rosemary Morris. University Park: Pennsylvania State University Press, 1995.

———. *Vivre dans la rue à Paris au XVIIIe siècle.* Paris: Gallimard/Julliard, 1979.

Farge, Arlette, and Jacques Revel. *The Vanishing Children of Paris: Rumor and Politics before the French Revolution.* Trans. Claudia Miéville. Cambridge: Harvard University Press, 1991.

Fogel, Michèle. *Les Cérémonies de l'information dans la France du XVIe au XVIIe siècles.* Paris: Fayard, 1989.

Fournel, Victor. *Curiosités théâtrales, anciennes et modernes, françaises et étrangères. Nouvelle édition, revue, corrigée, et très-augmentée.* Paris: Garnier frères, 1878.

Fried, Michael. *Absorption and Theatricality: Painting and Beholder in the Age of Diderot.* Berkeley: University of California Press, 1980.

Friedland, Paul. "Representation and Revolution: The Theatricality of Politics and the Politics of Theater in France, 1789–1794." Ph.D. diss., University of California, Berkeley, 1995.

Fuchs, Max. *La Vie théâtrale en province au XVIIIe siècle.* Paris: Droz, 1933.

Funck-Brentano, Frantz. *La Bastille des comédiens. Le For l'Evêque.* Paris: Minerva, 1903.

Garrioch, David. *Neighbourhood and Community in Paris, 1740–1790.* Cambridge: Cambridge University Press, 1986.

———. "The People of Paris and Their Police in the Eighteenth Century: Reflections on the Introduction of a 'Modern' Police Force." *European History Quarterly* 24 (1994): 511–35.

Gelbart, Nina Rattner. *Feminine and Opposition Journalism in Old Regime France: Le Journal des Dames.* Berkeley: University of California Press, 1987.

Goffman, Erving. *The Presentation of Self in Everyday Life.* Garden City: Double-day, 1959.

Goodman, Dena. *The Republic of Letters: A Cultural History of the Enlighten-ment.* Ithaca: Cornell University Press, 1994.

Gordon, Daniel. *Citizens without Sovereignty: Equality and Sociability in French Thought, 1670–1789.* Princeton: Princeton University Press, 1994.

Gordon, Mel. *Lazzi: The Comic Routines of the Commedia dell'arte.* New York: Performing Arts Journal Publications, 1982.

Graham, Lisa Jane. "Crimes of Opinion: Policing the Public in Eighteenth-Century Paris." In *Visions and Revisions of Eighteenth-Century France,* edited by Chris-tine Adams, Jack Censer, and Lisa Jane Graham. University Park: Pennsylvania State University Press, 1997.

———. "If the King Only Knew: Popular Politics and Absolutism in the Reign of Louis XV, 1744–1774." Ph.D. diss., Johns Hopkins University, 1993.

Habermas, Jürgen. *The Structural Transformation of the Public Sphere: An Inquiry into a Category of Bourgeois Society.* Trans. Thomas Burger with the assistance of Frederick Lawrence. Cambridge: MIT Press, 1989.

Hanley, Sarah. "Engendering the State: Family Formation and State Building in Early Modern France." *French Historical Studies* 16 (Spring 1989): 4–27.

———. "Social Sites of Political Practice in France: Lawsuits, Civil Rights, and the Separation of Powers in Domestic and State Government, 1500–1800." *Ameri-can Historical Review* 102 (1997): 27–52.

Hemmings, F. W. J. *Theatre and State in France, 1760–1905.* Cambridge: Cam-bridge University Press, 1994.

Hesse, Carla. *Publishing and Cultural Politics in Revolutionary Paris, 1789–1810.* Berkeley: University of California Press, 1991.

Huet, Marie-Hélène. *Rehearsing the Revolution: The Staging of Marat's Death.* Trans. Robert Hurley. Berkeley: University of California Press, 1982.

Hunt, Lynn Avery. *The Family Romance of the French Revolution.* Berkeley: Uni-versity of California Press, 1992.

———. *Politics, Culture and Class in the French Revolution.* Berkeley: University of California Press, 1984.

———, ed. *The New Cultural History.* Berkeley: University of California Press, 1989.

Isherwood, Robert. *Farce and Fantasy: Popular Entertainment in Eighteenth-Century Paris.* Oxford: Oxford University Press, 1986.

———. *Music in the Service of the King: France in the Seventeenth Century.* Ithaca: Cornell University Press, 1973.

Johnson, James H. *Listening in Paris: A Cultural History.* Berkeley: University of California Press, 1995.

Kaplan, Steven L. *Bread, Politics, and Political Economy in the Reign of Louis XV.* 2 vols. The Hague: Martinus Nijhoff, 1976.

———. "Notes sur les commissaires de police de Paris au XVIIIe siècle." *Revue d'histoire moderne et contemporaine* 28 (October–December 1981): 669–86.

Kerckhove, Derrick de. "Des Bancs et du parterre: la réception du spectacle drama-tique au XVIIIe siècle." In *L'Age du théâtre en France,* edited by David Trott and Nicole Boursier, 311–24. Edmonton: Academic Printing & Publishing, 1988.

Kirsop, Wallace. "Nouveautés: théâtre et roman." In *Histoire de l'édition française*, edited by Henri-Jean Martin and Roger Chartier, 2:218–24. Paris: Promodis, 1984.

Lagrave, Henri. *Le Théâtre et le public à Paris de 1715 à 1750*. Paris: Klincksieck, 1972.

Lagrave, Henri, et al. *La Vie théâtrale à Bordeaux des origines à nos jours. Tome 1, Des origines à 1799*. Paris: Editions du CNRS, 1985.

Lancaster, Henry Carrington. *The Comédie-Française, 1680–1701: Plays, Actors, Spectators, Finances*. Baltimore: Johns Hopkins University Press, 1941.

———. *The Comédie-Française, 1701–1774: Plays, Actors, Spectators, Finances*. Philadelphia: American Philosophical Society, 1951.

Landes, Joan. *Women and the Public Sphere in the Age of the French Revolution*. Ithaca, Cornell University Press, 1988.

Lawrenson, T. E. *The French Stage in the Seventeenth Century: A Study in the Advent of the Italian Order*. Manchester: Manchester University Press, 1957.

Le Dantec, Denise, and Jean-Pierre Le Dantec. *Reading the French Garden: Story and History*. Trans. Jessica Levine. Cambridge: MIT Press, 1990.

Lough, John. *Paris Theatre Audiences in the Seventeenth and Eighteenth Centuries*. London: Oxford University Press, 1957.

———. "A Paris Theatre in the Eighteenth Century." *University of Toronto Quarterly* 27 (April 1958): 289–304.

Maslan, Susan. "Resisting Representation: Theater and Democracy in Revolutionary France." *Representations* 52 (Fall 1995): 27–51.

Mason, Laura. *Singing the French Revolution: Popular Culture and Politics, 1787–1799*. Ithaca: Cornell University Press, 1996.

Maza, Sarah. *Private Lives and Public Affairs: The 'Causes Célèbres' of Prerevolutionary France*. Berkeley: University of California Press, 1993.

McKenzie, Donald W. "Typography and Meaning: The Case of William Congreve." In *Buch und Buchhandel in Europa im achtzehnten Jahrhundert*, edited by Giles Barber and Bernhard Fabian, 81–125. Hamburg: Dr. Ernst Hauswedell & Co., 1977.

McManners, John. *Abbés and Actresses: The Church and the Theatrical Profession in Eighteenth-Century France*. Oxford: Clarendon Press, 1986.

Mélèse, Pierre. *Répertoire analytique des documents contemporains d'information et de critique concernant le théâtre à Paris sous Louis XIV, 1659–1715*. Paris: E. Droz, 1934.

———. *Le Théâtre et le public à Paris sous Louis XIV, 1659–1715*. Paris: E. Droz, 1934.

Merlin, Hélène. *Public et littérature en France au XVIIe siècle*. Paris: Les Belles Lettres, 1994.

Merrick, Jeffrey W. *The Desacralization of the French Monarchy in the Eighteenth Century*. Baton Rouge: Louisiana State University Press, 1990.

Mittman, Barbara. *Spectators on the Paris Stage in the Seventeenth and Eighteenth Centuries*. Ann Arbor: UMI Press, 1984.

Moffat, Margaret M. *Rousseau et la querelle du théâtre au XVIIIe siècle*. Paris: E. de Boccard, 1930.

Murray, Timothy C. "Richelieu's Theatre: The Mirror of a Prince." *Renaissance Drama*, n.s. 8 (1977): 275–98.

————. *Theatrical Legitimation: Allegories of Genius in Seventeenth-Century France and England.* Oxford: Oxford University Press, 1987.

Ozouf, Mona. "'Public Opinion' at the End of the Old Regime." *Journal of Modern History* 60, suppl. (September 1988): S1–S21.

Payne, Harry C. *The Philosophes and the People.* New Haven: Yale University Press, 1976.

Piasenza, Paolo. "Juges, Lieutenants de Police, et Bourgeois à Paris aux XVIIe et XVIIIe siècles." *Annales ESC* 45 (September–October 1990): 1189–1215.

Prat, Aristide. "Le Parterre au XVIIIe siècle." *La Quinzaine* 68 (February 1906): 388–412.

Ravel, Jeffrey S. "Actress to Activist: Mlle Clairon in the Public Sphere of the 1760s." *Theatre Survey* 35 (May 1994): 73–86.

————. "Language and Authority in the Comedies of Edme Boursault." *Papers on French Seventeenth-Century Literature* 28 (1988): 177–99.

————. "*La Reine boit!* Print, Performance, and Theater Publics in France, 1724–1725." *Eighteenth-Century Studies* 29 (Summer 1996): 391–411.

————. "Rousseau and the Construction of French Provincial Playhouses." *Pensée Libre* 6 (1997): 183–90.

————. "Seating the Public: Spheres and Loathing in the Paris Theaters, 1777–1788." *French Historical Studies* 18 (Spring 1993): 173–210.

Roach, Joseph. *The Player's Passion: Studies in the Science of Acting.* Newark: University of Delaware Press, 1985.

Roddick, Nick. "From Siege to Lock-out: An Actors' Strike at the Comédie-Française in 1765." *Theatre Research International* n.s. 4 (October 1978): 45–58.

Root-Bernstein, Michèle. *Boulevard Theater and Revolution in Eighteenth-Century Paris.* Ann Arbor: UMI Press, 1984.

————. "The Moral Criminality of the Popular Actor in Eighteenth-Century Paris." *Eighteenth-Century Life* n.s. 10 (January 1986): 48–70.

Rougemont, Martine de. *La Vie théâtrale en France au XVIIIe siècle.* Paris: Champion, 1988.

Scott, Virginia. *The Commedia dell'arte in Paris, 1644–1697.* Charlottesville: University of Virginia Press, 1990.

————. "The *Jeu* and the *Rôle*: Analysis of the Appeals of the Italian Comedy in France in the Time of Arlequin-Dominique." In *Western Popular Theatre*, edited by David Mayer and Kenneth Richards, 1–27. London: Methuen, 1977.

Sennett, Richard. *The Fall of Public Man.* New York: Knopf, 1977.

Spaziani, Marcello. *Gli Italiani alla 'Foire': Quattro Studi con Due Appendici.* Rome: Edizioni di Storia e Letteratura, 1982.

————. "Per una Storia della Commedia 'Foraine.'" In *Studi in Onore di Carlo Pellegrini*, 255–77. Turin: Società Editrice Internationale, 1963.

————. *Il Teatro della Foire.* Rome: Edizioni dell'Ateneo, 1965.

————. *Il Théâtre Italien di Gherardi.* Rome: Edizioni dell'Ateneo, 1966.

Striker, Ardelle. "A Curious Form of Protest Theater: The *pièce à écriteaux.*" *Theatre Survey* 14 (1973): 55–71.

Trott, David. "A Dramaturgy of the Unofficial Stage: the Non-Texts of Louis Fuzelier." In *The Age of Theatre in France*, edited by David Trott and Nicole Boursier, 209–18. Edmonton: Academic Printing and Publishing, 1987.

Van Kley, Dale. *The Damiens Affair and the Unraveling of the Ancien Régime.* Princeton: Princeton University Press, 1984.

Viala, Alain. *Naissance de l'écrivain: Sociologie de la littérature à l'âge classique.* Paris: Editions de minuit, 1985.

Weber, William. "L'Institution et son public. L'Opéra à Paris et à Londres au XVIIIe siècle." *Annales ESC* 48 (November–December 1993): 1519–39.

———. "Learned and General Music Taste in Eighteenth-Century France." *Past and Present* 89 (November 1980): 58–85.

———. "*La Musique ancienne* in the Waning of the Ancien Régime." *Journal of Modern History* 56 (March 1984): 58–88.

Wikander, Matthew. *Princes to Act: Royal Audience and Royal Performance, 1578–1792.* Baltimore: Johns Hopkins University Press, 1993.

Wiley, William L. *The Early Public Theater in France.* Cambridge: Harvard University Press, 1960.

Williams, Alan. *The Police of Paris, 1718–1789.* Baton Rouge: Louisiana State University Press, 1979.

Zanger, Abby. "Paralyzing Performance: Sacrificing Theater on the Altar of Publication." *Stanford French Review* 12 (Fall-Winter 1988): 169–85.

Index

Page numbers in boldface type refer to illustrations. Page numbers followed by *n* indicate footnotes.